# HIKING THE PACIFIC CREST TRAIL – CALIFORNIA

## PCT – CAMPO TO CASTELLA

by David Jordan

JUNIPER HOUSE, MURLEY MOSS,
OXENHOLME ROAD, KENDAL, CUMBRIA LA9 7RL
www.cicerone.co.uk

First edition 2025
ISBN: 978 1 78631 213 6

Printed in China on responsibly sourced paper on behalf of Latitude Press Ltd.
A catalogue record for this book is available from the British Library.
All photographs are by the author unless otherwise stated.

Route mapping by Lovell Johns www.lovelljohns.com
Contains OpenStreetMap.org data © OpenStreetMap contributors, CC-BY-SA.
NASA relief data courtesy of ESRI

## Updates to this guide

While every effort is made by our authors to ensure the accuracy of guidebooks as they go to print, changes can occur during the lifetime of an edition. Any updates that we know of for this guide will be on the Cicerone website (www.cicerone.co.uk/1212/updates), so please check before planning your trip. We also advise that you check information about such things as transport, accommodation and shops locally. Even rights of way can be altered over time. We are always grateful for information about any discrepancies between a guidebook and the facts on the ground, sent by email to updates@cicerone.co.uk.

**Register your book:** To sign up to receive free updates, special offers and GPX files where available, create a Cicerone account and register your purchase via the 'My Account' tab at www.cicerone.co.uk

*Front cover:* Looking out across Desolation Wilderness from Dick's Pass (Stage 42)

# CONTENTS

*Late lying snow obscures the trail in upper Evolution Basin in Stage 33 (photo: James Humenansky)*

## Warning

The Pacific Crest Trail is designed as a summer trail to be hiked when it is free of snow and the creeks are relatively low. You should be aware that navigation could be difficult and the trail could be dangerous when there is snow in the mountains or when the creeks are running high because of snowmelt. The maps in this guide will not be adequate for navigation when snow covers the trail. If you hike the PCT you will be going into high mountains, wilderness areas and deserts. You might be faced with severe storms, fording unbridged creeks, wildfires, burned areas and hiking through long waterless sections in high temperatures. Mountains and wilderness trekking can be dangerous, carrying the risk of personal injury or death.

## Note on mapping

The route maps in this guide are derived from publicly available data, databases and crowd-sourced data. As such they have not been through the detailed checking procedures that would generally be applied to a published map from an official mapping agency. However, we have reviewed them closely in the light of local knowledge as part of the preparation of this guide.

# Mountain safety

Every mountain walk has its dangers, and those described in this guidebook are no exception. All who walk or climb in the mountains should recognise this and take responsibility for themselves and their companions along the way. The author and publisher have made every effort to ensure that the information contained in this guide was correct when it went to press, but, except for any liability that cannot be excluded by law, they cannot accept responsibility for any loss, injury or inconvenience sustained by any person using this book.

**International distress signal** *(emergency only)*
Six blasts on a whistle (and flashes with a torch after dark) spaced evenly for one minute, followed by a minute's pause. Repeat until an answer is received. The response is three signals per minute followed by a minute's pause.

**Helicopter rescue**
The following signals are used to communicate with a helicopter:

Help needed: raise both arms above head to form a 'Y'

Help not needed: raise one arm above head, extend other arm downward

**Emergency telephone numbers**
In the US the Nationwide Emergency Number is 911

Be prepared to confirm:
1. The location of the emergency
2. The phone number you are calling from
3. The type of the emergency
4. The detail of the emergency

The operator will then transfer you to the appropriate response team.

**Weather reports**
*National Weather Service: www.weather.gov*
*Mountain Weather: www.mountain-forecast.com*

**Mountain rescue can be very expensive – be adequately insured.**

*Trail sign in Sequoia National Park (Stage 28)*

# ROUTE SUMMARY TABLE

## (FROM THE SOUTHERN TERMINUS TO INTERSTATE 5 AT CASTELLA)

| No. | Stage | Distance (miles) | Total ascent (feet) | Total descent (feet) | Duration (hr:min) | Page |
|---|---|---|---|---|---|---|
| **Section 1** | | | | | | |
| 1 | Southern Terminus – Lake Morena | 20.0 | 2451 | 2260 | 9:00 | 19 |
| 2 | Lake Morena – Mount Laguna | 22.6 | 3865 | 971 | 10:30 | 21 |
| 3 | Mount Laguna – Scissors Crossing | 34.7 | 2034 | 5692 | 14:15 | 23 |
| 4 | Scissors Crossing – Warner Springs | 32.2 | 3635 | 2831 | 13:30 | 25 |
| 5 | Warner Springs – Chihuahua Valley Rd | 17.8 | 2927 | 942 | 8:00 | 27 |
| 6 | Chihuahua Valley Rd – Hwy 74 | 24.6 | 3110 | 3228 | 11:10 | 29 |
| 7 | Hwy 74 – Saddle Junction | 27.5 | 6791 | 3586 | 14:15 | 31 |
| 8 | Saddle Junction – San Gorgonio Pass | 30.1 | 2431 | 9206 | 15:50 | 33 |
| 9 | San Gorgonio Pass – Onyx Summit | 42.6 | 10853 | 3652 | 20:00 | 35 |
| 10 | Onyx Summit – Van Dusen Canyon | 23.0 | 1742 | 3018 | 10:30 | 37 |
| **Totals** | | **275.1** | **39,839** | **35,386** | **126:30** | |
| **Section 2** | | | | | | |
| 11 | Van Dusen Canyon – Hwy 173 | 39.2 | 3432 | 7503 | 14:30 | 45 |
| 12 | Hwy 173 – Hwy 138 | 14.8 | 1266 | 974 | 6:00 | 46 |
| 13 | Hwy 138 – Cajon Pass | 12.9 | 1302 | 1690 | 5:40 | 49 |
| 14 | Cajon Pass – Hwy 2 Inspiration Point | 27.4 | 6263 | 1916 | 14:15 | 51 |
| 15 | Hwy 2 Inspiration Point – Hwy 2 Islip Saddle | 16.6 | 3714 | 4413 | 8:40 | 53 |
| 16 | Hwy 2 Islip Saddle – Mill Crk Summit | 32.6 | 5525 | 7320 | 14:40 | 55 |
| 17 | Mill Crk Summit – North Fork Ranger Station | 17.5 | 2867 | 3609 | 7:30 | 57 |
| 18 | North Fork Ranger Station – Agua Dulce | 18.4 | 1965 | 3612 | 8:00 | 56 |
| **Totals** | | **179.4** | **26,334** | **31,037** | **79:15** | |

| No. | Stage | Distance (miles) | Total ascent (feet) | Total descent (feet) | Duration (hr:min) | Page |
|---|---|---|---|---|---|---|
| **Section 3** | | | | | | |
| 19 | Agua Dulce – Lake Hughes Rd | 31.2 | 5092 | 4554 | 14:30 | 64 |
| 20 | Lake Hughes Rd – Hwy 138 | 31.9 | 4619 | 4639 | 14:30 | 66 |
| 21 | Hwy 138 – Cottonwood Creek | 17.3 | 548 | 495 | 6:35 | 69 |
| 22 | Cottonwood Crk – Tehachapi Pass | 31.5 | 4849 | 4137 | 14:50 | 71 |
| 23 | Tehachapi Pass – Piute Mountain Rd | 42.9 | 7444 | 5036 | 19:20 | 73 |
| 24 | Piute Mountain Rd – Bird Spring Pass | 22.7 | 2992 | 3862 | 9:40 | 76 |
| 25 | Bird Spring Pass – Walker Pass | 21.2 | 3222 | 3314 | 9:10 | 78 |
| 26 | Walker Pass – Chimney Creek CG | 28.9 | 5115 | 4826 | 13:30 | 81 |
| 27 | Chimney Creek CG – Kennedy Meadows | 21.3 | 3153 | 2703 | 9:40 | 83 |
| **Totals** | | **248.9** | **37,034** | **33,566** | **111:45** | |
| **Section 4** | | | | | | |
| 28 | Kennedy Meadows – Trail Pass | 43.1 | 7972 | 3494 | 21:45 | 91 |
| 29 | Trail Pass – Crabtree Meadow | 21 | 2756 | 2887 | 9:30 | 95 |
| 30 | Crabtree Meadow – Kearsarge Pass Trail | 22.6 | 5394 | 5016 | 12:50 | 96 |
| 31 | Kearsarge Pass Trail – Taboose Pass Trail | 21.3 | 4780 | 4728 | 13:15 | 101 |
| 32 | Taboose Pass Trail – Bishop Pass Trail | 20.8 | 2759 | 4790 | 10:00 | 103 |
| 33 | Bishop Pass Trail – Piute Pass Trail | 24.9 | 3379 | 4052 | 12:20 | 105 |
| 34 | Piute Pass Trail – Bear Ridge Trail | 18.6 | 4049 | 2231 | 10:10 | 107 |
| 35 | Bear Ridge Trail – Red's Meadow | 32.1 | 5604 | 7792 | 14:45 | 108 |
| 36 | Red's Meadow – Tuolumne Meadows | 35.9 | 4990 | 4094 | 16:25 | 110 |
| **Totals** | | **240.3** | **41,683** | **39,084** | **121:00** | |

| No. | Stage | Distance (miles) | Total ascent (feet) | Total descent (feet) | Duration (hr:min) | Page |
|---|---|---|---|---|---|---|
| **Section 5** | | | | | | |
| 37 | Tuolumne Meadows – Bear Valley Trail | 37.2 | 6775 | 7372 | 19:00 | 119 |
| 38 | Bear Valley Trail – Sonora Pass | 37.2 | 6348 | 4689 | 18:50 | 123 |
| 39 | Sonora Pass – Ebbetts Pass | 31.5 | 5384 | 6335 | 14:45 | 124 |
| 40 | Ebbetts Pass – Carson Pass | 28.3 | 4285 | 4432 | 12:10 | 129 |
| 41 | Carson Pass – Echo Lake | 15.5 | 2018 | 3150 | 6:45 | 131 |
| 42 | Echo Lake – Barker Pass | 32.6 | 4908 | 4485 | 14:50 | 133 |
| 43 | Barker Pass – Interstate 80 | 32.2 | 5236 | 5659 | 14:50 | 134 |
| **Totals** | | **214.5** | **34,954** | **36,122** | **101:10** | |
| **Section 6** | | | | | | |
| 44 | Interstate 80 – Hwy 49 Sierra City | 38.4 | 4547 | 7205 | 16:20 | 145 |
| 45 | Hwy 49 Sierra City – Quincy LaPorte Road | 39.4 | 7664 | 5712 | 18:35 | 146 |
| 46 | Quincy/LaPorte Road – Big Creek Road | 28.7 | 5023 | 5984 | 12:40 | 151 |
| 47 | Big Creek Road – Hwy 70 Belden | 23.4 | 2300 | 5627 | 9:45 | 153 |
| 48 | Hwy 70 Belden – Humboldt Summit | 24.7 | 6811 | 2356 | 13:45 | 152 |
| 49 | Humboldt Summit – Hwy 36 nr Chester | 19.5 | 2218 | 3819 | 8:20 | 157 |
| 50 | Hwy 36 nr Chester – Hat Creek Resort | 42.1 | 4455 | 4961 | 18:15 | 156 |
| 51 | Hat Creek Resort – Road 22 | 20.1 | 1112 | 1066 | 8:00 | 163 |
| 52 | Road 22 – Burney Falls | 25.5 | 669 | 2323 | 9:50 | 165 |
| 53 | Burney Falls – Bartle Gap | 27 | 4678 | 2510 | 13:00 | 167 |
| 54 | Bartle Gap – McCloud River | 25 | 2612 | 5302 | 10:20 | 169 |
| 55 | McCloud River – I-5 (Castella) | 30.2 | 5039 | 5335 | 13:35 | 171 |
| **Totals** | | **344** | **47,128** | **52,200** | **152:25** | |

# INTRODUCTION

Starting from the Mexican border, at a monument around 50 miles east of San Diego, the Pacific Crest Trail (PCT) meanders its way north for around 2655 miles, through the combined length of California, Oregon and Washington, all the way to a corresponding monument at the Canadian Border about 100 miles east of Vancouver, British Columbia. As the name suggests, it follows the crest of the mountains, rising and falling with the watershed divide, exploring the panorama that becomes visible, only from the higher ground.

This is book two in a series that also includes: book one – *Hiking the Pacific Crest Trail* and book three – *Hiking the Pacific Crest Trail – Oregon and Washington*. The guide has been presented as three booklets to enable the hiker to keep weight to the absolute minimum, while still carrying a physical guide and maps that can both supplement, and if necessary, replace a digital mapping app.

In planning terms, the PCT is too long to think about in its entirety, not least as it includes incredibly diverse landscapes and conditions, which affect choices of gear, time of year, when and where to resupply, right down to where to camp and find adequate water. It is necessary to break the trail down into manageable chunks, to facilitate hiking in sections, or as a way of planning the logistics of a thru-hike.

This guide divides the trail into one hundred stages grouped into eleven sections. The structure hopes to offer the section hiker an easier way to plan and think about smaller hikes, that can easily be 'chunked' together when more time is available for longer outings. At the same time the thru-hiker might appreciate the manageable scale that encourages them to think, typically a day or two ahead in each stage while tent sites and water sources are the priority, yet still relate to a larger structure in which opportunities for rest and resupply become the priority.

This book commences in Southern California, where Sections 1–3 take the hiker across the desert, from the Southern Terminus to Kennedy Meadows South, just before the Sierra Nevada mountains. These sections break, first at Van Dusen Canyon where there is good access to Big Bear Lake, and second at Agua Dulce, just off Highway 14 between Santa Clarita and Palmdale. Sections 4 and 5 take the hiker across the Sierra Nevada range, breaking at Tuolumne Meadows and then at Interstate 80 outside of Truckee. Section 6 covers Northern California as far as the first crossing of Interstate 5, at Castella, not too far from Mount Shasta.

Camp in Domeland Wilderness before the final desert stage to Kennedy Meadows (Stage 27)

## USING THIS GUIDE

This, book two of the guide, is intended to be used by the hiker who has first read book one, *Hiking the Pacific Crest Trail*. There you will find a more detailed explanation of the trail structure, history, timings, permits required, navigation and how to approach a hike on the PCT, whether a thru-hike or a shorter section.

The route maps are presented at 1:100,000 scale, sufficient to navigate from topography and major features most of the time. Smaller details that might be required to navigate in poor conditions will not be present. Mapping is continuous throughout each booklet, and mileage is given cumulatively from 0–2655. Stage timings are indicative only, and do not include breaks. Individuals will hike faster or slower than the suggested timings. The water sources indicated can vary greatly from year to year. Many will dry up during the season, earlier some years than others. Water caches are indicated where commonly seen, but should never be relied upon.

The PCT Water Report is an invaluable crowd-sourced project managed by volunteers. It provides updates regarding water sources, fires, passes, and fords. You can access it at www.pctwater.com, on Instagram @pctwater, or on Facebook. You can also download it in several formats for offline use. Please contribute updates whenever you can.

# SECTION 1 – SOUTHERN TERMINUS TO VAN DUSEN CANYON

| | Stage | Distance (miles) | Total ascent (feet) | Total descent (feet) | Duration (hr:min) | Page |
|---|---|---|---|---|---|---|
| 1 | Southern Terminus – Lake Morena | 20.0 | 2451 | 2260 | 9:00 | 19 |
| 2 | Lake Morena – Mount Laguna | 22.6 | 3865 | 971 | 10:30 | 21 |
| 3 | Mount Laguna – Scissors Crossing | 34.7 | 2034 | 5692 | 14:15 | 23 |
| 4 | Scissors Crossing – Warner Springs | 32.2 | 3635 | 2831 | 13:30 | 25 |
| 5 | Warner Springs – Chihuahua Valley Rd | 17.8 | 2927 | 942 | 8:00 | 27 |
| 6 | Chihuahua Valley Rd – Hwy 74 | 24.6 | 3110 | 3228 | 11:10 | 29 |
| 7 | Hwy 74 – Saddle Junction | 27.5 | 6791 | 3586 | 14:15 | 31 |
| 8 | Saddle Junction – San Gorgonio Pass | 30.1 | 2431 | 9206 | 15:50 | 33 |
| 9 | San Gorgonio Pass – Onyx Summit | 42.6 | 10853 | 3652 | 20:00 | 35 |
| 10 | Onyx Summit – Van Dusen Canyon | 23.0 | 1742 | 3018 | 10:30 | 37 |
| **Totals** | | **275.1** | **39,839** | **35,386** | **126:30** | |

## WHAT TO EXPECT

The archetypal desert environment from the start, with alternating rocky and sandy trail, manzanita, cacti and scrub oak typical of a chaparral landscape, Section 1 does not disappoint. Stretching from Campo, within touching distance of the Mexican border fence, to the slopes north of Big Bear Lake, this is a varied section that is demanding of the hiker.

With an altitude range of 1000–9000ft, and temperatures that can soar above 100°F (38°C), then sink below freezing at night, it is important to resist the temptation to under-estimate the challenge. Thru-hikers may want to start with the lightest pack possible, to build fitness before taking on equipment needed for the 'bigger' mountains, especially if you are starting early in the season. However, this is an area where you will be grateful for an extra layer to put on, and where you may also really appreciate an umbrella, less for the occasional shower, than as shade against the unrelenting sun that will bear down on you from dawn until dusk most days.

Snow can be a problem. You are unlikely to see more than a few patches when you climb into the Laguna Mountains in Stage 2, but when you reach Mount San Jacinto in Stage 8 you can need micro-spikes or

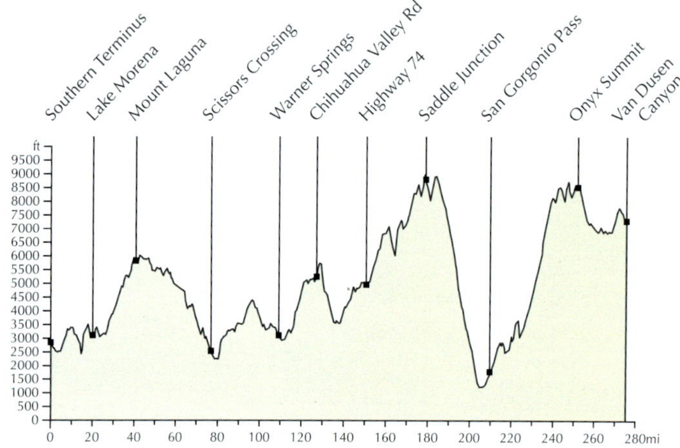


crampons, and possibly an ice-axe to safely negotiate the stage in a higher snow year. In between these high points, and especially in a dry year, heat and water shortage will be your biggest challenges.

Whether hiking a section, or starting a northbound thru-hike, mid-April is the ideal time to start. With the permit system now spreading hikers out, those with an earlier start date can expect cooler, wetter weather, and a greater challenge on Mount San Jacinto; those starting later will face more problems with heat, and long, heavy water carries, but may also breeze over Mount San Jacinto and arrive at Kennedy Meadows at a better time for entering the Sierra Nevada range. Autumn can also be a pleasant time to hike, but you need to be much more self-reliant in terms of water as most creeks and springs will be completely dry.

Resupply is not difficult in this section, with regular access to post offices, communities and small towns, so with a little planning you should not need to carry more than a few days' food. There are also plenty of people around to help out in this first section: sometimes other, more experienced, hikers, but also kind souls who act as unofficial trail angels providing rides into town, or perhaps you may walk into a picnic area or trailhead and find someone offering cold drinks, hotdogs or other very welcome fare.

# RESUPPLY OPTIONS

| Stage | Trail mile | Place | Off trail (miles) | Description | Facilities |
|---|---|---|---|---|---|
| 1 | 1.4 | Campo | 0.2 N | Small town with basic facilities and hiker-focused store and deli | |
| 1 | 20 | Lake Morena | 0.4 SE | Oak Shores Malt Shop, store/café/deli | |
| 2 | 41.5 | Mount Laguna | 0.4 W | Lodge and hiker-focused store, plus nearby PO | |
| 3 | 77.3 | Stagecoach RV Park | 4 SE | Tent sites, cabins, pool, showers and store | |
| 3 | 77.3 | Julian | 12 W | Hiker friendly town, famed for apple pie | |
| 4 | 101.2 | Ranchita Bodega | 4 E | Hiker-focused small store, a few rooms, showers, kitchen | |
| 4 | 109.5 | Warner Springs Ranch | 1.2 E | Community center, resort and mini-mart at gas station | |
| 6 | 151.9 | Paradise Valley Café | 1 W | Famed diner, tap/faucet outside, also accepts packages | |
| 6 | 151.9 | Anza | 6.8 SW | Small town with usual facilities | |
| 7 | 179.4 | Idyllwild | 5.1 W | Hiker friendly town, good resupply stop and state park campground | |
| 8 | 209.5 | Cabazon | 4.5 W | Small community store & post office | |
| 10 | 266.1 | Big Bear City | 5.4 SW | Smaller of the two 'Big Bear' towns, free mountain transit bus runs between them | |
| 10 | 275.1 | Big Bear Lake | 4 SE | Popular Big Bear Hostel, several supermarkets, hospital | |

*Crossing the rail tracks north of Campo Creek (Stage 1)*

## PERMITS

Permits are required for some or all of stages 1, 7 and 8.

Stage 1 – The Cleveland National Forest PCT Permit is valid for all portions of the Cleveland National Forest: PCT mile 13.5 to mile 53.2 (north of Pioneer Mail Picnic Area), and mile 112.7 to mile 124.8.

To obtain a permit visit: www.recreation.gov/permits/445862

For more information call the Descanso Ranger District Office at (619) 445-6235 or visit: www.fs.usda.gov/detail/cleveland/home/?cid=FSEPRD488307

Stages 7 and 8 – San Jacinto Wilderness permits are free for both federal and state wilderness areas. Both the National Forest and State Park honor each other's day use permit so visitors only need to obtain one for both wilderness areas. PCT mile 167.3 to mile 205.0.

*Cholla Cactus in Anza-Borrego Desert State Park (Stage 4)*

To obtain a permit visit: Idyllwild Ranger Station in person where self-issued permits are available 24/7: 25905 Highway 243, Idyllwild, CA 92549 (located on a permit desk in front of office).

## MAIL DROP INFORMATION

Laguna Mountain Lodge
10678 Sunrise Hwy POB 146
Mount Laguna, CA 91948
Hold for 'Your Name'
'Your Phone Number'
ETA: 'Your ETA'
They are open: 9am–5pm, seven days a week
Phone them on: (619) 473-8533
Visit them at:
www.lagunamountain.com

Paradise Valley Café
'Your Name Here'
c/o Paradise Corner Café
61721 Hwy 74
Mountain Center, CA 92561
They are open: Mon–Tue 8am–3pm, Wed–Sat 8am–8pm, Sun 8am–7pm
Phone them on: (951) 659-3663
Visit them at:
www.theparadisevalleycafe.com

## POST OFFICE INFORMATION

'Your Name Here'
c\o General Delivery
Campo, CA 91906
Located at: 951 Jeb Stuart Road
Phone them on: (619) 478-5466

'Your Name Here'
c\o General Delivery
Mt Laguna, CA 91948
Located at: 810 Sunrise Highway
Phone them on: (619) 473-8341

'Your Name Here'
c\o General Delivery
Julian, CA 92036
Located at: 1785 Highway 78
Phone them on: (760) 765-3648

'Your Name Here'
c\o General Delivery
Warner Springs, CA 92086
Located at: 31650 Highway 79
Phone them on: (760) 782-3166

'Your Name Here'
c\o General Delivery
Anza, CA 92539
Located at: 38775 Contreras Road
Phone them on: (951) 763-2074

'Your Name Here'
c\o General Delivery
Idyllwild, CA 92549
Located at: 54391 Village Center Drive
Phone them on: (951) 659-9719

'Your Name Here'
c\o General Delivery
Cabazon, CA 92230
Located at: 50360 Ramona Street
Phone them on: (951) 849-6233

'Your Name Here'
c\o General Delivery
Big Bear City, CA 92314
Located at: 120 West Country Club Boulevard
Phone them on: (909) 585-7132

'Your Name Here'
c/o General Delivery
Big Bear Lake, CA 92315
Located at: 472 Pine Knot Boulevard
Phone them on: (909) 866-1035

## Stage 1 route waypoints

From the Southern Terminus head north-west initially, passing first PCT trail sign

**1** **0.6mi, 0:10hr**
Pass Camp Lockett Campground campsite on R

**2** **1.2mi, 0:25hr**
Water tap behind Juvenile Ranch sign board

**3** **1.4mi, 0:30hr**
Keep L on trail from Forest Gate Rd (Campo facilities 0.2mi N)

**4** **2.3mi, 0:50hr**
Cross Hwy 94

**5** **2.6mi, 0:55hr**
Cross Campo Crk (possible water early season)

**6** **3.0mi, 1:10hr**
Cross rail track and through gate

**7** **8.8mi, 3:55hr**
Pass through gates and across two dirt roads

**8** **14.0mi, 6:00hr**
Turn R on dirt boundary road

**9** **14.7mi, 6:15hr**
Turn L off dirt road

**10** **15.4mi, 6:30hr**
Cross Hauser Crk (possible water early season)

**11** **20.0mi, 9:00hr**
Lake Morena Trailhead (Oak Shores Malt Shop 0.4mi SE)

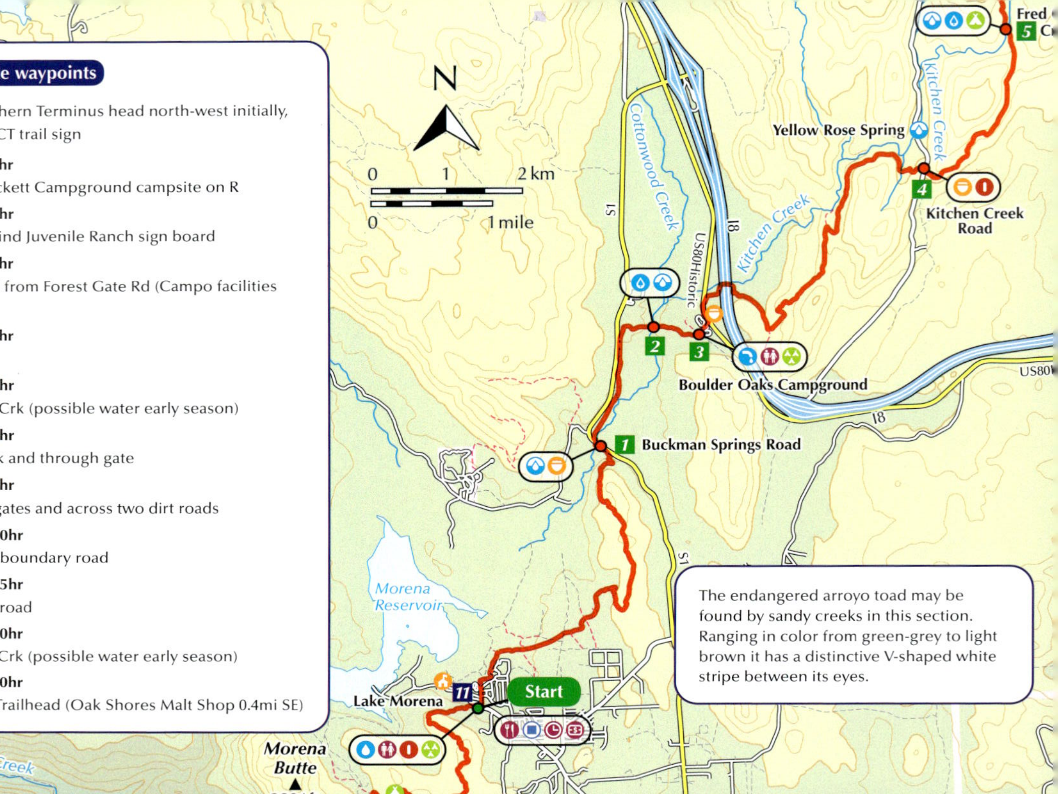


The endangered arroyo toad may be found by sandy creeks in this section. Ranging in color from green-grey to light brown it has a distinctive V-shaped white stripe between its eyes.

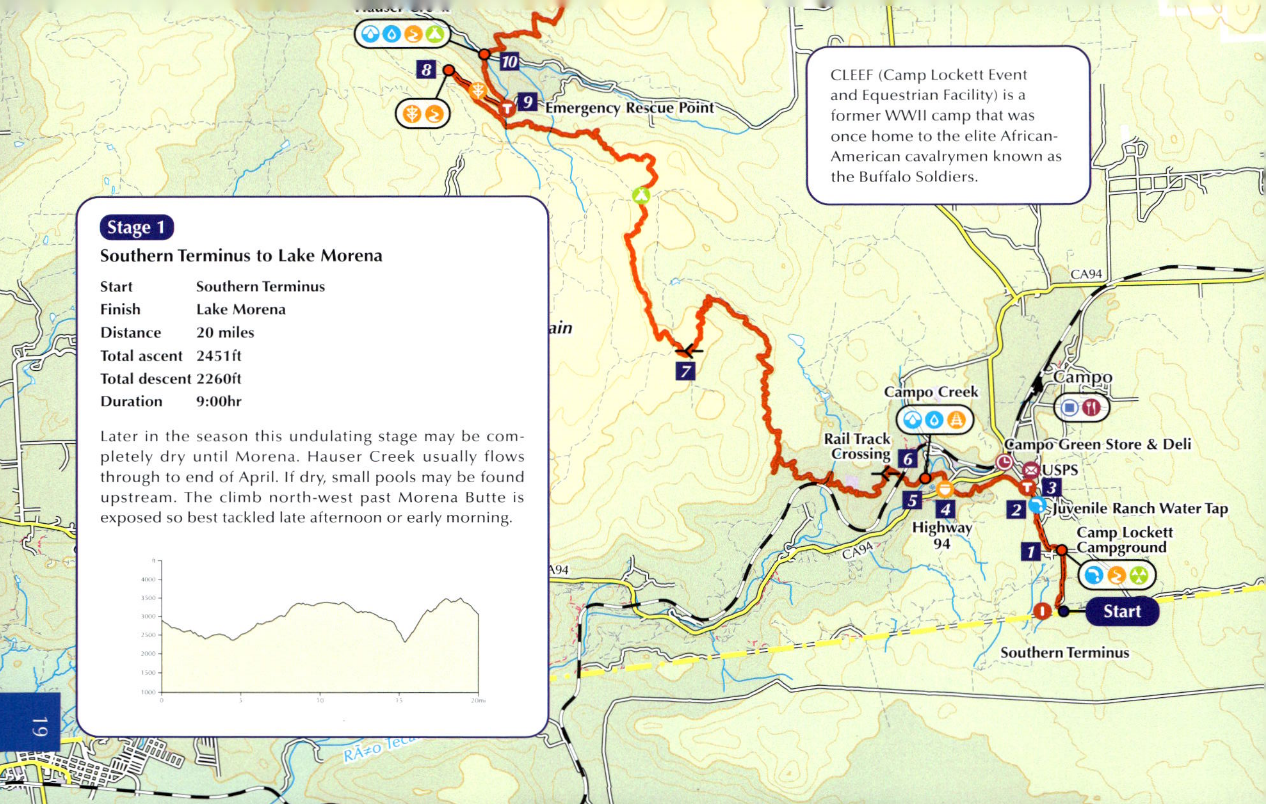


CLEEF (Camp Lockett Event and Equestrian Facility) is a former WWII camp that was once home to the elite African-American cavalrymen known as the Buffalo Soldiers.

**Stage 1**

## Southern Terminus to Lake Morena

| | |
|---|---|
| **Start** | **Southern Terminus** |
| **Finish** | **Lake Morena** |
| **Distance** | **20 miles** |
| **Total ascent** | **2451ft** |
| **Total descent** | **2260ft** |
| **Duration** | **9:00hr** |

Later in the season this undulating stage may be completely dry until Morena. Hauser Creek usually flows through to end of April. If dry, small pools may be found upstream. The climb north-west past Morena Butte is exposed so best tackled late afternoon or early morning.

## Stage 2 route waypoints

**1 24.1mi, 1:40hr**
Pass under Buckman Springs Rd and ford creek if running

**2 25.5mi, 2:25hr**
Ford Cottonwood Crk

**3 26.0mi, 2:35hr**
Pass through Boulder Oaks Campground to the road and turn L for 0.5mi to find underpass below I-8

**4 30.2mi, 4:25hr**
Cross Kitchen Creek Rd

**5 32.0mi, 5:15hr**
Cross Fred Canyon Crk (usually dry)

**6 32.6mi, 5:35hr**
Cross Fred Canyon Rd providing access (0.7mi L) to Cibbets Flat Campground

**7 37.7mi, 8:00hr**
Cross Long Canyon Crk (sometimes dry)

**8 39.9mi, 9:35hr**
Cross Morris Ranch Rd with access left to Lower Morris Meadow Spring Trail

**9 41.5mi, 10:00hr**
Southern boundary of Burnt Rancheria Campground (Mount Laguna facilities 0.4mi W)

**10 42.6mi, 10:30hr**
Desert View Picnic Area at Mount Laguna

Among the Jeffrey Pines you may see acorn woodpeckers, a medium-sized bird, mainly black and white with a red crown. They cache acorns under the bark of these pine trees.

**Stage 2**

## Lake Morena to Mount Laguna

| | |
|---|---|
| **Start** | Lake Morena |
| **Finish** | Mount Laguna |
| **Distance** | 22.6 miles |
| **Total ascent** | 3865ft |
| **Total descent** | 971ft |
| **Duration** | 10:30hr |

This stage follows the marshy foreshore of Lake Morena before a long, exposed climb into the Laguna Mountains. The last reliable water before the climb will be at Boulder Oaks Campground.

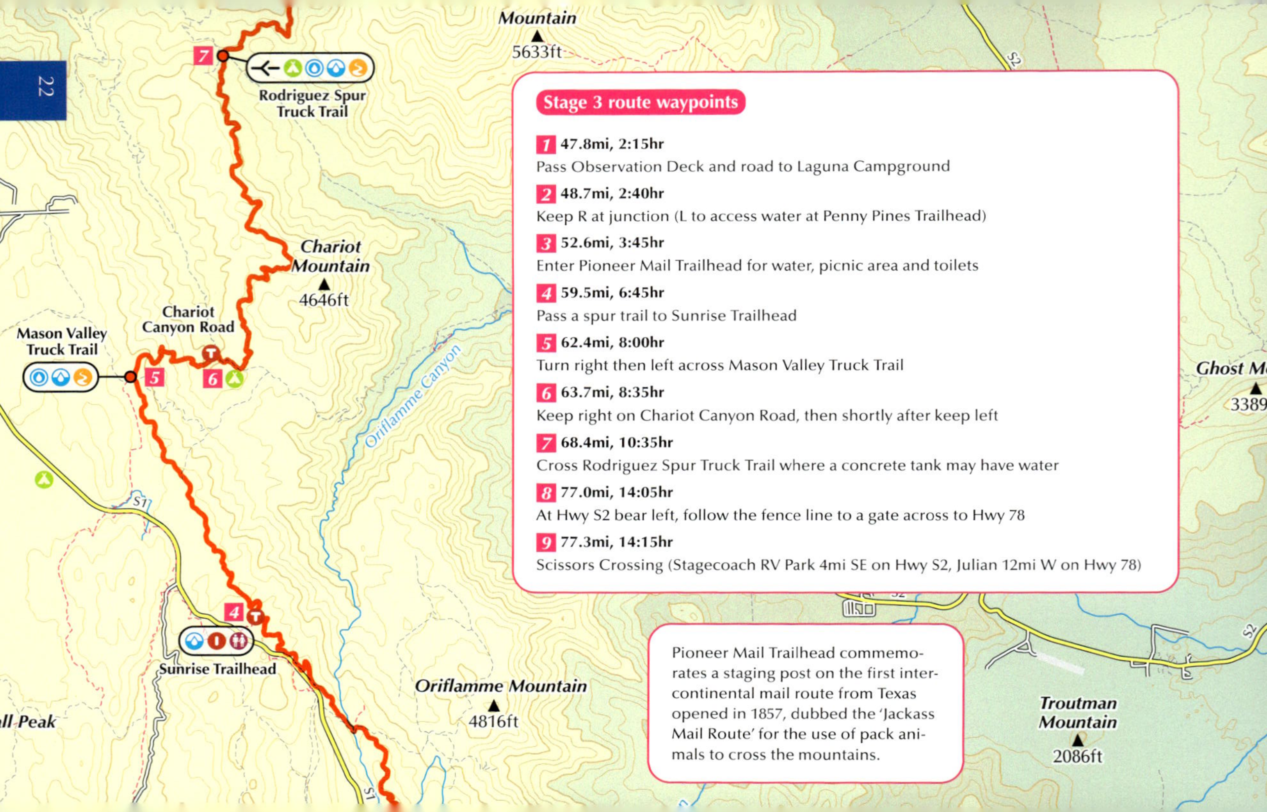


## Stage 3 route waypoints

**1** **47.8mi, 2:15hr**
Pass Observation Deck and road to Laguna Campground

**2** **48.7mi, 2:40hr**
Keep R at junction (L to access water at Penny Pines Trailhead)

**3** **52.6mi, 3:45hr**
Enter Pioneer Mail Trailhead for water, picnic area and toilets

**4** **59.5mi, 6:45hr**
Pass a spur trail to Sunrise Trailhead

**5** **62.4mi, 8:00hr**
Turn right then left across Mason Valley Truck Trail

**6** **63.7mi, 8:35hr**
Keep right on Chariot Canyon Road, then shortly after keep left

**7** **68.4mi, 10:35hr**
Cross Rodriguez Spur Truck Trail where a concrete tank may have water

**8** **77.0mi, 14:05hr**
At Hwy S2 bear left, follow the fence line to a gate across to Hwy 78

**9** **77.3mi, 14:15hr**
Scissors Crossing (Stagecoach RV Park 4mi SE on Hwy S2, Julian 12mi W on Hwy 78)

Pioneer Mail Trailhead commemorates a staging post on the first intercontinental mail route from Texas opened in 1857, dubbed the 'Jackass Mail Route' for the use of pack animals to cross the mountains.

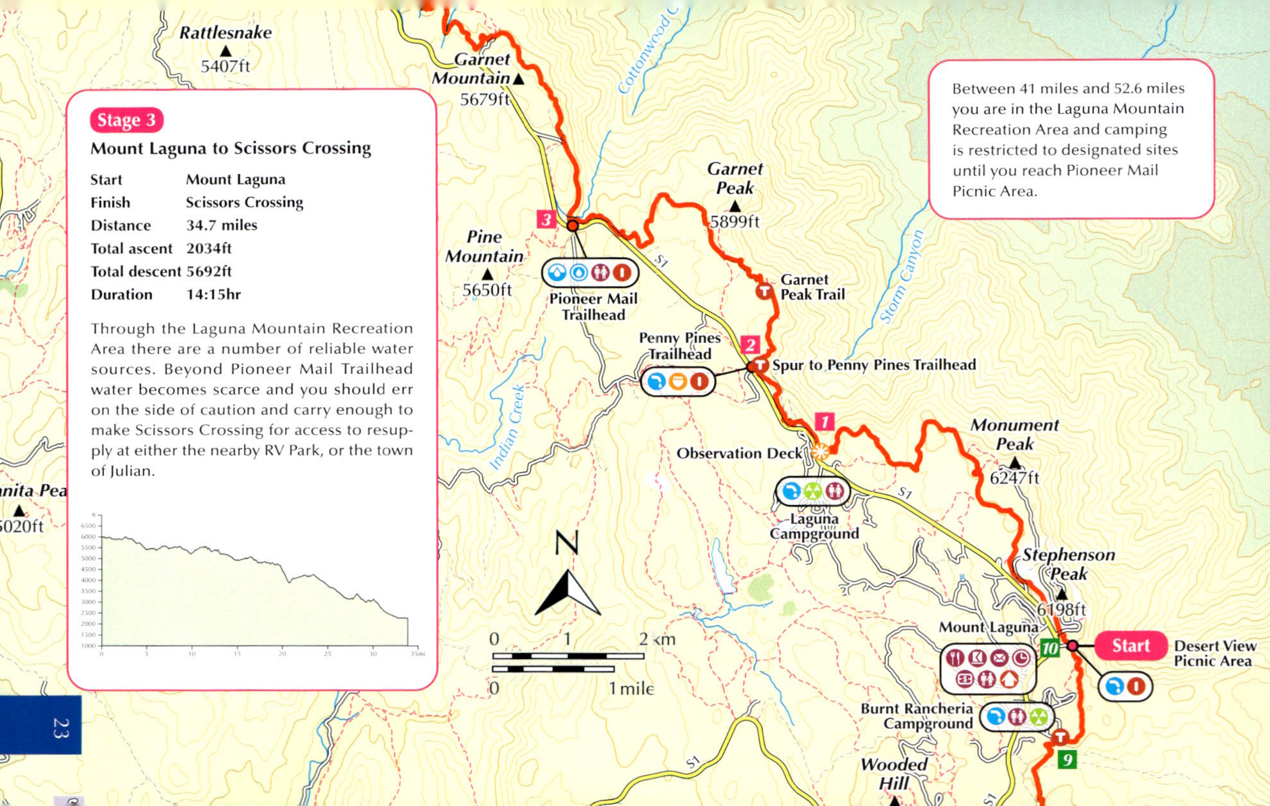


Between 41 miles and 52.6 miles you are in the Laguna Mountain Recreation Area and camping is restricted to designated sites until you reach Pioneer Mail Picnic Area.

**Stage 3**

## Mount Laguna to Scissors Crossing

| | |
|---|---|
| **Start** | **Mount Laguna** |
| **Finish** | **Scissors Crossing** |
| **Distance** | **34.7 miles** |
| **Total ascent** | **2034ft** |
| **Total descent** | **5692ft** |
| **Duration** | **14:15hr** |

Through the Laguna Mountain Recreation Area there are a number of reliable water sources. Beyond Pioneer Mail Trailhead water becomes scarce and you should err on the side of caution and carry enough to make Scissors Crossing for access to resupply at either the nearby RV Park, or the town of Julian.

## Stage 4 route waypoints

Follow Hwy 78 a short way NE to where trail resumes NW

**1 86.0mi, 3:45hr**
Pass through first pipe gate

**2 91.2mi, 5:00hr**
Approaching ridge, pass tent site then find the spur trail 0.3mi E downhill to third gate water cache

**3 101.1mi, 9:30hr**
Reach the Barrel Spring alongside the trail and just beyond cross Hwy S22, Montezuma Valley Rd (Ranchita Bodega 4mi E)

**4 105.0mi, 11:25hr**
Cross San Ysidro Crk which may have water

**5 109.5mi, 13:30hr**
Reach Hwy 79 for Warner Springs (1.2mi E)

The semi-arid regions crossed by the PCT are home to the short-horned lizard which looks a little like a toad, but with a crown of horns on its head and protective spines along its back.

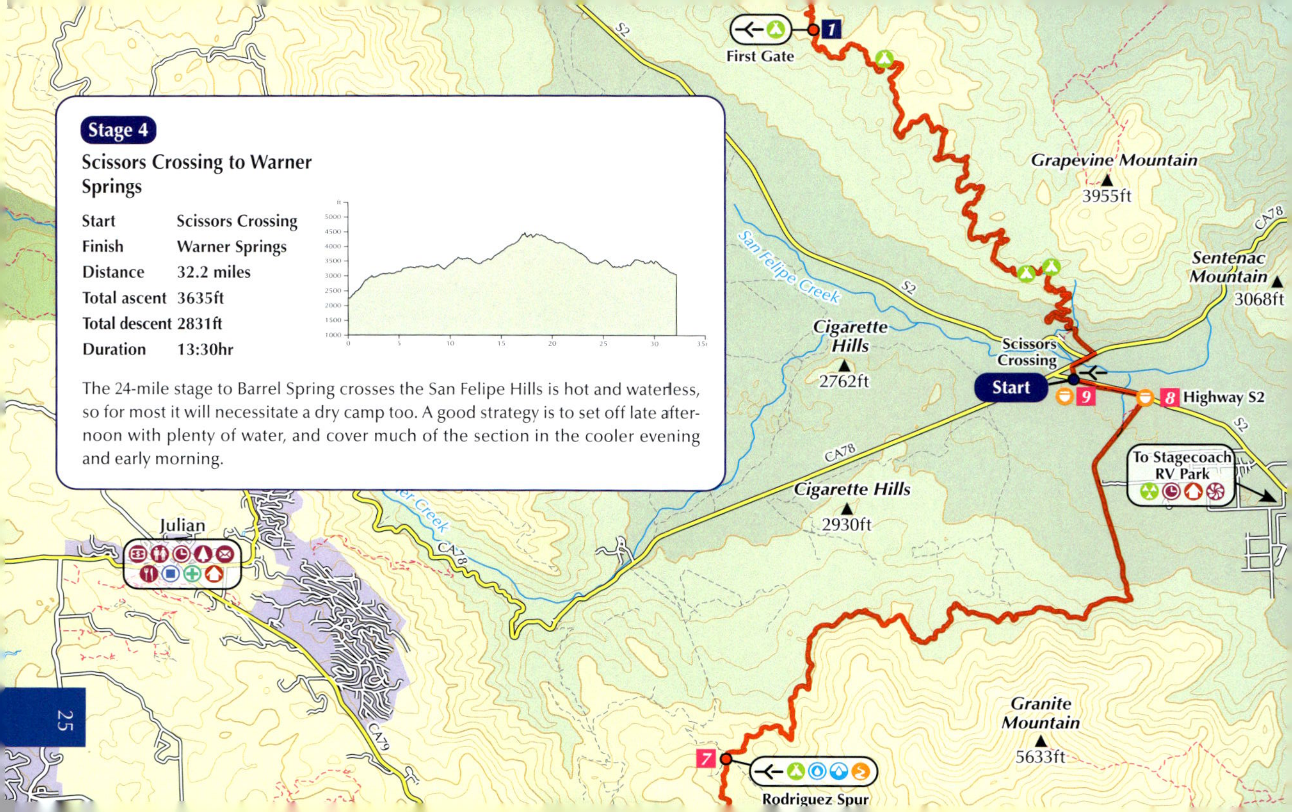


## Stage 4

### Scissors Crossing to Warner Springs

| | |
|---|---|
| Start | Scissors Crossing |
| Finish | Warner Springs |
| Distance | 32.2 miles |
| Total ascent | 3635ft |
| Total descent | 2831ft |
| Duration | 13:30hr |

The 24-mile stage to Barrel Spring crosses the San Felipe Hills is hot and waterless, so for most it will necessitate a dry camp too. A good strategy is to set off late afternoon with plenty of water, and cover much of the section in the cooler evening and early morning.

## Stage 5 route waypoints

**1 111.4mi, 0:50hr**
Bridge under Hwy 79 (second crossing)

**2 112.6mi, 1:25hr**
Cross Agua Caliente Crk (flows here early season)

**3 114.7mi, 2:25hr**
Cross creek several times (usually better flow here)

**4 116.2mi, 3:05hr**
If possible collect water before climbing away from creek

**5 119.6mi, 4:35hr**
Spur trail to Lost Valley Spring (0.2mi NW)

**6 127.3mi, 8:00hr**
Chihuahua Valley Road (Mike's Place 0.2mi E)

Mike's Place is a rambling and quirky private property, the owner of which has been a long-time supporter of hikers on the PCT. A water tank is provided, and hikers are welcome to stay on the property.

## Stage 5

### Warner Springs to Chihuahua Valley Road

| | |
|---|---|
| Start | Warner Springs |
| Finish | Chihuahua Valley Road |
| Distance | 17.8 miles |
| Total ascent | 2927ft |
| Total descent | 942ft |
| Duration | 8:00hr |

Stage 5 is a steady climb with little shade and water sources can dry up so check water availability ahead or carry enough. Mike's Place, close to the stage end, is usually a reliable water source but check in advance at Warner Springs Community Center if there is any doubt.

The old stagecoach that sits outside Warner Springs Ranch Resort is a nod to its history as a staging post on the Butterfield Overland Mail Line between 1858 and 1861. The hot springs however were in use long before this time, by the Cahuilla and Cupeño indigenous people.

Nearby Anza is an early settler town bearing the name of Captain Juan Bautista de Anza who first set foot there in 1774 while scouting a route from Sonora to San Francisco. He returned a year later with some 200 settlers and cattle and the town was born.

## Stage 6 route waypoints

**1 129.2mi, 0:55hr**
Combs Peak Ridge, a short side trail leads to the summit

**2 137.0mi, 4:25hr**
Tule Canyon Truck Trail. Turn R for Tule Spring and tent sites (0.25mi E)

**3 139.7mi, 5:40hr**
Cross Coyote Canyon (dirt) Rd. Just before the road is a concrete cistern that may yield some water, just after is a tiny creek in early season

**4 143.1mi, 7:10hr**
Cross Table Mountain Truck Trail before dropping steeply into the dry Alkali Wash (or turn L to follow dirt roads 6.2mi into Anza for PO and resupply)

**5 151.9mi, 11:10hr**
At Hwy 74 a short dogleg right then left crosses the highway. Alternatively turn L for 1mi NW to Paradise Valley Café and options to hitch beyond for resupply

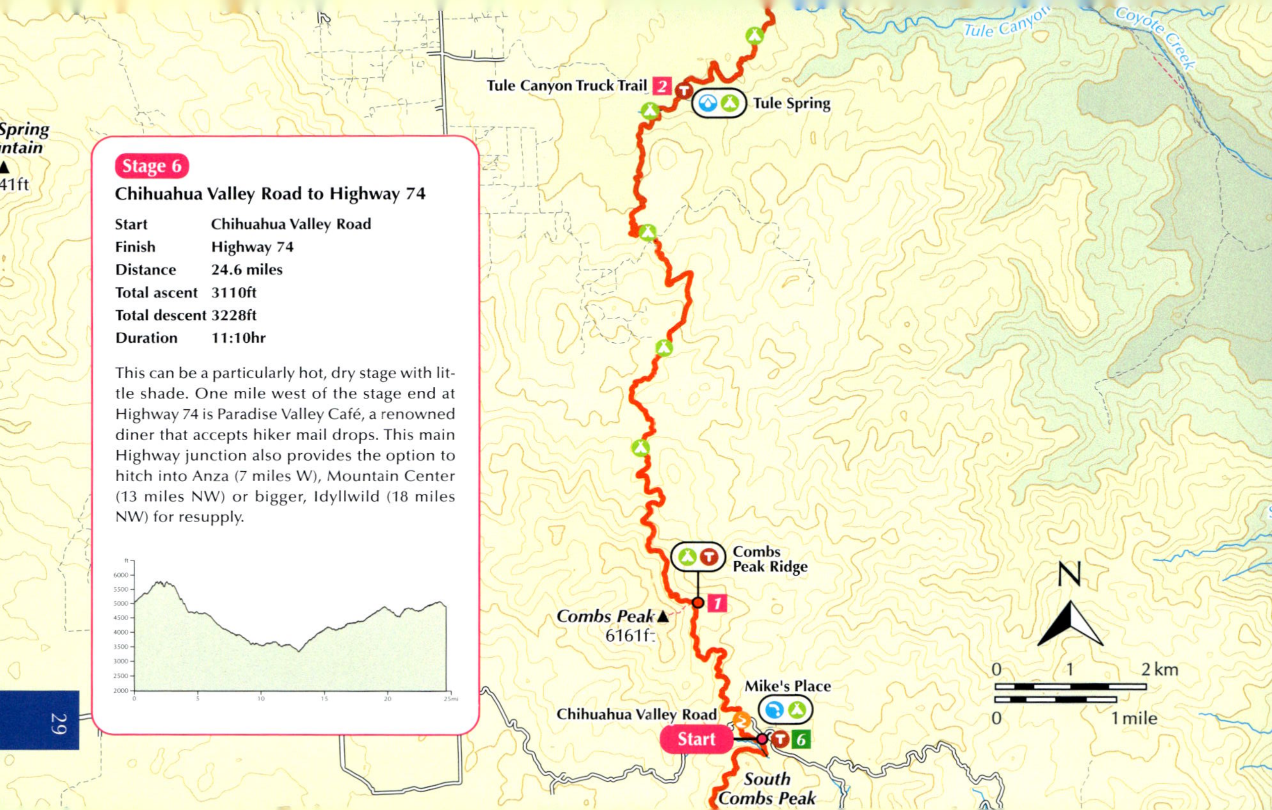


## Stage 6

### Chihuahua Valley Road to Highway 74

| | |
|---|---|
| **Start** | **Chihuahua Valley Road** |
| **Finish** | **Highway 74** |
| **Distance** | **24.6 miles** |
| **Total ascent** | **3110ft** |
| **Total descent** | **3228ft** |
| **Duration** | **11:10hr** |

This can be a particularly hot, dry stage with little shade. One mile west of the stage end at Highway 74 is Paradise Valley Café, a renowned diner that accepts hiker mail drops. This main Highway junction also provides the option to hitch into Anza (7 miles W), Mountain Center (13 miles NW) or bigger, Idyllwild (18 miles NW) for resupply.

## Stage 7 route waypoints

**1 158.4mi, 3:25hr**
At trail junction on saddle 2 potential water options: 0.3mi W steeply down to Tunnel Spring, or 1mi E on graded trail to Live Oak Spring and tent site

**2 162.6mi, 5:35hr**
At Cedar Spring Trail junction, trail N descends 1mi to reliable spring and tent sites (recommended). If snow is a problem here, descend SW 2.3mi to Morris Ranch Road then 3.7mi to Hwy 74

**3 166.5mi, 7:45hr**
Keep ahead at Fobes Trail junction. 0.6mi descent SW is a small unreliable spring

**4 169.2mi, 9:20hr**
Just before the trail skirts R around Apache Peak a small trail R descends 0.5mi NE to Apache Peak Spring

**5 177.3mi, 12:45hr**
Tahquitz Crk: if dry, water may be found downstream descending via Tahquitz Valley Trail, then turn L to return to PCT at Saddle Junction via Caramba Trail

Even though hot, dry desert conditions may have preceded, hazards such as snow, ice and rockslides can still present a challenge crossing San Jacinto. The trail climbs steeply around Spitler and Apache Peaks, then follows an exposed path under the granite buttresses of Antsell Rock. Ice here may require the use of an axe and crampons. The steep slopes beyond are prone to rockslides.

## Stage 7

### Highway 74 to Saddle Junction

| | |
|---|---|
| Start | Highway 74 |
| Finish | Saddle Junction |
| Distance | 27.5 miles |
| Total ascent | 6791ft |
| Total descent | 3586ft |
| Duration | 14:15hr |

Stages 7 and 8 present the first significant challenge to hikers in early season or a high snow year. The route across Mount San Jacinto climbs to almost 9000ft and follows ridgelines and exposed slopes. If significant snow remains, hikers not confident on winter mountain terrain would be well advised to detour by road from Hwy 74 to Idyllwild then rejoin the PCT by Black Mountain Road. There is no water on the main ridges so side trails down to nearby springs must be used.

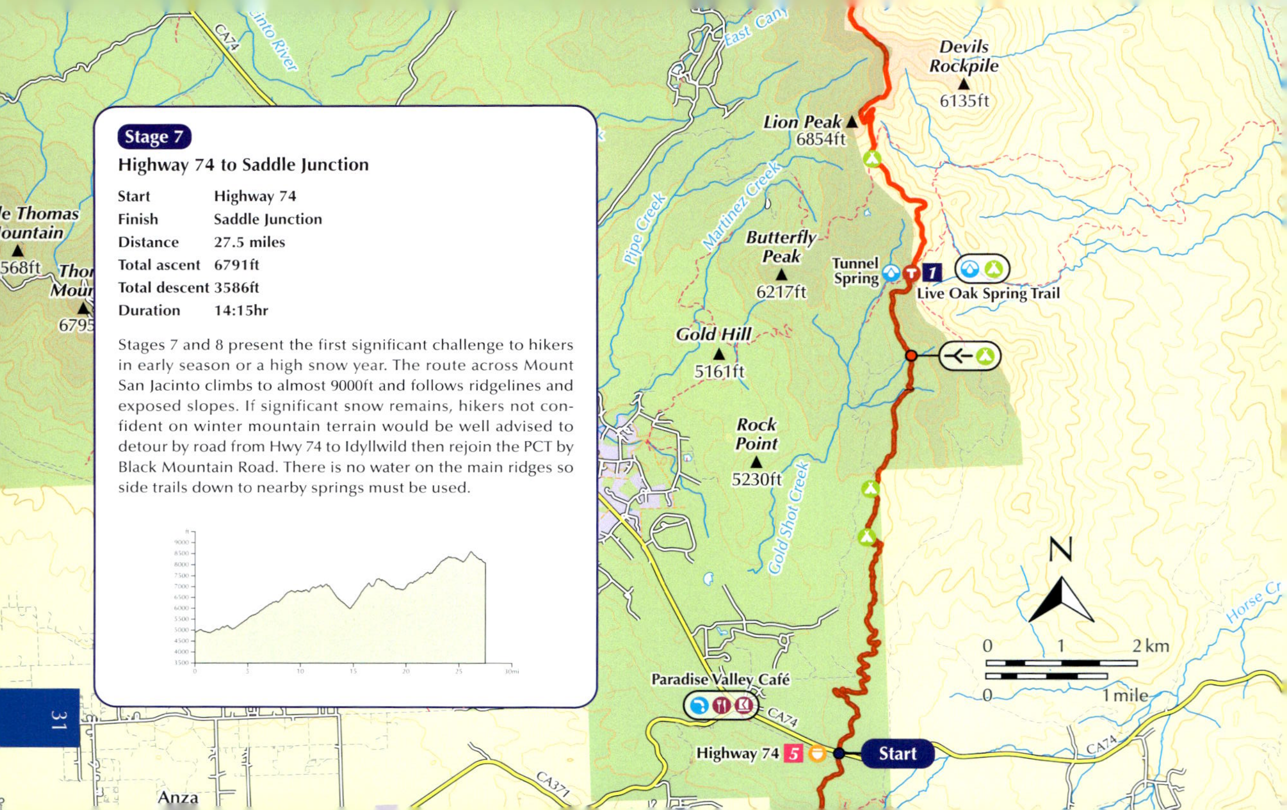

## Stage 8 route waypoints

**1 181.2mi, 1:00hr**
Bear L at Wellman Divide Trail unless detouring to summit San Jacinto

**2 183.5mi, 2:20hr**
Cross into State Park at designated Strawberry Junction Campground, then keep R at Deer Springs Trail (S)

**3 185.6mi, 3:30hr**
Cross head of North Fork San Jacinto River (last water for 22mi) then along Fuller Ridge Trail, keeping L at Deer Springs Trail (N)

**4 190.5mi, 6:10hr**
Pass through Fuller Ridge Trailhead and campground then cross Black Mountain Road commencing steep descent

**5 192.6mi, 7:25hr**
Cross switchback on dirt road

**6 205.7mi, 13:55hr**
Water tap/faucet at base of climb, then turn L on Falls Creek Road

**7 207.1mi, 14:40hr**
Cross Snow Creek Rd onto trail heading N. Indistinct at times cross several dirt roads and washes heading for Hwy I10

**8 209.5mi, 15:50hr**
Reach underpass under Hwy I10 (a popular trail magic cache). Trail continues N across Tamarack Road and through residential area (Cabazon PO 4.5mi W, larger town of Banning 10mi W)

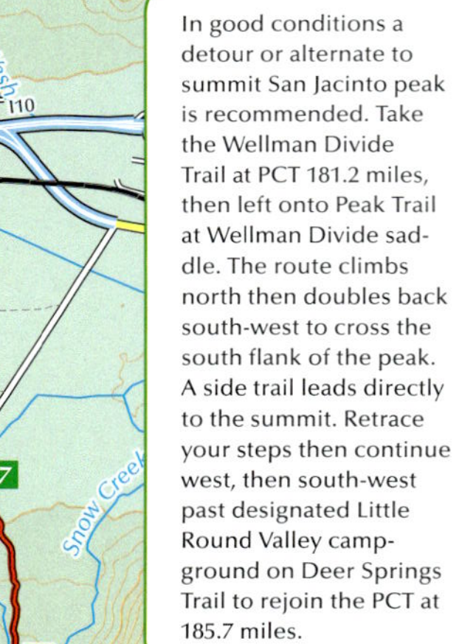


In good conditions a detour or alternate to summit San Jacinto peak is recommended. Take the Wellman Divide Trail at PCT 181.2 miles, then left onto Peak Trail at Wellman Divide saddle. The route climbs north then doubles back south-west to cross the south flank of the peak. A side trail leads directly to the summit. Retrace your steps then continue west, then south-west past designated Little Round Valley campground on Deer Springs Trail to rejoin the PCT at 185.7 miles.

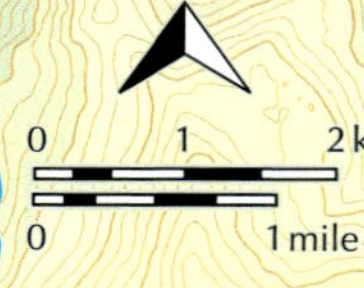

## Stage 7 route waypoints – continued

**6 178.0mi, 13:25hr**
Keep R at Tahquitz Peak Trail (0.3mi summit detour is recommended)

**7 179.4mi, 14:15hr**
Reach Saddle Junction. Devils Slide Trail descends 2.5mi W to Humber Park Trailhead, then 2.6mi by road to Idyllwild

## Stage 8

### Saddle Junction to San Gorgonio Pass

| | |
|---|---|
| **Start** | Saddle Junction |
| **Finish** | San Gorgonio Pass |
| **Distance** | 30.1 miles |
| **Total ascent** | 2431ft |
| **Total descent** | 9206ft |
| **Duration** | 15:50hr |

Navigating the trail as it skirts below the peak of San Jacinto and out onto the Fuller Ridge can be extremely challenging if there is snowpack. In these conditions allow extra time. Other than designated campgrounds, camping is prohibited inside the State Park, from 183.4 miles to 188.7 miles. Water is scarce for 22 miles from North Fork San Jacinto River to Snow Canyon in the valley.

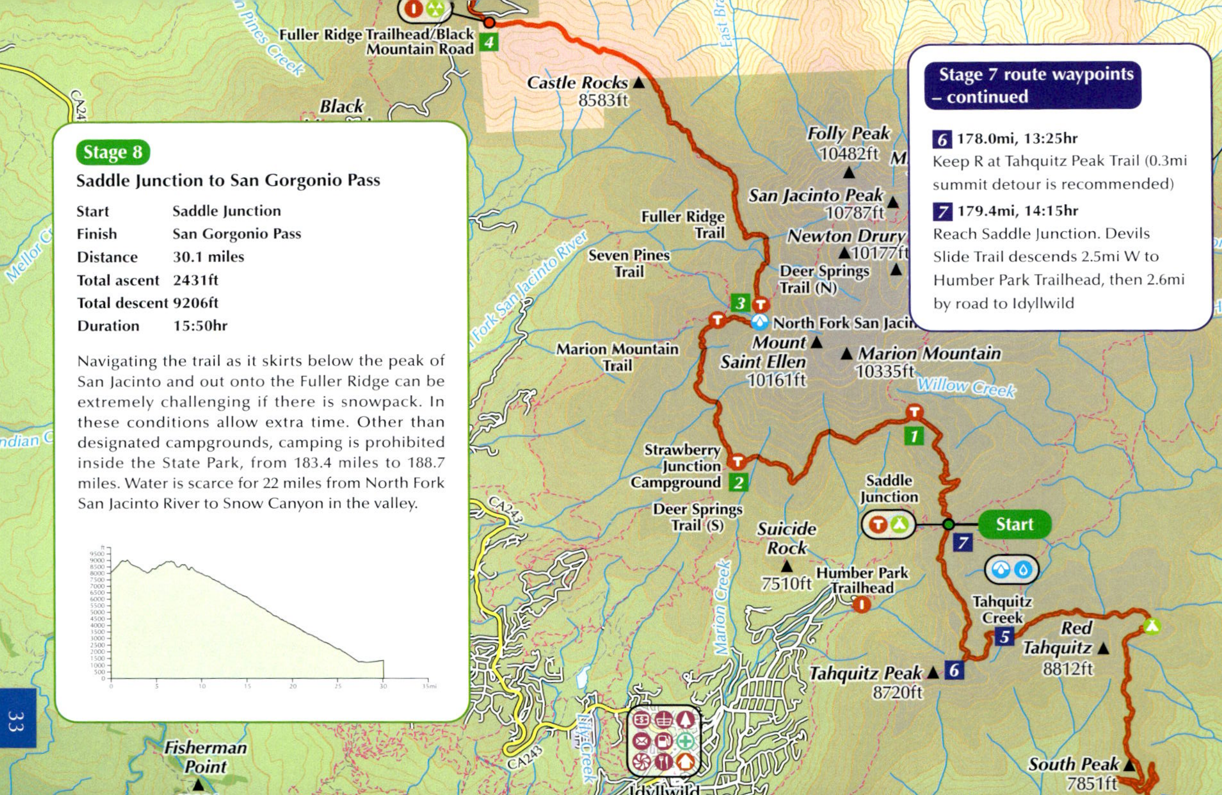

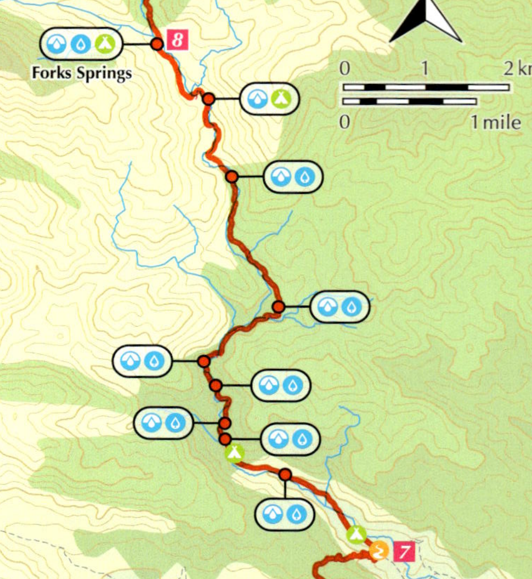


## Stage 9 route waypoints – continued

**5 220.3mi, 5:25hr**
Cross Whitewater River, usually a series of manageable channels

**6 221.7mi, 6:05hr**
Cross West Fork Mission Crk and dirt road, E through narrow canyon

**7 225.7mi, 8:00hr**
Abandoned East Fork Mission Creek Rd. Continue NW to follow Mission Crk upstream crossing 20–30 times depending on flow and erosion

**8 232.1mi, 11:00hr**
Forks Springs, in a dry year likely last water

**9 239.9mi, 14:25hr**
Pass sign for Mission Springs Campground (spring-fed trough usually running) then cross several dirt roads

**10 246.4mi, 17:25hr**
Cross dirt road at Coon Creek Campground

**11 250.0mi, 18:55hr**
Cross Rainbow Lane and keep ahead

**12 252.1mi 20:00hr**
Dirt road just E of Hwy 38 and Onyx Summit. Trail continues ahead alongside then crossing forest road 1N01

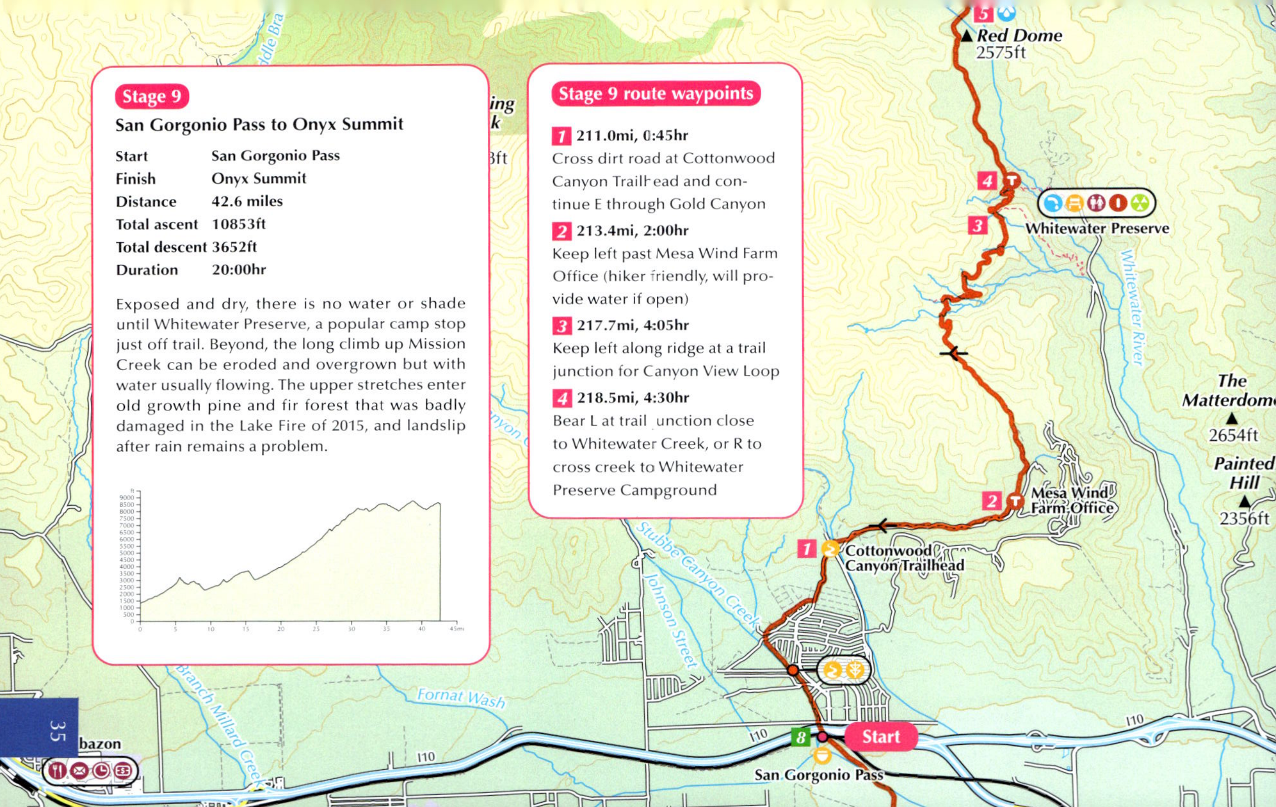


## Stage 9

### San Gorgonio Pass to Onyx Summit

| | |
|---|---|
| **Start** | San Gorgonio Pass |
| **Finish** | Onyx Summit |
| **Distance** | 42.6 miles |
| **Total ascent** | 10853ft |
| **Total descent** | 3652ft |
| **Duration** | 20:00hr |

Exposed and dry, there is no water or shade until Whitewater Preserve, a popular camp stop just off trail. Beyond, the long climb up Mission Creek can be eroded and overgrown but with water usually flowing. The upper stretches enter old growth pine and fir forest that was badly damaged in the Lake Fire of 2015, and landslip after rain remains a problem.

### Stage 9 route waypoints

**1 211.0mi, 0:45hr**
Cross dirt road at Cottonwood Canyon Trailhead and continue E through Gold Canyon

**2 213.4mi, 2:00hr**
Keep left past Mesa Wind Farm Office (hiker friendly, will provide water if open)

**3 217.7mi, 4:05hr**
Keep left along ridge at a trail junction for Canyon View Loop

**4 218.5mi, 4:30hr**
Bear L at trail junction close to Whitewater Creek, or R to cross creek to Whitewater Preserve Campground

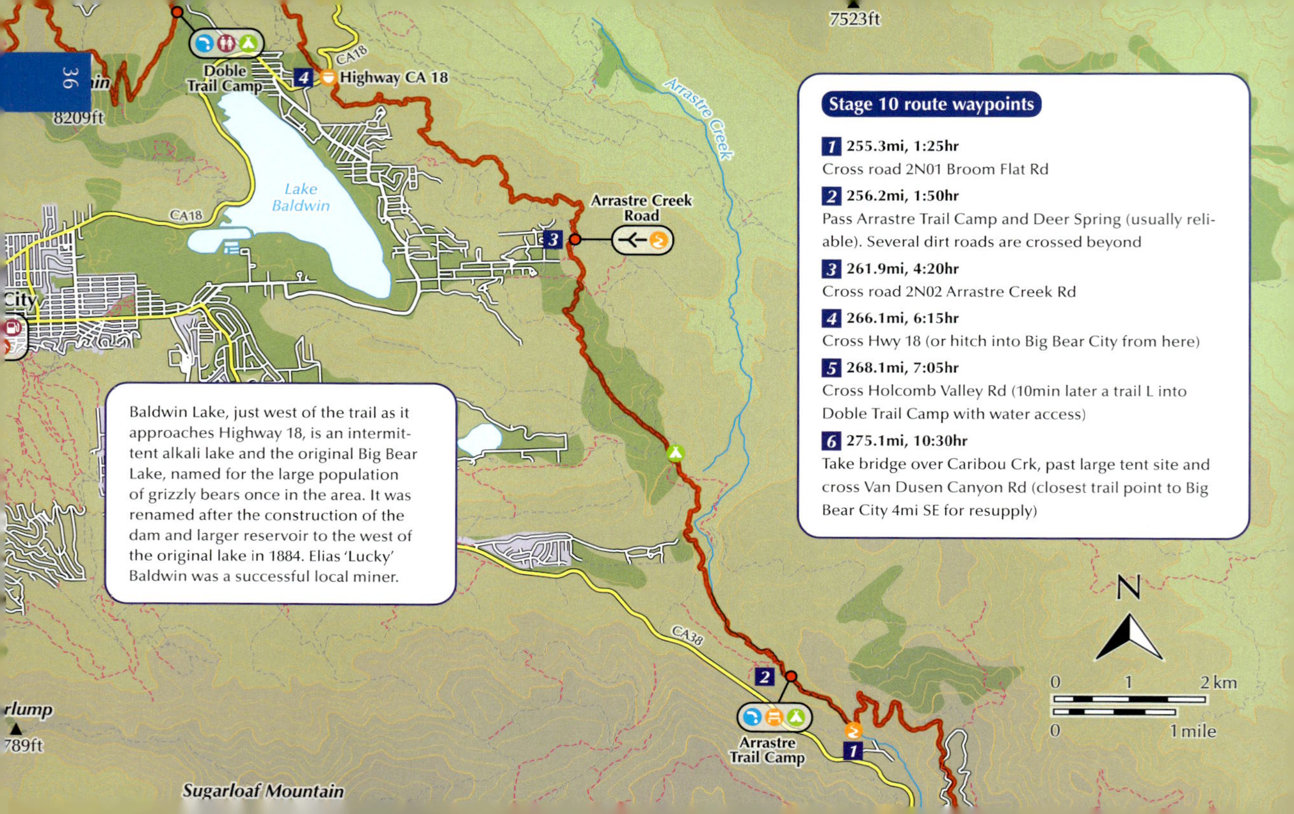

## Stage 10 route waypoints

**1 255.3mi, 1:25hr**
Cross road 2N01 Broom Flat Rd

**2 256.2mi, 1:50hr**
Pass Arrastre Trail Camp and Deer Spring (usually reliable). Several dirt roads are crossed beyond

**3 261.9mi, 4:20hr**
Cross road 2N02 Arrastre Creek Rd

**4 266.1mi, 6:15hr**
Cross Hwy 18 (or hitch into Big Bear City from here)

**5 268.1mi, 7:05hr**
Cross Holcomb Valley Rd (10min later a trail L into Doble Trail Camp with water access)

**6 275.1mi, 10:30hr**
Take bridge over Caribou Crk, past large tent site and cross Van Dusen Canyon Rd (closest trail point to Big Bear City 4mi SE for resupply)

Baldwin Lake, just west of the trail as it approaches Highway 18, is an intermittent alkali lake and the original Big Bear Lake, named for the large population of grizzly bears once in the area. It was renamed after the construction of the dam and larger reservoir to the west of the original lake in 1884. Elias 'Lucky' Baldwin was a successful local miner.

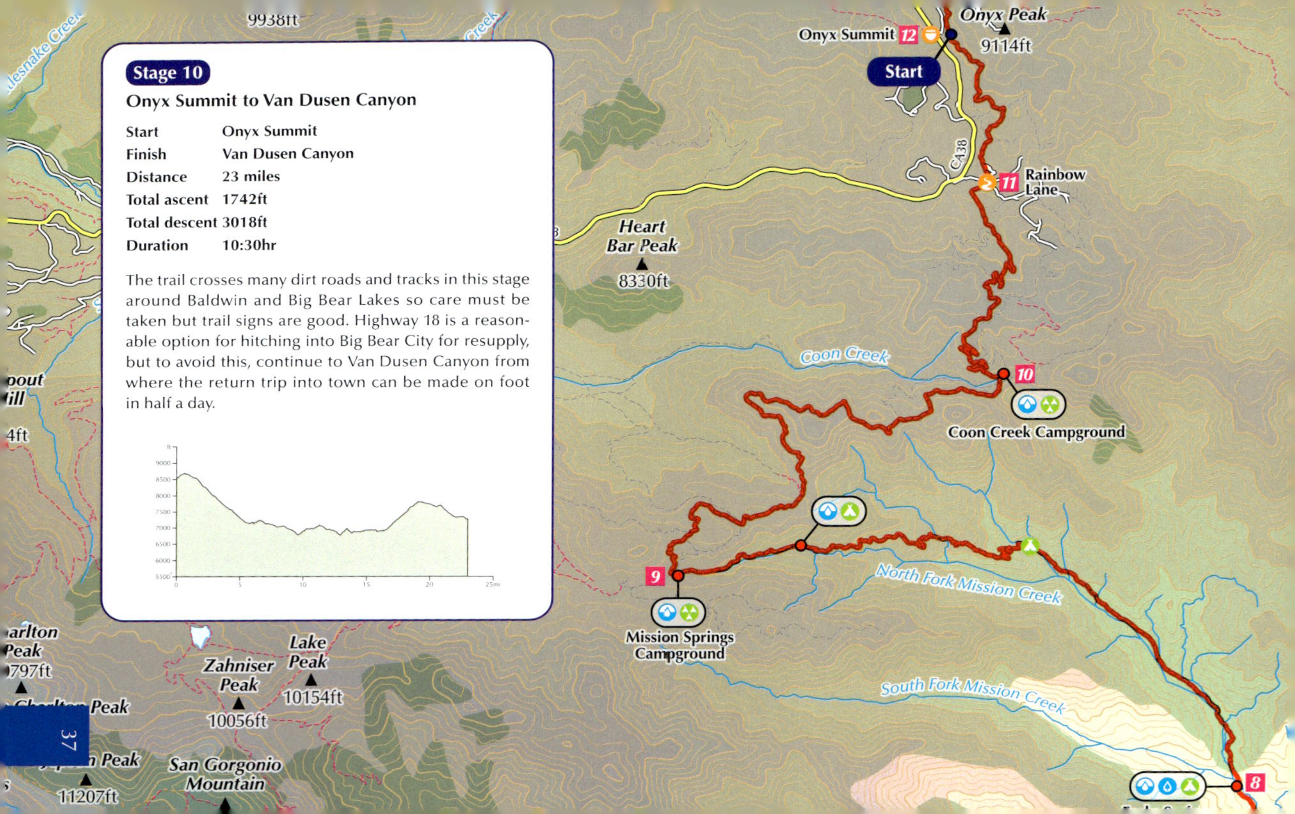

**Stage 10**

## Onyx Summit to Van Dusen Canyon

| | |
|---|---|
| Start | Onyx Summit |
| Finish | Van Dusen Canyon |
| Distance | 23 miles |
| Total ascent | 1742ft |
| Total descent | 3018ft |
| Duration | 10:30hr |

The trail crosses many dirt roads and tracks in this stage around Baldwin and Big Bear Lakes so care must be taken but trail signs are good. Highway 18 is a reasonable option for hitching into Big Bear City for resupply, but to avoid this, continue to Van Dusen Canyon from where the return trip into town can be made on foot in half a day.

N
0
1
2 km
0
1 mile
Van Dusen Canyon Road
6
Start
Caribou Creek
Bertha Peak
8199ft
1
Polique Canyon Road 2N09
Gold Mountain
8209ft
5
Doble Trail Camp
4
Highway CA 18
CA18
Arrastre Creek
Lake Baldwin
CA18
Arrastre Creek Road
3
Big Bear City
CA38
CA18
CA38
Lake
Big Bear Lake
CA18
Snow

# SECTION 2 – VAN DUSEN CANYON TO AGUA DULCE

| | Stage | Distance (miles) | Total ascent (feet) | Total descent (feet) | Average duration (hr:min) | Page |
|---|---|---|---|---|---|---|
| 11 | Van Dusen Canyon – Highway 173 | 39.2 | 3432 | 7503 | 14:30 | 45 |
| 12 | Hwy 173 – Hwy 138 | 14.8 | 1266 | 974 | 6:00 | 46 |
| 13 | Hwy 138 – Cajon Pass | 12.9 | 1302 | 1690 | 5:40 | 49 |
| 14 | Cajon Pass – Hwy 2 Inspiration Point | 27.4 | 6263 | 1916 | 14:15 | 51 |
| 15 | Hwy 2 Inspiration Point – Hwy 2 Islip Saddle | 16.6 | 3714 | 4413 | 8:40 | 53 |
| 16 | Hwy 2 Islip Saddle – Mill Crk Summit | 32.6 | 5525 | 7320 | 14:40 | 55 |
| 17 | Mill Crk Summit – North Fork Ranger Station | 17.5 | 2867 | 3609 | 7:30 | 57 |
| 18 | North Fork Ranger Station – Agua Dulce | 18.4 | 1965 | 3612 | 8:00 | 56 |
| **Totals** | | **179.4** | **26,334** | **31,037** | **79:15** | |

## *WHAT TO EXPECT*

Now heading west, the PCT follows the ridges of the San Bernardino Mountains, among Pinyon Pine, the nuts of which are an indigenous diet staple. Tree cover remains sparse, and the influence of the Mojave can be seen among flora and fauna. Water can be scarce here despite the initial proximity of creeks and lakes which can either dry out or remain frustratingly out of reach.

For many Deep Creek Hot Springs will be a highlight at the end of a long, exposed stretch. Beyond you cross the San Andreas Fault zone and a keen geologist will spot where the rock has been transported out of place. Cajon Pass may not be attractive, but it is useful. The infamous McDonalds will be welcome as much for its air-conditioning as its food, and the small businesses a little further up the road are equally valuable, for beyond is a long, dry and exposed climb.

Anyone with connections to the worldwide scouting movement will appreciate the ascent of Mount Baden-Powell, named in honor of the movement's founder. From the wind-swept summit, at 9399ft, it is possible to see as far as the Sierra Nevada on a clear day. In early season most years will see the hiker tackling snow on

Cajon summit, close to Wrightwood (Stage 14)

the back of the mountain in descent. In a higher snow year the switchbacks that climb to the summit spur could be buried and will require care, and possibly traction.

Beyond Mount Baden-Powell water sources dry up again quickly and, unless the situation changes, a detour along the highway is required around a long-term closure that protects the mountain yellow-legged frog.

It is worth taking your time through Vasquez Rocks. The area is most famed for its use in numerous films, from westerns to *Star Trek*, but should be enjoyed in its own right for the fascinating and dramatic rock formations, cool canyons and, until mid-season, welcome water sources.

The ideal hiking season doesn't differ significantly for day-, section- or thru-hikes. The thru-hikers will likely be here first and in a wetter year those with more choice might wait a little into May and June. Beyond June, the lower elevations will be getting quite hot. Check local water sources carefully here before setting out. They may differ greatly between years.

There are fewer resupply options close to trail in this section. Most will descend from the trail into Wrightwood for resupply in the middle of the section. It is a popular mountain town, extremely welcoming to hikers and supplying most things you might need. At the end of the section, Agua Dulce used to be a key resupply stop with a wonderful trail angel house supporting hikers by taking packages, and even providing transport to REI. Since that ceased operation, Acton has become an important resupply stop with two good independent markets, a growing network of trail angels and a campsite near the trail that will take packages.

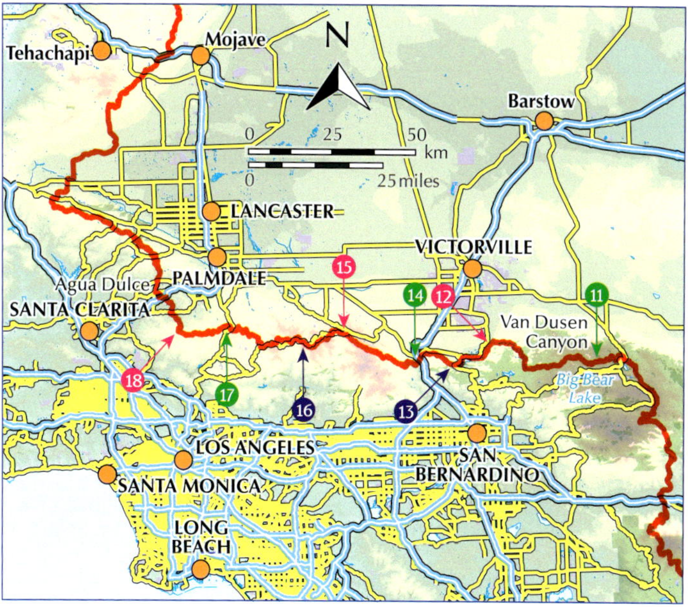

Tehachapi
Mojave
N
Barstow
0 25 50 km
0 25 miles
LANCASTER
VICTORVILLE
PALMDALE
15
Agua Dulce
14
12
11
SANTA CLARITA
Van Dusen Canyon
18
Big Bear Lake
17
16
13
LOS ANGELES
SAN BERNARDINO
SANTA MONICA
LONG BEACH

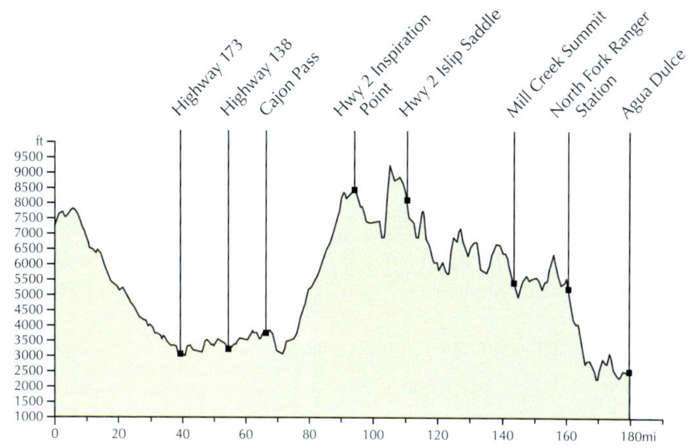
Highway 173
Highway 138
Cajon Pass
Hwy 2 Inspiration Point
Hwy 2 Islip Saddle
Mill Creek Summit
North Fork Ranger Station
Agua Dulce
ft
9500
9000
8500
8000
7500
7000
6500
6000
5500
5000
4500
4000
3500
3000
2500
2000
1500
1000
0
20
40
60
80
100
120
140
160
180mi

## RESUPPLY OPTIONS

| Stage | Trail mile | Place | Off trail (miles) | Description | Facilities |
|---|---|---|---|---|---|
| 11 | 278.6 | Fawnskin | 5.6 SW | Lakeside community with basic facilities | |
| 13 | 342 | Cajon Pass | 0.5 N | Highway intersection with friendly inn and McDonalds | |
| 14 | 363.4 | Wrightwood | 4 N | Popular town with PCT trail angel hub at hardware store | |
| 14 | 369.4 | Wrightwood | 5.5 E | Popular town with PCT trail angel hub at hardware store | |
| 18 | 444.2 | Acton LA RV Resort | 0.2 E | Campsite with showers, laundry, small store, accepts packages | |
| 18 | 444.2 | Acton | 5.9 E | Small town, good resupply, with two markets, popular 49er Saloon | |
| 18 | 454.5 | Agua Dulce | On trail | No longer a hostel here, hardware store, and fast food only | |

### PERMITS

No permits are required.

### MAIL DROP INFORMATION

Hold for 'Your Name'
Mountain Hardware
1390 Highway 2 PO Box 398
Wrightwood, California 92397
ETA: 'Your ETA'
They are open: 9am–5pm, seven days a week
Phone them on: (760) 249-3653
Visit them at: https://mtnhardware.com

'Your Name Here'
c/o LA RV Resort
7601 Soledad Canyon Road
Acton, CA 93510
Your ETA Here
They are open: 9am–5pm, seven days a week
Phone them on: (661) 268-1214
Visit them at: https://larvresort.com

*You may recognise Vasquez Rocks that have been used as a set for many famous movies (Stage 18)*

## POST OFFICE INFORMATION

'Your Name Here'
c\o General Delivery
Fawnskin, CA 92333
Located at: 39132 N Shore Drive
Phone them on: (909) 866-3245

'Your Name Here'
c\o General Delivery
Wrightwood, CA 92397
Located at: 1440 State Highway 2
Phone them on: (760) 249-8882

'Your Name Here'
c\o General Delivery
Acton, CA 93510
Located at: 3632 Smith Avenue
Phone them on: (661) 269-8618

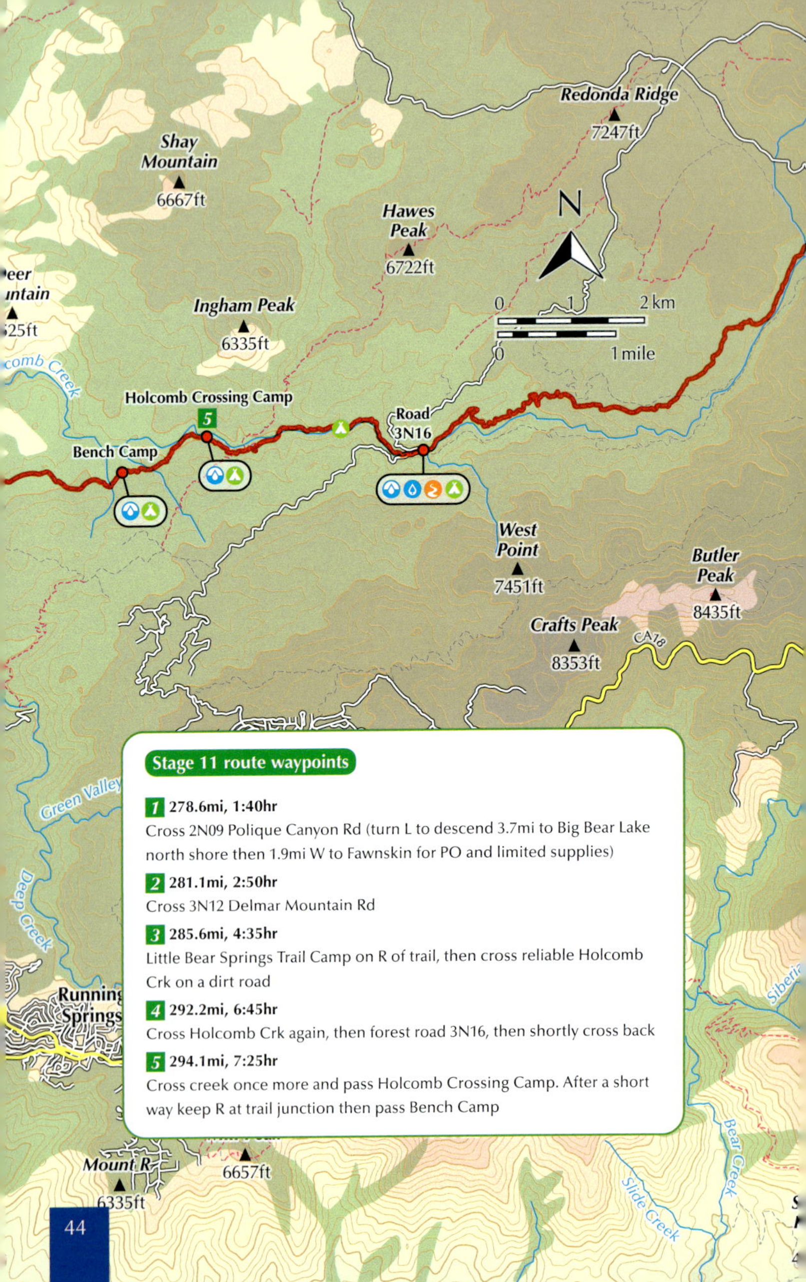


## Stage 11 route waypoints

**1 278.6mi, 1:40hr**
Cross 2N09 Polique Canyon Rd (turn L to descend 3.7mi to Big Bear Lake north shore then 1.9mi W to Fawnskin for PO and limited supplies)

**2 281.1mi, 2:50hr**
Cross 3N12 Delmar Mountain Rd

**3 285.6mi, 4:35hr**
Little Bear Springs Trail Camp on R of trail, then cross reliable Holcomb Crk on a dirt road

**4 292.2mi, 6:45hr**
Cross Holcomb Crk again, then forest road 3N16, then shortly cross back

**5 294.1mi, 7:25hr**
Cross creek once more and pass Holcomb Crossing Camp. After a short way keep R at trail junction then pass Bench Camp

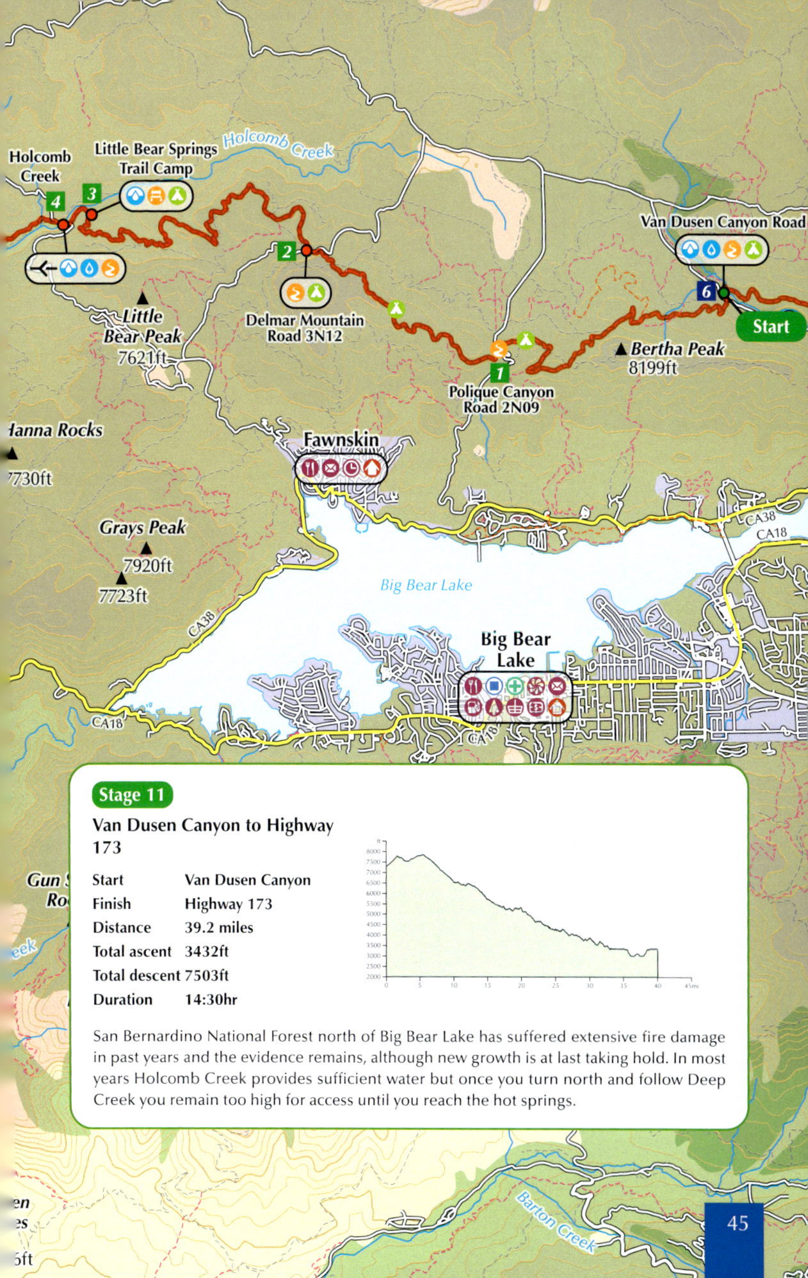


## Stage 11

### Van Dusen Canyon to Highway 173

| | |
|---|---|
| Start | Van Dusen Canyon |
| Finish | Highway 173 |
| Distance | 39.2 miles |
| Total ascent | 3432ft |
| Total descent | 7503ft |
| Duration | 14:30hr |

San Bernardino National Forest north of Big Bear Lake has suffered extensive fire damage in past years and the evidence remains, although new growth is at last taking hold. In most years Holcomb Creek provides sufficient water but once you turn north and follow Deep Creek you remain too high for access until you reach the hot springs.

## Stage 12

### Highway 173 to Highway 138

| | |
|---|---|
| **Start** | **Highway 173** |
| **Finish** | **Highway 138** |
| **Distance** | **14.8 miles** |
| **Total ascent** | **1266ft** |
| **Total descent** | **974ft** |
| **Duration** | **6:00hr** |

This short, undulating stage presents little challenge except perhaps remaining exposed and largely dry. Silverwood Lake presents a swimming opportunity, but check local signage for information on water quality which varies through the year.

The hot spring pools of Deep Creek look inviting and have a long history of skinny-dipping but be aware that they also contain a rare and sometimes fatal disease called primary amebic meningoencephalitis. The disease originates in contaminated soil and thrives in the warm water. It is advisable not to submerse your head. Human and organic pollution are increasing in the drainage too. High fecal coliform counts are also found in the Hot Springs area, so filter water well before drinking.

## Stage 11 route waypoints – continued

**6** **298.5mi, 9:00hr**
Cross high above Deep Crk on steel bridge, then take trail R heading N

**7** **307.9mi, 12:20hr**
Deep Creek Hot Springs. Camping is officially not permitted within 1mi of pools, but the area is popular at weekends, and many do camp

**8** **310.0mi, 13:00hr**
Trail switches back and down to an arch bridge. Take this across Deep Creek then turn L along North bank

**9** **313.0mi, 14:00hr**
Mojave Forks Dam. Descend L to ford Deep Crk here. If impassable, cross the dam to Arrowhead Rd and walk the road to Hwy 173 Trailhead

**10** **0 314.3mi, 14:30hr**
Hwy 173 Trailhead car park (Joshua Inn 3.0mi N is hiker friendly)

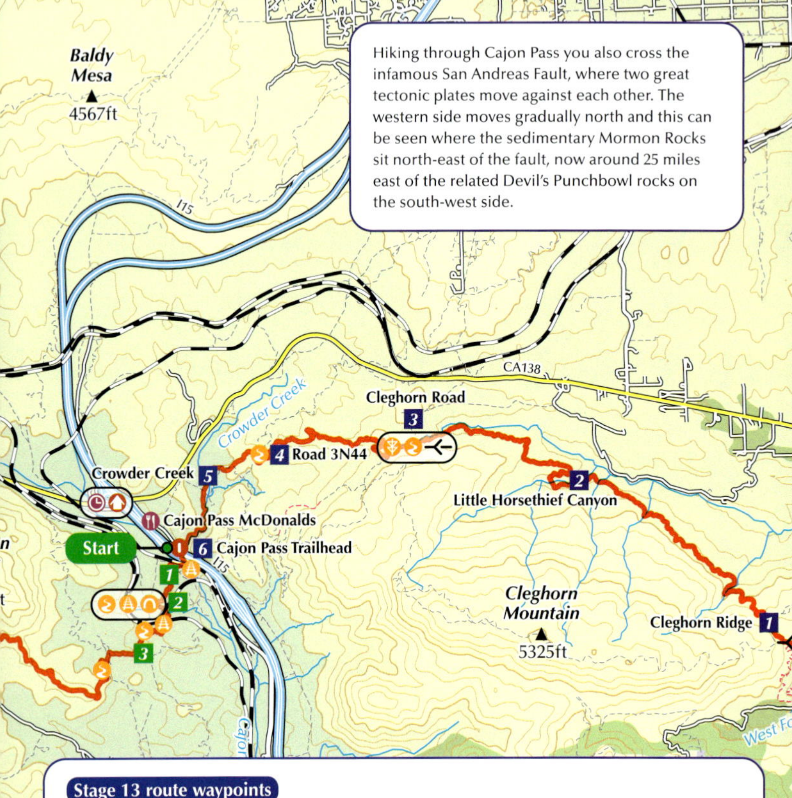


## Stage 13 route waypoints

**1 332.2mi, 1:40hr**
Turn R along a dirt road atop the scenic Cleghorn Ridge for a short way then trail resumes L

**2 335.6mi, 3:05hr**
Third of three small creek tributaries crossed in Little Horsethief Canyon may have a small flow in early season. Several tent sites nearby

**3 338.1mi, 4:10hr**
Cross Cleghorn Rd under powerlines

**4 340.4mi, 5:00hr**
Cross Forest Rd 3N44 followed by two further dirt tracks

**5 341.4mi, 5:25hr**
Cross and then parallel Crowder Crk (last water for 28.9mi)

**6 342.0mi, 5:40hr**
Interstate 15 just S of Cajon Pass (0.5mi N fast food, a convenience store and accommodation)

## Stage 12 route waypoints

**1 317.6mi, 1:30hr**
Turn off for Mojave River Forks Campground (tent sites and showers for a fee). Short way beyond is Grass Valley Crk (usually reliable into the summer)

**2 323.8mi, 3:50hr**
After crossing several dirt roads, a paved road leads to Hwy 173 and crossing of Cedar Springs Dam slipway

**3 328.7mi, 5:30mi**
A two-lane bike track leads 0.2mi E to Cleghorn picnic area (piped water, toilets, picnic benches)

**4 329.1mi, 6:00hr**
Exit Silverwood Lake Recreation Area entrance and cross the road passing under Hwy 138

## Stage 13

### Highway 138 to Cajon Pass

| | |
|---|---|
| Start | Highway 138 |
| Finish | Cajon Pass |
| Distance | 12.9 miles |
| Total ascent | 1302ft |
| Total descent | 1690ft |
| Duration | 5:40hr |



Another dry, exposed stage, the trail intersects numerous unmapped dirt tracks and trails, but signage is present to keep you on track.

**Stage 14 route waypoints – continued**

**5 351.8mi, 5:10hr**
Cross Sharpless Ranch Rd 3N29

**6 356.2mi, 7:40hr**
Cross Sheep Creek Truck Trail 3N31

**7 363.4mi, 12:00hr**
Acorn Trail junction (descend to Wrightwood for resupply 4mi N)

**8 364.4mi, 12:35hr**
Guffy Campground (unreliable spring 0.1mi N down Flume Canyon)

**9 367.3mi, 13:30hr**
Blue Ridge Campground

**10 0 369.4mi, 14:15hr**
Angeles Crest Hwy 2, Inspiration Point Trailhead (Wrightwood 5.5mi E)

From Guffy Campground to Inspiration Point the trail criss-crosses East Blue Ridge Road. If snow remains between Guffy and Blue Ridge camps it can be advantageous to keep to the clearer road on the south side of the ridge. As you descend from Blue Ridge's high point you pass an enclosed artificial lake, one of two used for snow-making in the Mountain High ski area.

## Stage 14

### Cajon Pass to Highway 2 Inspiration Point

| | |
|---|---|
| Start | Cajon Pass |
| Finish | Highway 2 Inspiration Point |
| Distance | 27.4 miles |
| Total ascent | 6263ft |
| Total descent | 1916ft |
| Duration | 14:15hr |

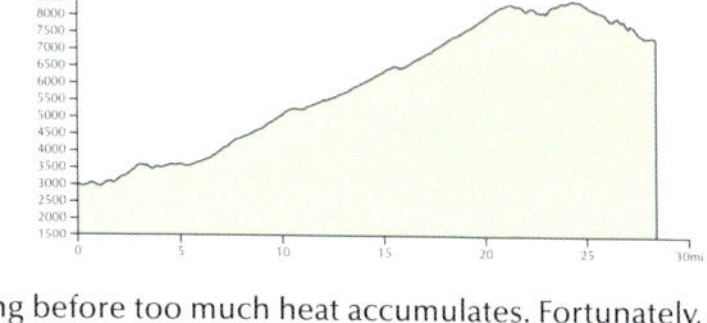


This long, dry climb is best tackled early morning before too much heat accumulates. Fortunately, at the foot of the climb, Swarthout Canyon Road offers some good tent sites along with a fairly reliable water cache, making this easier.

## Stage 14 route waypoints

**1 342.1mi, 0:05**

From Sante Fe and Salt Lake Trail monument, trail descends under I-15 freeway and rail tracks before turning W on a dirt track where signage resumes

**2 342.9mi, 0:35hr**

Cross a dirt road then descend under railway culvert at Sullivan's Curve, a historical railway grade, then turn R uphill to cross further rail track

**3 344.3mi, 1:15hr**

Cross a dirt road, then soon another

**4 347.3mi, 2:25hr**

Reach Swarthout Canyon Rd, numerous tent sites and possible water cache. Avoid Biker Springs, 10min further on – believed polluted

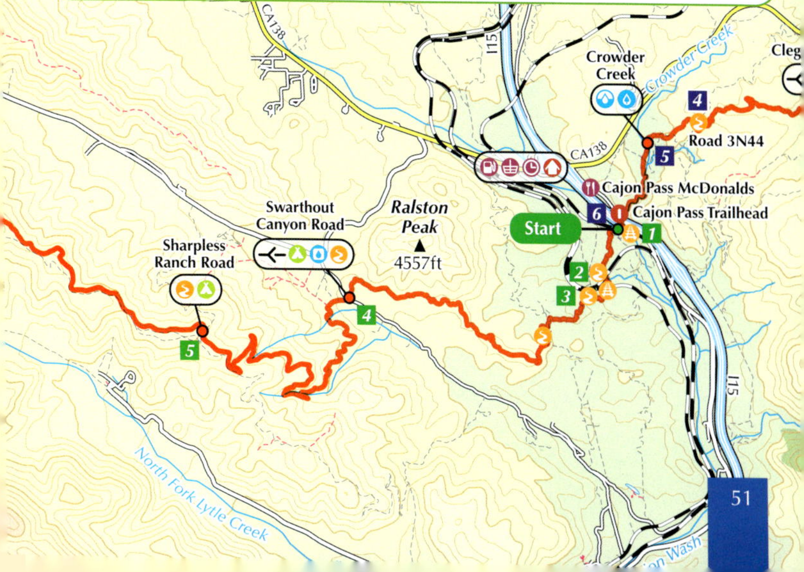

CA138
I15
Crowder Creek
Crowder Creek
Cleg
4
Road 3N44
5
CA138
Cajon Pass McDonalds
6
Cajon Pass Trailhead
Start
1
2
3
Swarthout Canyon Road
Ralston Peak
4557ft
Sharpless Ranch Road
4
5
I15
North Fork Lytle Creek
on Wash

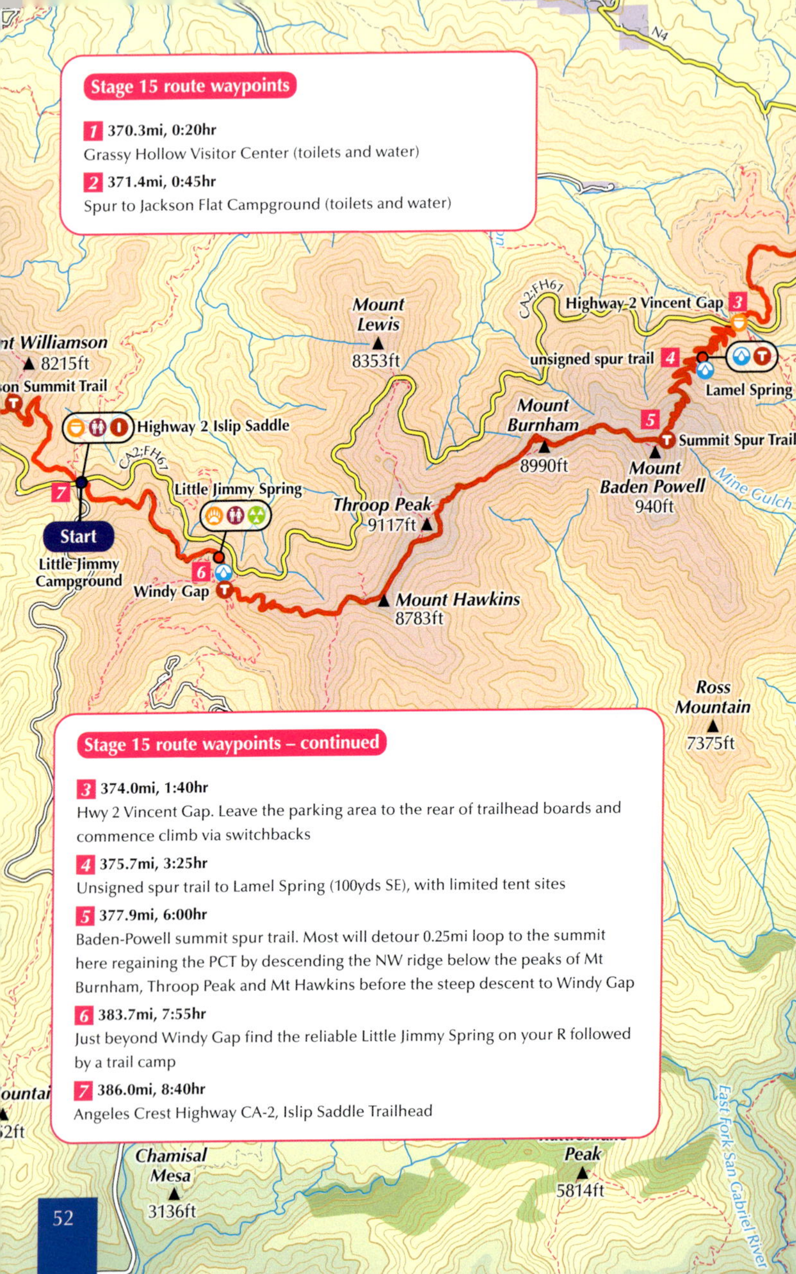


## Stage 15 route waypoints

**1** **370.3mi, 0:20hr**
Grassy Hollow Visitor Center (toilets and water)

**2** **371.4mi, 0:45hr**
Spur to Jackson Flat Campground (toilets and water)

## Stage 15 route waypoints – continued

**3** **374.0mi, 1:40hr**
Hwy 2 Vincent Gap. Leave the parking area to the rear of trailhead boards and commence climb via switchbacks

**4** **375.7mi, 3:25hr**
Unsigned spur trail to Lamel Spring (100yds SE), with limited tent sites

**5** **377.9mi, 6:00hr**
Baden-Powell summit spur trail. Most will detour 0.25mi loop to the summit here regaining the PCT by descending the NW ridge below the peaks of Mt Burnham, Throop Peak and Mt Hawkins before the steep descent to Windy Gap

**6** **383.7mi, 7:55hr**
Just beyond Windy Gap find the reliable Little Jimmy Spring on your R followed by a trail camp

**7** **386.0mi, 8:40hr**
Angeles Crest Highway CA-2, Islip Saddle Trailhead

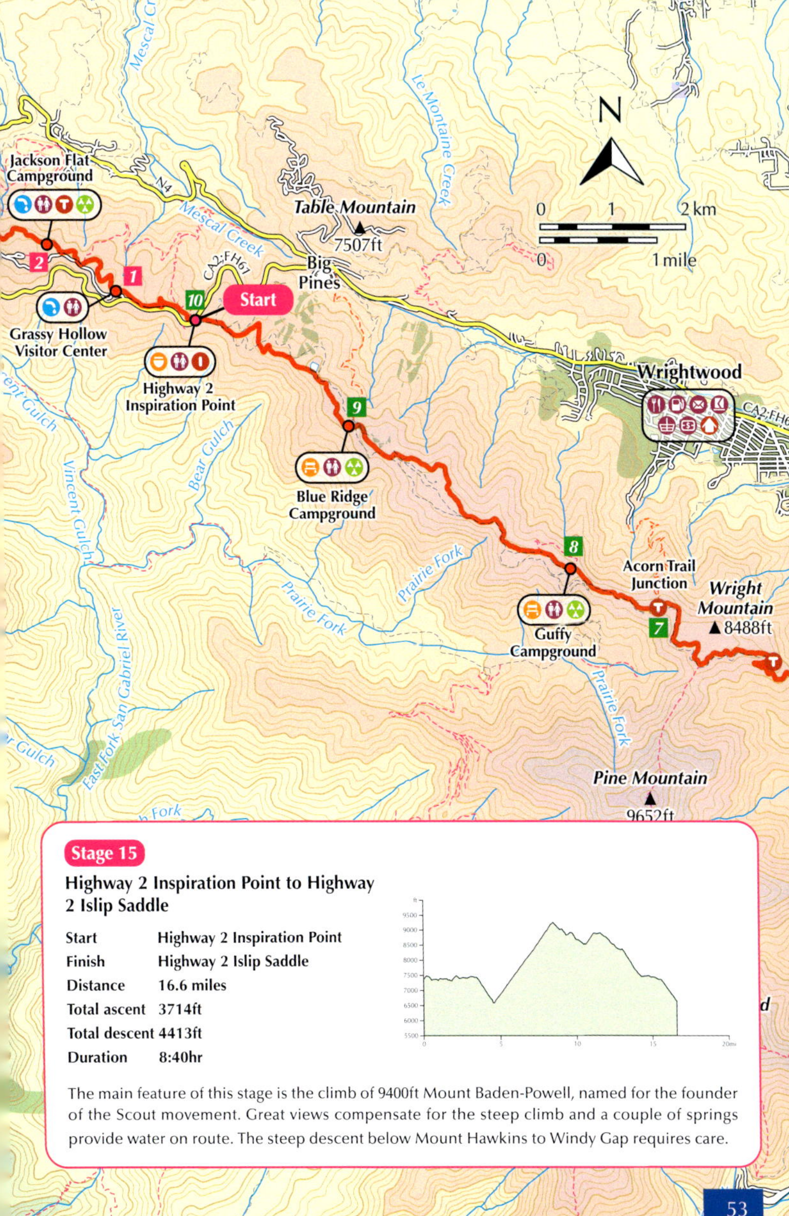


## Stage 15

### Highway 2 Inspiration Point to Highway 2 Islip Saddle

| | |
|---|---|
| Start | Highway 2 Inspiration Point |
| Finish | Highway 2 Islip Saddle |
| Distance | 16.6 miles |
| Total ascent | 3714ft |
| Total descent | 4413ft |
| Duration | 8:40hr |



The main feature of this stage is the climb of 9400ft Mount Baden-Powell, named for the founder of the Scout movement. Great views compensate for the steep climb and a couple of springs provide water on route. The steep descent below Mount Hawkins to Windy Gap requires care.

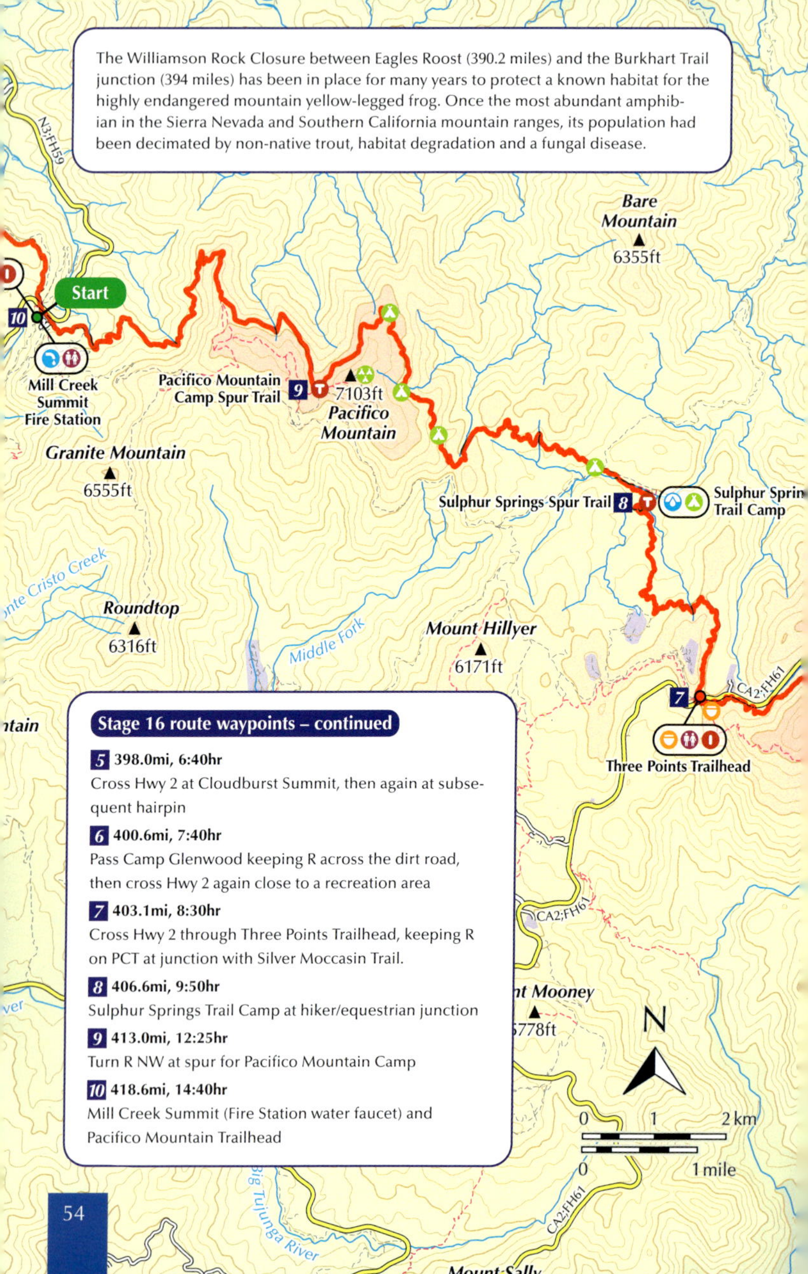


The Williamson Rock Closure between Eagles Roost (390.2 miles) and the Burkhart Trail junction (394 miles) has been in place for many years to protect a known habitat for the highly endangered mountain yellow-legged frog. Once the most abundant amphibian in the Sierra Nevada and Southern California mountain ranges, its population had been decimated by non-native trout, habitat degradation and a fungal disease.

## Stage 16 route waypoints – continued

**5 398.0mi, 6:40hr**
Cross Hwy 2 at Cloudburst Summit, then again at subsequent hairpin

**6 400.6mi, 7:40hr**
Pass Camp Glenwood keeping R across the dirt road, then cross Hwy 2 again close to a recreation area

**7 403.1mi, 8:30hr**
Cross Hwy 2 through Three Points Trailhead, keeping R on PCT at junction with Silver Moccasin Trail.

**8 406.6mi, 9:50hr**
Sulphur Springs Trail Camp at hiker/equestrian junction

**9 413.0mi, 12:25hr**
Turn R NW at spur for Pacifico Mountain Camp

**10 418.6mi, 14:40hr**
Mill Creek Summit (Fire Station water faucet) and Pacifico Mountain Trailhead

## Stage 16

### Highway 2 Islip Saddle to Mill Creek Summit

| | |
|---|---|
| Start | Highway 2 Islip Saddle |
| Finish | Mill Creek Summit |
| Distance | 32.6 miles |
| Total ascent | 5525ft |
| Total descent | 7320ft |
| Duration | 14:40hr |

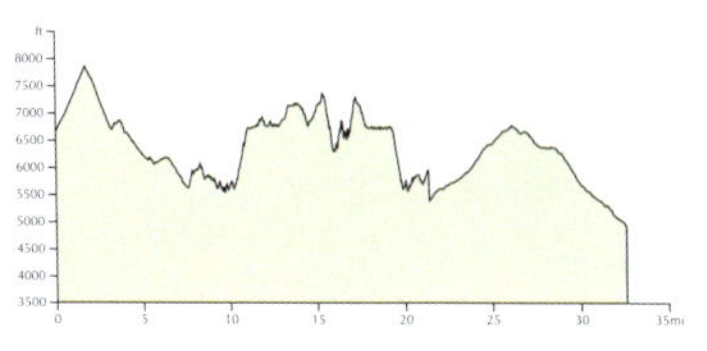


The stage criss-crosses Highway 2 and, unless reopened, also requires a 5.8 mile detour around the Williamson Rock Closure. There is substantial fire damage remaining, particularly on the detour along the Burkhart Trail. However, water sources are usually good here.

## Stage 16 route waypoints

The trail commences just W of parking area on Islip Saddle using the Mt Williamson Trail, keeping L at the summit trail junction.

**1 389.3mi, 2:05hr**

Cross Hwy 2 to the south side

**2 390.2mi, 2:35hr**

Eagles Roost Picnic Area. Trail commences NW of Hwy 2 but has been subject to long-term 'Williamson Rock Closure' to protect vulnerable habitat (check with PCTA for updates). Most detour 3.4mi SW along Hwy 2 (great care required) to Buckhorn Campground, then regain PCT via Burkhart Trail 2.4mi NE to Cooper Canyon

**3 394.0mi, 4:30hr**

Cross Little Rock Crk (reliable water) and head W (Burkhart Trail/PCT junction)

**4 395.2mi, 5:20hr**

Cooper Canyon Trail Camp, keep R heading NW at dirt road junction

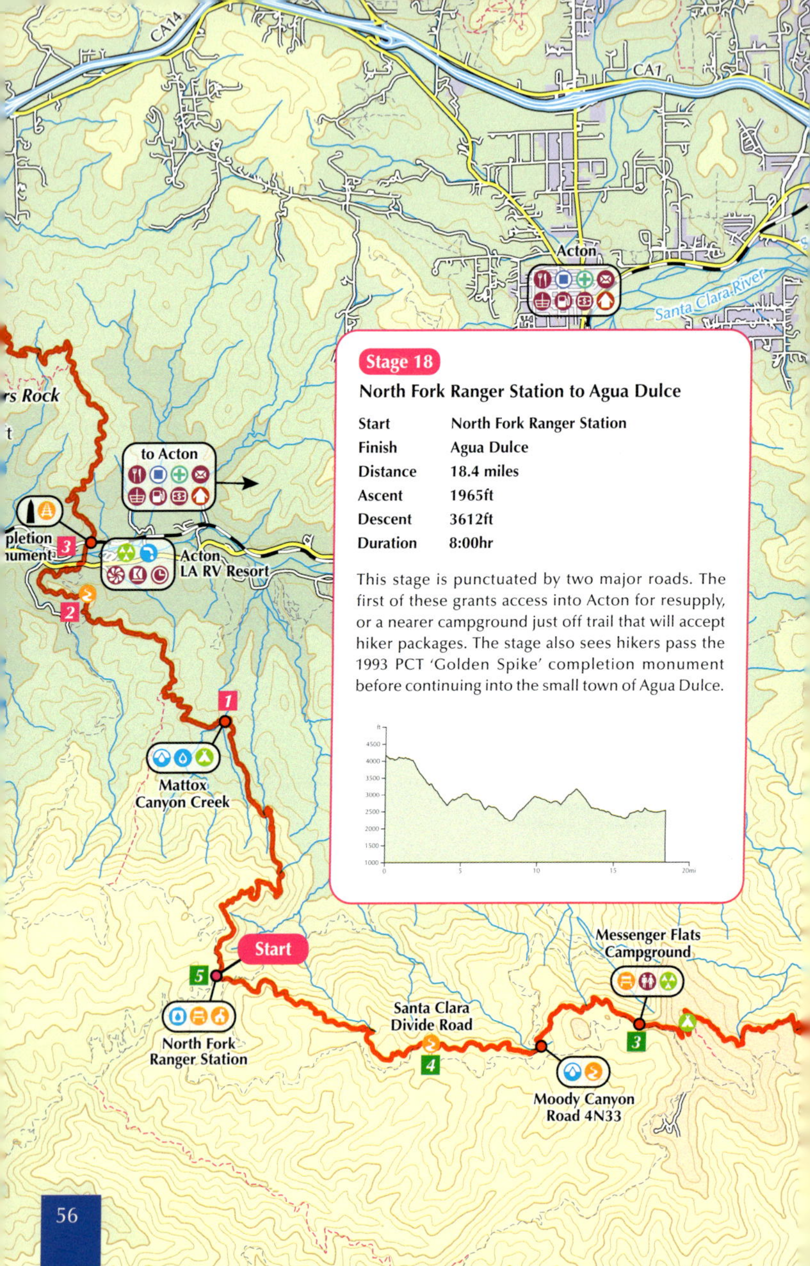


## Stage 18

### North Fork Ranger Station to Agua Dulce

| | |
|---|---|
| **Start** | North Fork Ranger Station |
| **Finish** | Agua Dulce |
| **Distance** | 18.4 miles |
| **Ascent** | 1965ft |
| **Descent** | 3612ft |
| **Duration** | 8:00hr |

This stage is punctuated by two major roads. The first of these grants access into Acton for resupply, or a nearer campground just off trail that will accept hiker packages. The stage also sees hikers pass the 1993 PCT 'Golden Spike' completion monument before continuing into the small town of Agua Dulce.

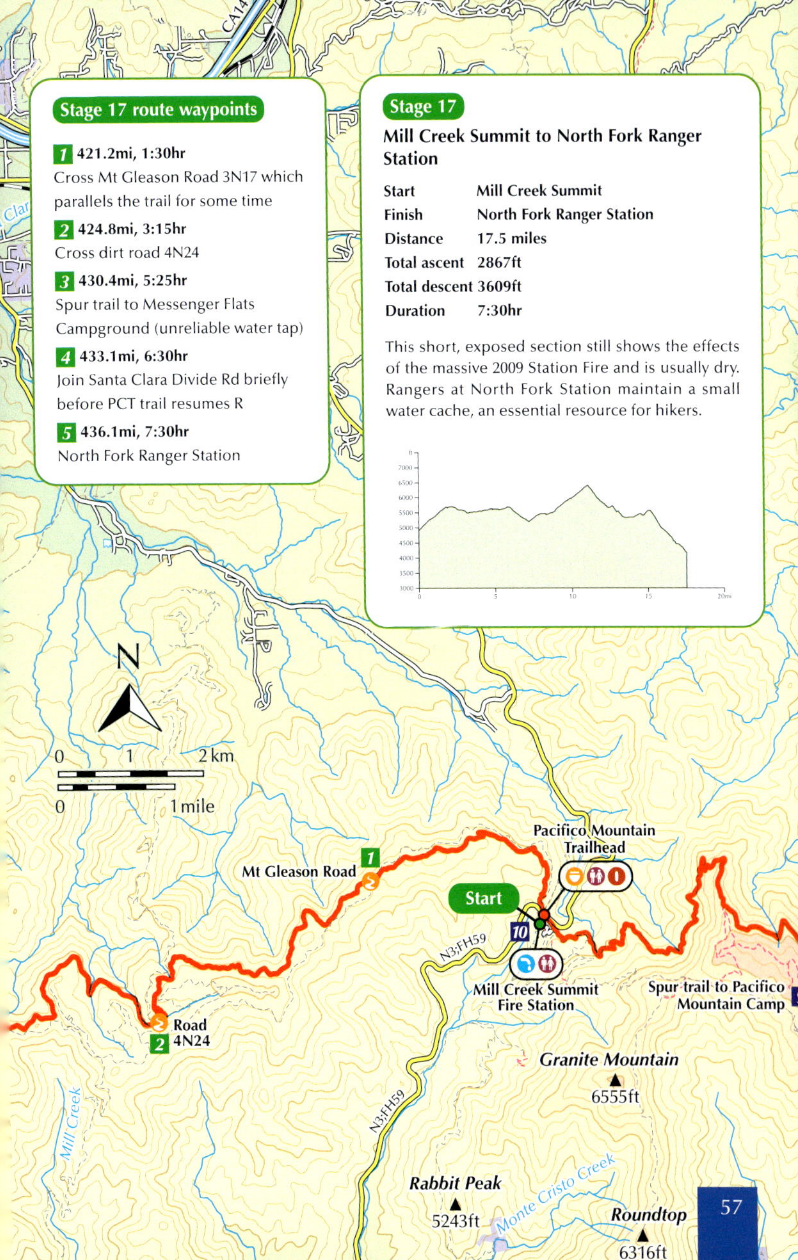


## Stage 17 route waypoints

**1 421.2mi, 1:30hr**
Cross Mt Gleason Road 3N17 which parallels the trail for some time

**2 424.8mi, 3:15hr**
Cross dirt road 4N24

**3 430.4mi, 5:25hr**
Spur trail to Messenger Flats Campground (unreliable water tap)

**4 433.1mi, 6:30hr**
Join Santa Clara Divide Rd briefly before PCT trail resumes R

**5 436.1mi, 7:30hr**
North Fork Ranger Station

## Stage 17

### Mill Creek Summit to North Fork Ranger Station

| | |
|---|---|
| **Start** | **Mill Creek Summit** |
| **Finish** | **North Fork Ranger Station** |
| **Distance** | **17.5 miles** |
| **Total ascent** | **2867ft** |
| **Total descent** | **3609ft** |
| **Duration** | **7:30hr** |

This short, exposed section still shows the effects of the massive 2009 Station Fire and is usually dry. Rangers at North Fork Station maintain a small water cache, an essential resource for hikers.

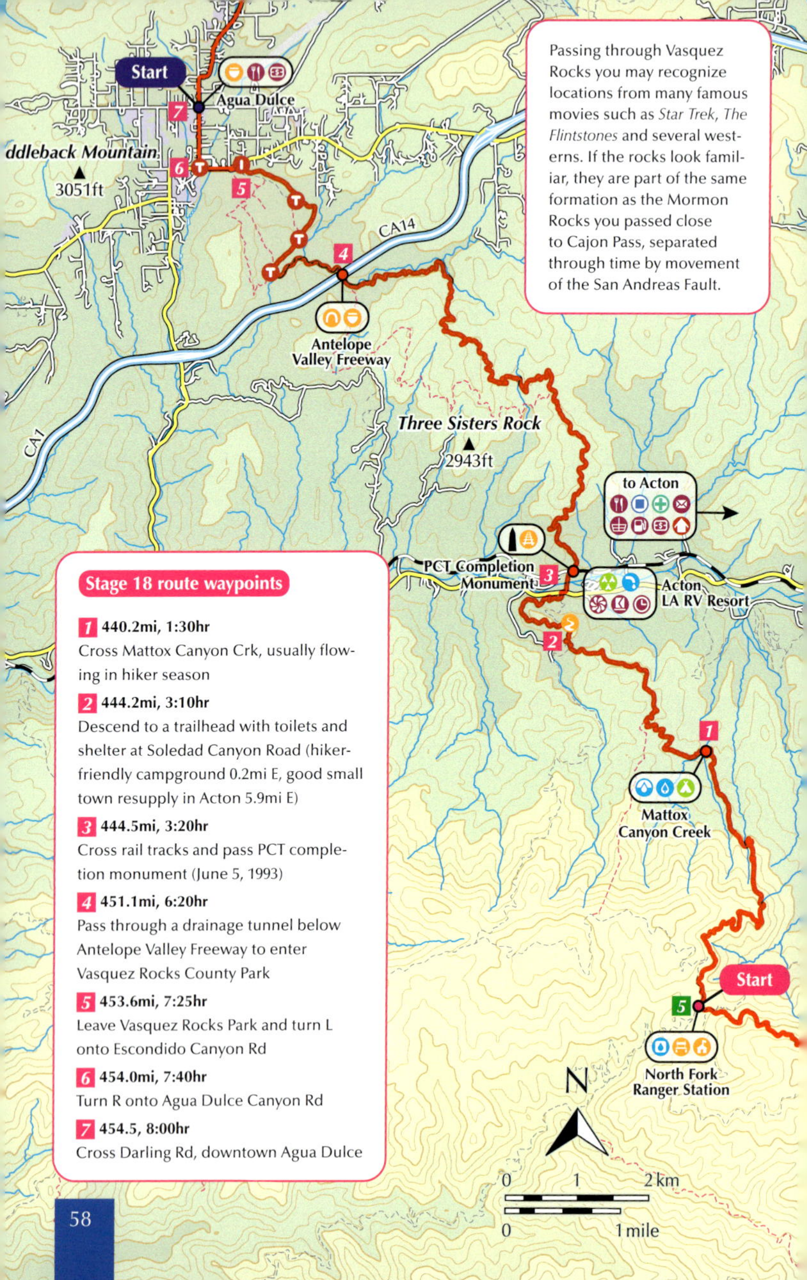


Passing through Vasquez Rocks you may recognize locations from many famous movies such as *Star Trek*, *The Flintstones* and several westerns. If the rocks look familiar, they are part of the same formation as the Mormon Rocks you passed close to Cajon Pass, separated through time by movement of the San Andreas Fault.

## Stage 18 route waypoints

**1 440.2mi, 1:30hr**
Cross Mattox Canyon Crk, usually flowing in hiker season

**2 444.2mi, 3:10hr**
Descend to a trailhead with toilets and shelter at Soledad Canyon Road (hiker-friendly campground 0.2mi E, good small town resupply in Acton 5.9mi E)

**3 444.5mi, 3:20hr**
Cross rail tracks and pass PCT completion monument (June 5, 1993)

**4 451.1mi, 6:20hr**
Pass through a drainage tunnel below Antelope Valley Freeway to enter Vasquez Rocks County Park

**5 453.6mi, 7:25hr**
Leave Vasquez Rocks Park and turn L onto Escondido Canyon Rd

**6 454.0mi, 7:40hr**
Turn R onto Agua Dulce Canyon Rd

**7 454.5, 8:00hr**
Cross Darling Rd, downtown Agua Dulce

# SECTION 3 – AGUA DULCE TO KENNEDY MEADOWS

| | Stage | Distance (miles) | Total ascent (feet) | Total descent (feet) | Average duration (hr:min) | Page |
|---|---|---|---|---|---|---|
| 19 | Agua Dulce – Lake Hughes Rd | 31.2 | 5092 | 4554 | 14:30 | 64 |
| 20 | Lake Hughes Rd – Hwy 138 | 31.9 | 4619 | 4639 | 14:30 | 66 |
| 21 | Hwy 138 – Cottonwood Creek | 17.3 | 548 | 495 | 6:35 | 69 |
| 22 | Cottonwood Crk – Tehachapi Pass | 31.5 | 4849 | 4137 | 14:50 | 71 |
| 23 | Tehachapi Pass – Piute Mountain Rd | 42.9 | 7444 | 5036 | 19:20 | 73 |
| 24 | Piute Mountain Rd – Bird Spring Pass | 22.7 | 2992 | 3862 | 9:40 | 76 |
| 25 | Bird Spring Pass – Walker Pass | 21.2 | 3222 | 3314 | 9:10 | 78 |
| 26 | Walker Pass – Chimney Creek CG | 28.9 | 5115 | 4826 | 13:30 | 81 |
| 27 | Chimney Creek CG – Kennedy Meadows | 21.3 | 3153 | 2703 | 9:40 | 83 |
| **Totals** | | **248.9** | **37,034** | **33,566** | **111:45** | |

## WHAT TO EXPECT

Manzanita, cacti and yucca are your companions through this sparse, dusty and exceptionally dry landscape. In Section 3 the PCT completes its traverse along the ridges of the south-western edge of the Mojave Desert before turning north and cutting directly across its scorched and barren western corner to gain the ridges to the north among the massive windfarms that are characteristic of the area. These take advantage of the warm winds that rise off the desert and are funnelled through the Tehachapi Pass at great speed. The ground near here is predominantly sandy and the combination can prove quite challenging for pitching a tent.

While there have long been plans to re-route the PCT a little further west at this point, and keep it to the ridges, there is no sign of this happening in the near future and in the meantime the desert crossing has become quite a feature of the hike. In a warmer year, arrive here after May and this stretch becomes extremely hot during the day. There are many strategies to this desert crossing and it is here that many will try their first night-hike.

On the whole the hiking across this section is not hard and the elevation change is quite manageable. Water management is the primary challenge with long stretches between water sources. Mapping shows many small creeks but most dry up in early season. Landers Meadow near Piute Mountain Road in the middle of the section provides welcome relief with a little more shade and a piped spring that is fairly reliable.

Walker Pass is a notable milestone, not only as a major highway from which resupply towns can be reached, and an historical route along which hundreds of pioneers made their way into California during the Gold Rush years from 1848 to 1855, but also as the geological start of the Sierra Nevada. That said, you are unlikely to notice a significant a change in the landscape, which continues in much the same vein. However, as you gradually ascend from here into the Owens Peak Wilderness you are subtly acclimatizing for the bigger mountains ahead. Section hikers proposing to tackle Section 4 might consider starting at Walker Pass to enable effective acclimatization and minimize the possibility of problems with altitude.

Resupply in the early part of the section is a little sparse with primarily small gas station mini-marts with limited food options. Most will resupply in Tehachapi which has a full range of main stores but does suffer from being quite spread-out and difficult to cover on foot. Beyond Tehachapi,

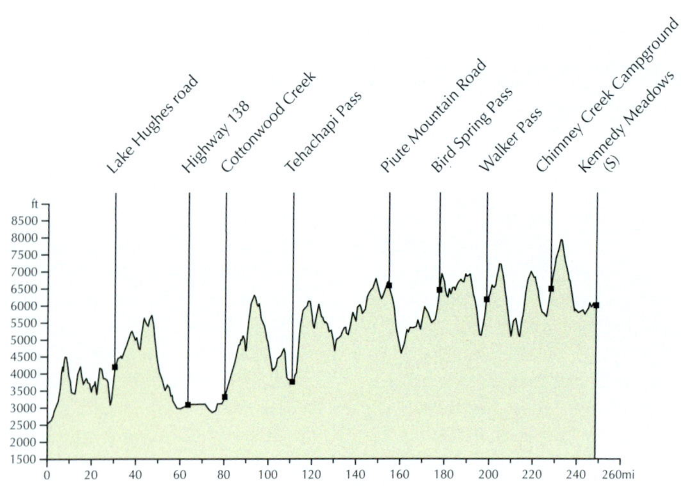

a full resupply could be achieved by hitching east or west from Walker Pass to either Lake Isabella or Ridgecrest. Traditionally most would send a box ahead to Kennedy Meadows from perhaps Tehachapi or Ridgecrest, but in recent years the arrival of the excellent Triple Crown Outfitters at Kennedy Meadows has meant this isn't wholly necessary.

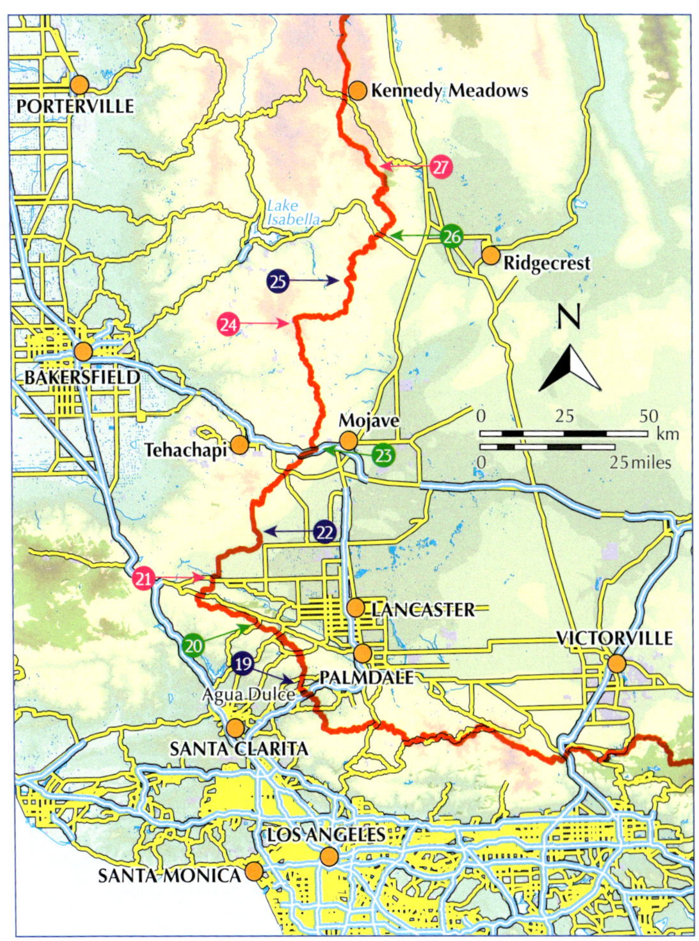

# RESUPPLY OPTIONS

| Stage | Trail mile | Place | Off trail (miles) | Description | Facilities |
|---|---|---|---|---|---|
| 19 | 478.2 | Green Valley | 2.0 SW | Well stocked gas station mini-mart | |
| 19 | 485.7 | Lake Hughes | 2.1 N | Small community, diner has some rooms | |
| 20 | 517.6 | Hikertown | On trail | Quirky hiker hostel, accepts packages ($) | |
| 20 | 517.6 | Neenach Café/ Market | 4.0 E | Small hiker-focused mini-mart, gas and deli | |
| 20 | 517.6 | Wee Vill Market | 8.0 E | Very friendly market and burrito grill with hang-out area | |
| 22 | 558.5 | Tehachapi | 10.0 NW | Full service town, hospital, Big 5 store, trail angels | |
| 22 | 556.4 | Mojave | 11.5 E | Smaller town, regular bus runs to/from Tehachapi | |
| 25 | 653.2 | Onyx | 17.7 W | Small community, post office, no longer a store | |
| 25 | 653.2 | Ridgecrest | 28.0 E | Sprawling military town, hospital and multiple supermarkets | |
| 25 | 653.2 | Lake Isabella | 37.0 W | Small town, campsites by lake, good stores | |
| 27 | 703.4 | Kennedy Meadows | 0.6–2.0 E | General Store (accepts packages $), restaurant & outfitters | |

## PERMITS

No permits are required.

## MAIL DROP INFORMATION

'Your Name Here'
c/o Hikertown
26803 W. Avenue C-15
Lancaster, CA 93536
ETA: 'Your ETA'
They are open: seven days a week
Email them at: highway138@gmail.com

'Your Name Here'
c/o Kennedy Meadows General Store
96740 Beach Meadow Road
Inyokern CA 93527
ETA: 'Your ETA'
They are open: seven days a week
Phone them on: (559) 850-5647 or email at: pcthikerstuff@gmail.com.
Visit them at:
www.kennedymeadowsgeneralstore.com

'Your Name Here'
c/o Grumpy Bear's Retreat
98887 Kennedy Meadows Road
Inyokern, CA 93527
ETA: 'Your ETA'
They are open: seven days a week
Phone them on: (559) 850-2327 or email at: info@grumpybearsretreat.com
Visit them at:
www.grumpybearsretreat.com

## POST OFFICE INFORMATION

'Your Name Here'
c\o General Delivery
Lake Hughes, CA 93532
Located at: 16817 Elizabeth Lake Road
Phone them on: (661) 724-9281

'Your Name Here'
c\o General Delivery
Tehachapi, CA 93561
Located at: 1085 Voyager Drive
Phone them on: (661) 822-0279

'Your Name Here'
c\o General Delivery
Mojave, CA 93501
Located at: 2053 Belshaw Street
Phone them on: (661) 824-3502

'Your Name Here'
c\o General Delivery
Onyx, CA 93255
Located at: 8275 Easy Street
Phone them on: (760) 378-2121

'Your Name Here'
c\o General Delivery
Ridgecrest, CA 93555
Located at: 101 E Coso Avenue
Phone them on: (760) 375-1939

'Your Name Here'
c\o General Delivery
Lake Isabella, CA 93240
Located at: 6441 Lake Isabella Boulevard.
Phone them on: (760) 379-8755

## Stage 19

### Agua Dulce to Lake Hughes Road

| | |
|---|---|
| Start | Agua Dulce |
| Finish | Lake Hughes Road |
| Distance | 31.2 miles |
| Total ascent | 5092ft |
| Total descent | 4554ft |
| Duration | 14:30hr |

There's a succession of small climbs on this section and little shade. Bear Spring and Green Valley Ranger Station provide the main water, with Green Valley and Lake Hughes not far off route for food/drinks and limited resupply. You may find small water caches.

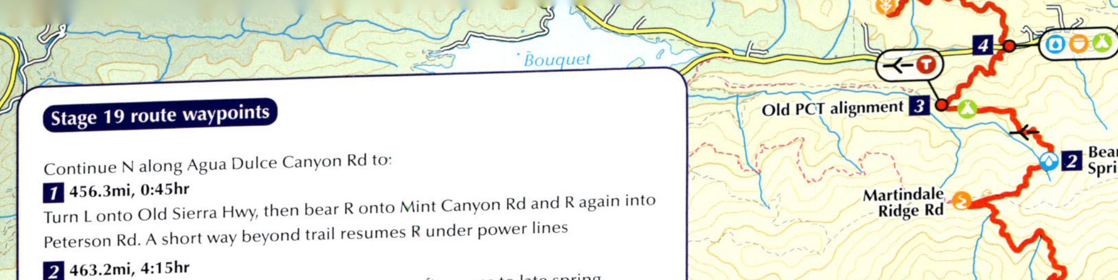


## Stage 19 route waypoints

Continue N along Agua Dulce Canyon Rd to:

**1 456.3mi, 0:45hr**
Turn L onto Old Sierra Hwy, then bear R onto Mint Canyon Rd and R again into Peterson Rd. A short way beyond trail resumes R under power lines

**2 463.2mi, 4:15hr**
Piped Bear Spring, above the trail among trees, often runs to late spring

**3 464.5mi, 5:00hr**
Keep R at old PCT alignment and through subsequent gate

**4 465.5mi, 5:30hr**
Cross Bouquet Canyon Rd where you may find a creek running, if not, sometimes a water cache

**5 471.5mi, 8:35hr**
Cross Spunky Edison Rd (Green Valley can be accessed 1.7mi SW, then 2mi NW)

**6 478.2mi, 11:10hr**
Cross San Francisquito Canyon Rd. A two min walk SW of crossing to Green Valley Ranger Station (water tap usually on, but needs treating), continue 2mi SW to Green Valley for limited supplies

**7 479.8mi, 12:35hr**
Cross Grass Mountain Rd

**8 481.2mi, 13:10hr**
Cross a four-way junction on a saddle keeping S below main dirt road

**9 485.7mi, 14:30hr**
Lake Hughes Rd (small community of Lake Hughes 2mi NE)

## Stage 20

### Lake Hughes Road to Highway 138

| | |
|---|---|
| Start | Lake Hughes Road |
| Finish | Highway 138 |
| Distance | 31.9 miles |
| Total ascent | 4619ft |
| Total descent | 4639ft |
| Duration | 14:30hr |

Dry ravines, dense chaparral and, if the LA smog is light, great views abound as the trail snakes over Grass Mountain then Sawmill Mountain, crossing a succession of tracks and dirt roads. Several concrete or plastic tanks provide water, but this must be filtered and treated to be potable.

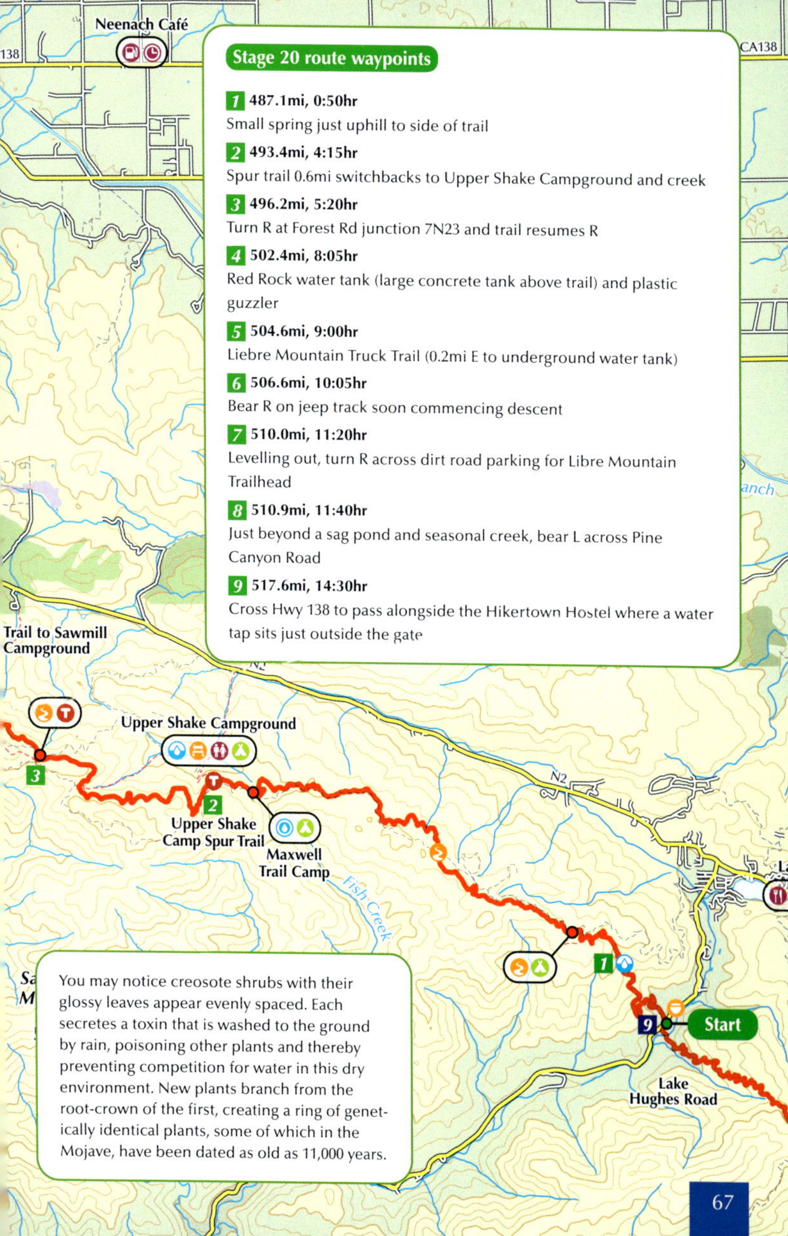


## Stage 20 route waypoints

**1 487.1mi, 0:50hr**
Small spring just uphill to side of trail

**2 493.4mi, 4:15hr**
Spur trail 0.6mi switchbacks to Upper Shake Campground and creek

**3 496.2mi, 5:20hr**
Turn R at Forest Rd junction 7N23 and trail resumes R

**4 502.4mi, 8:05hr**
Red Rock water tank (large concrete tank above trail) and plastic guzzler

**5 504.6mi, 9:00hr**
Liebre Mountain Truck Trail (0.2mi E to underground water tank)

**6 506.6mi, 10:05hr**
Bear R on jeep track soon commencing descent

**7 510.0mi, 11:20hr**
Levelling out, turn R across dirt road parking for Libre Mountain Trailhead

**8 510.9mi, 11:40hr**
Just beyond a sag pond and seasonal creek, bear L across Pine Canyon Road

**9 517.6mi, 14:30hr**
Cross Hwy 138 to pass alongside the Hikertown Hostel where a water tap sits just outside the gate

You may notice creosote shrubs with their glossy leaves appear evenly spaced. Each secretes a toxin that is washed to the ground by rain, poisoning other plants and thereby preventing competition for water in this dry environment. New plants branch from the root-crown of the first, creating a ring of genetically identical plants, some of which in the Mojave, have been dated as old as 11,000 years.

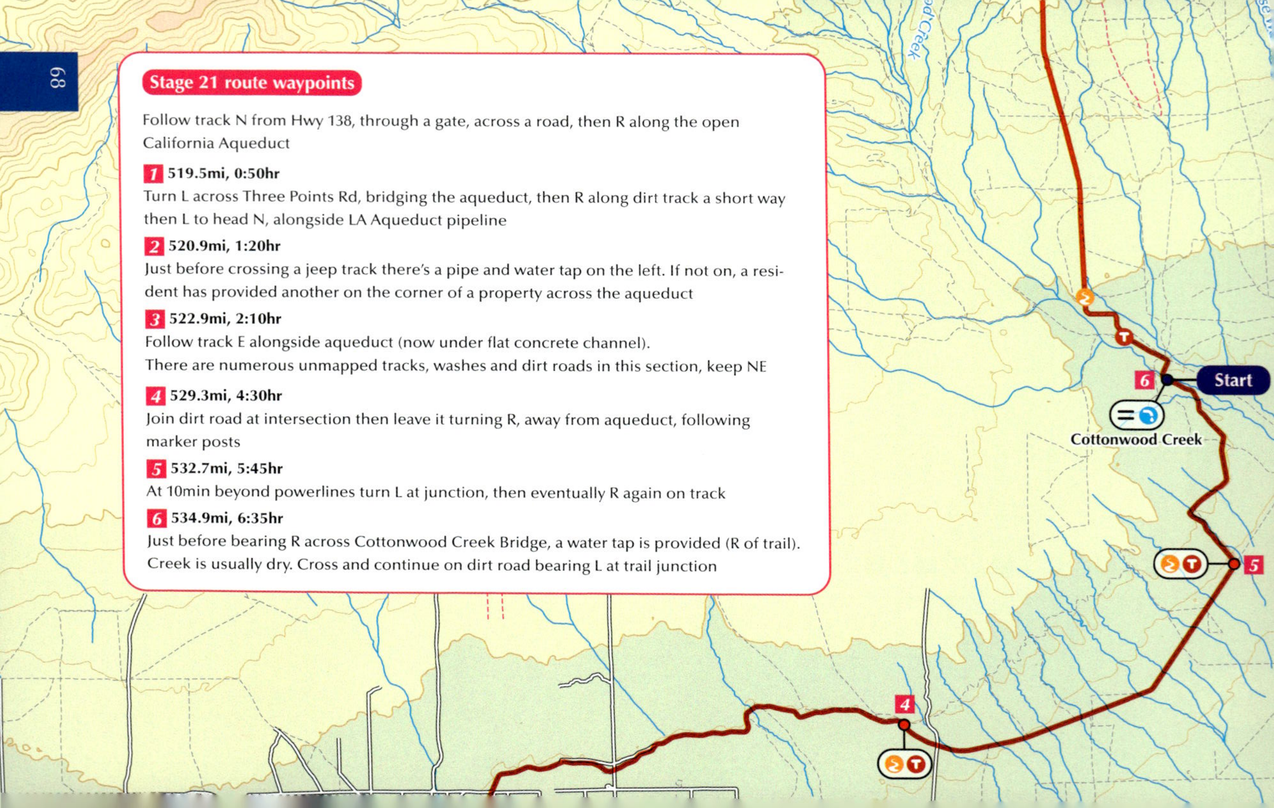


## Stage 21 route waypoints

Follow track N from Hwy 138, through a gate, across a road, then R along the open California Aqueduct

**1 519.5mi, 0:50hr**
Turn L across Three Points Rd, bridging the aqueduct, then R along dirt track a short way then L to head N, alongside LA Aqueduct pipeline

**2 520.9mi, 1:20hr**
Just before crossing a jeep track there's a pipe and water tap on the left. If not on, a resident has provided another on the corner of a property across the aqueduct

**3 522.9mi, 2:10hr**
Follow track E alongside aqueduct (now under flat concrete channel).
There are numerous unmapped tracks, washes and dirt roads in this section, keep NE

**4 529.3mi, 4:30hr**
Join dirt road at intersection then leave it turning R, away from aqueduct, following marker posts

**5 532.7mi, 5:45hr**
At 10min beyond powerlines turn L at junction, then eventually R again on track

**6 534.9mi, 6:35hr**
Just before bearing R across Cottonwood Creek Bridge, a water tap is provided (R of trail). Creek is usually dry. Cross and continue on dirt road bearing L at trail junction

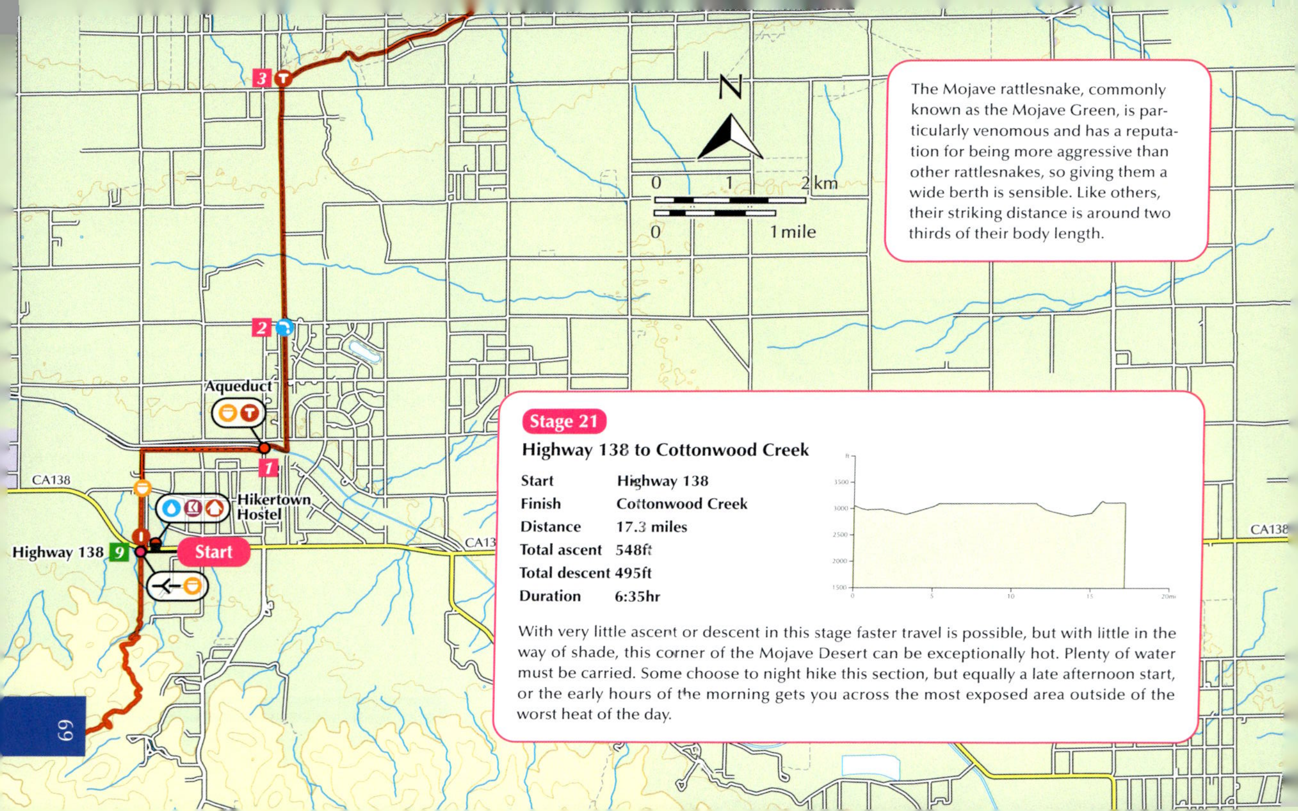


The Mojave rattlesnake, commonly known as the Mojave Green, is particularly venomous and has a reputation for being more aggressive than other rattlesnakes, so giving them a wide berth is sensible. Like others, their striking distance is around two thirds of their body length.

## Stage 21

### Highway 138 to Cottonwood Creek

| | |
|---|---|
| **Start** | **Highway 138** |
| **Finish** | **Cottonwood Creek** |
| **Distance** | **17.3 miles** |
| **Total ascent** | **548ft** |
| **Total descent** | **495ft** |
| **Duration** | **6:35hr** |

With very little ascent or descent in this stage faster travel is possible, but with little in the way of shade, this corner of the Mojave Desert can be exceptionally hot. Plenty of water must be carried. Some choose to night hike this section, but equally a late afternoon start, or the early hours of the morning gets you across the most exposed area outside of the worst heat of the day.

## Stage 22 route waypoints – continued

**4 553.6mi, 9:05hr**
Keep R at two successive trail forks

**5 558.2mi, 11:15hr**
Bear L across Oak Creek on a steel bridge

**6 558.5mi, 11:20hr**
Cross Tehachapi Willow Springs Rd (Tehachapi 10mi NW) and head NE through windfarms

**7 565.2mi, 14:25hr**
Descend to Cameron Canyon Rd, turn R, then across the subsequent rail tracks

**8 566.4mi, 14:50hr**
An overpass crosses the busy Hwy 58. Buses between Tehachapi and Mojave will stop here on request (telephone number online and posted nearby)

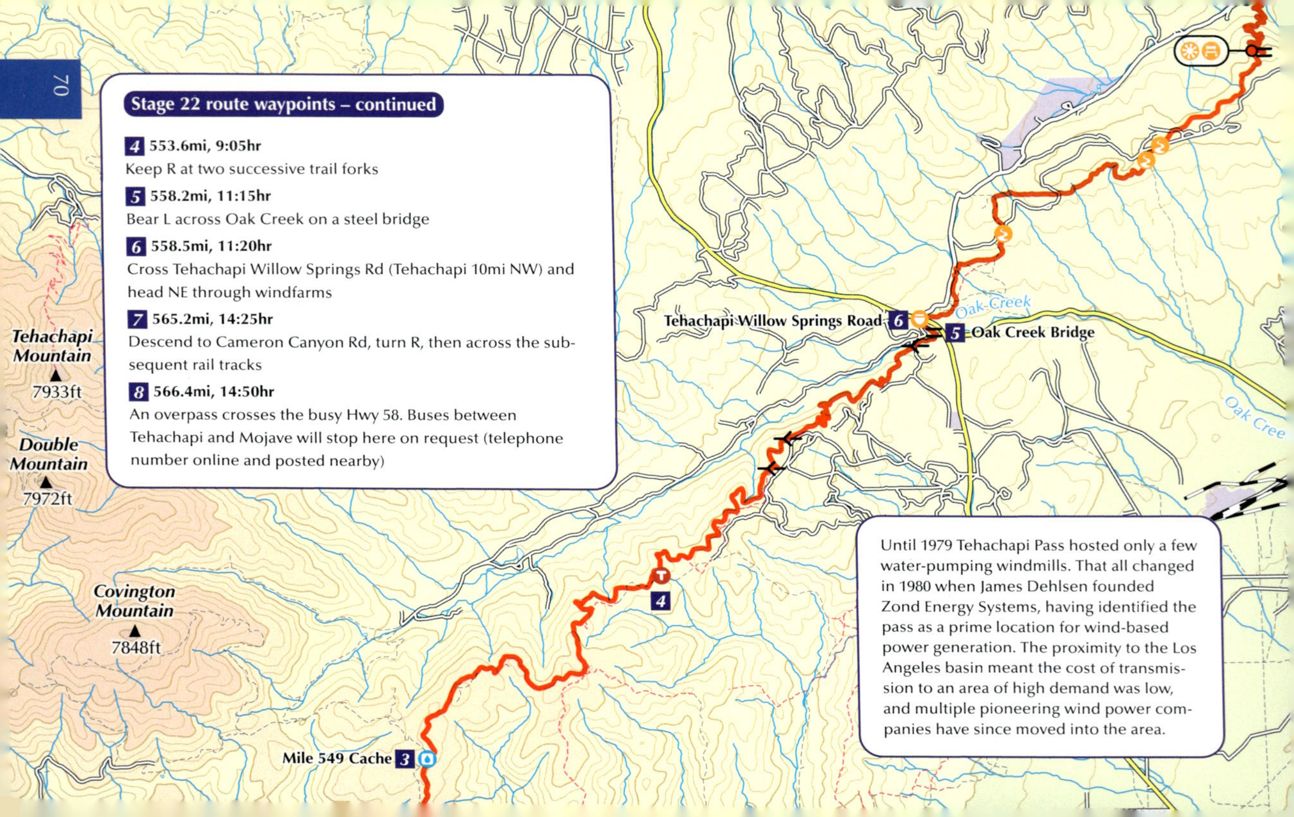


Until 1979 Tehachapi Pass hosted only a few water-pumping windmills. That all changed in 1980 when James Dehlsen founded Zond Energy Systems, having identified the pass as a prime location for wind-based power generation. The proximity to the Los Angeles basin meant the cost of transmission to an area of high demand was low, and multiple pioneering wind power companies have since moved into the area.

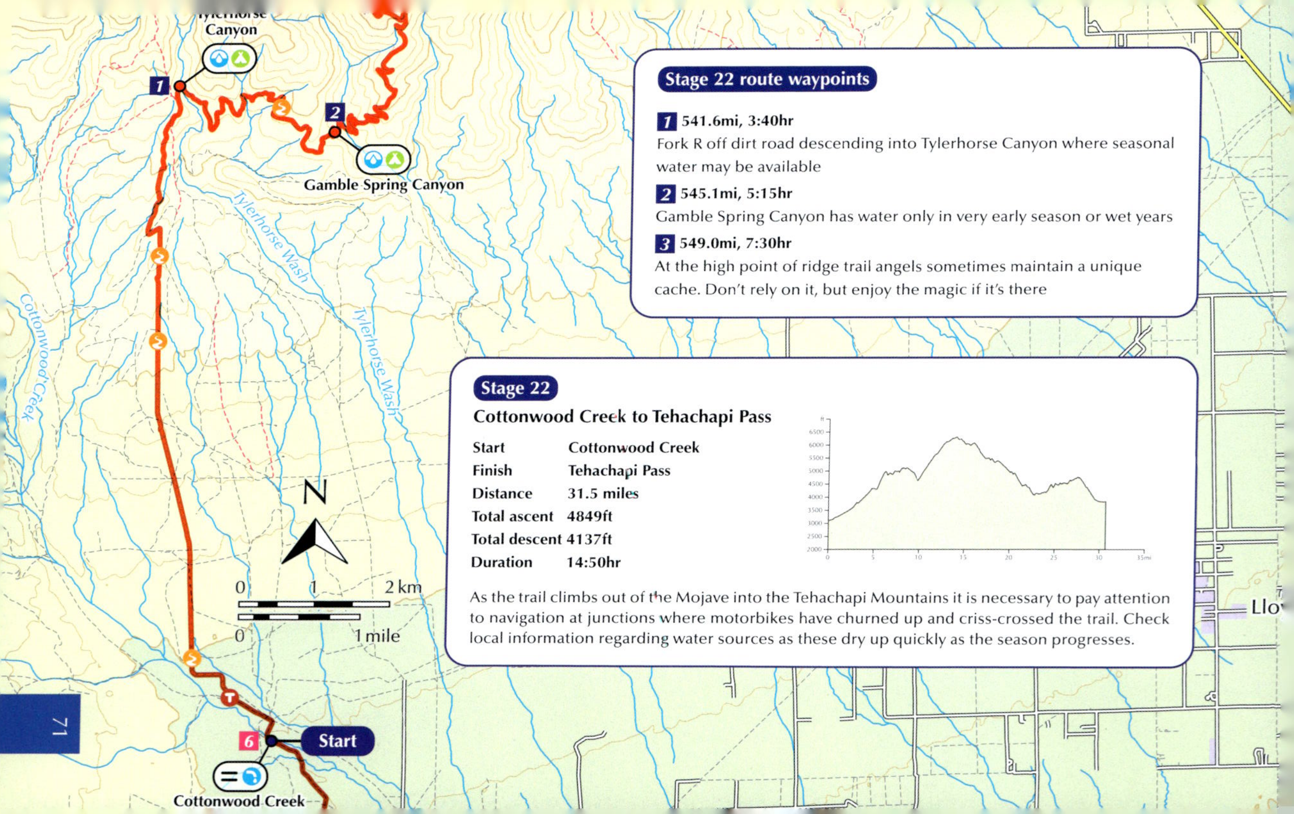


## Stage 22 route waypoints

**1** **541.6mi, 3:40hr**
Fork R off dirt road descending into Tylerhorse Canyon where seasonal water may be available

**2** **545.1mi, 5:15hr**
Gamble Spring Canyon has water only in very early season or wet years

**3** **549.0mi, 7:30hr**
At the high point of ridge trail angels sometimes maintain a unique cache. Don't rely on it, but enjoy the magic if it's there

## Stage 22

### Cottonwood Creek to Tehachapi Pass

| | |
|---|---|
| **Start** | **Cottonwood Creek** |
| **Finish** | **Tehachapi Pass** |
| **Distance** | **31.5 miles** |
| **Total ascent** | **4849ft** |
| **Total descent** | **4137ft** |
| **Duration** | **14:50hr** |



As the trail climbs out of the Mojave into the Tehachapi Mountains it is necessary to pay attention to navigation at junctions where motorbikes have churned up and criss-crossed the trail. Check local information regarding water sources as these dry up quickly as the season progresses.

## Stage 23 route waypoints

Follow the trail E through a gate, parallel to the N side of the CA Hwy 58

**1 575.1mi, 5:10hr**
At a second wooden equestrian gate turn L and join a dirt road for several miles

**2 579.5mi, 7:10hr**
At 0.2mi beyond a locked gated road, leave dirt road descending abruptly R then across several wind farm access tracks

**3 583.3mi, 8:40hr**
Cross a dirt road and descend to Golden Oaks Spring with shade and tent sites

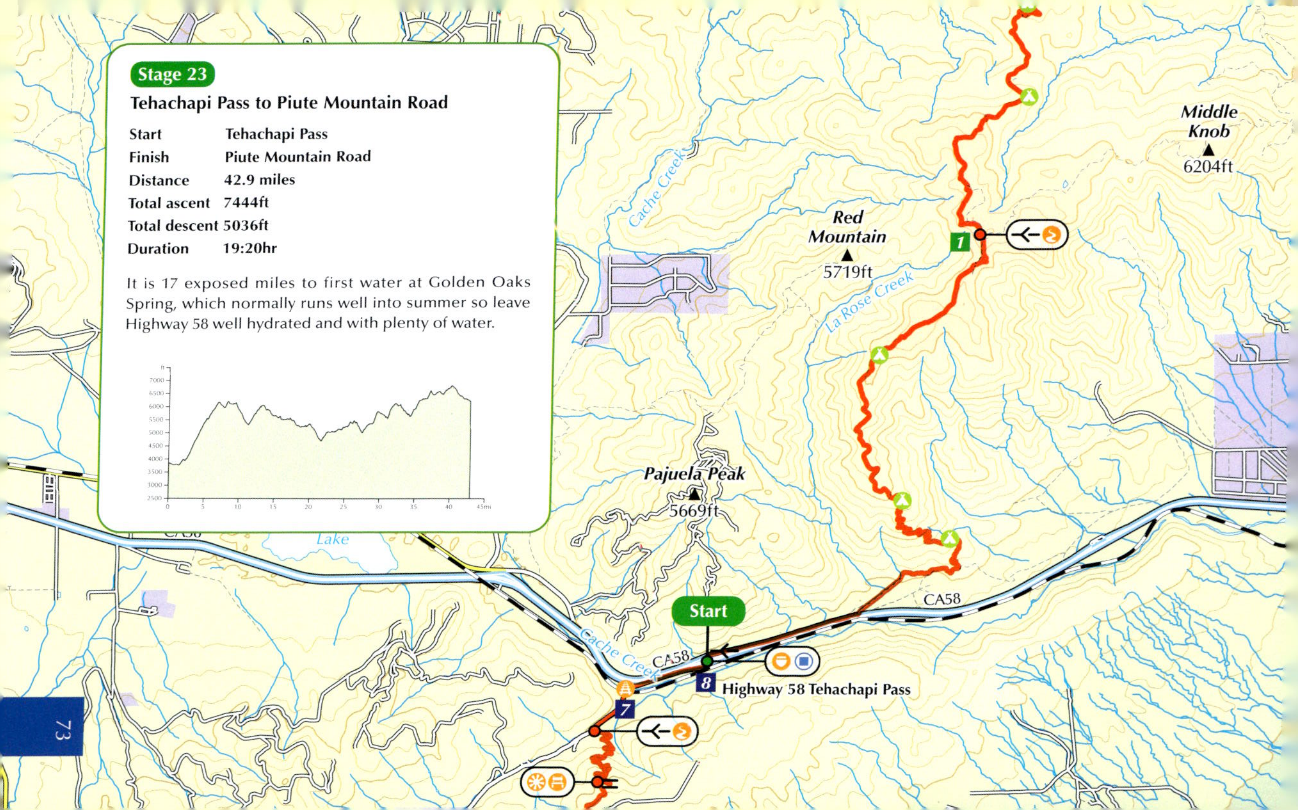


## Stage 23

### Tehachapi Pass to Piute Mountain Road

| | |
|---|---|
| Start | Tehachapi Pass |
| Finish | Piute Mountain Road |
| Distance | 42.9 miles |
| Total ascent | 7444ft |
| Total descent | 5036ft |
| Duration | 19:20hr |

It is 17 exposed miles to first water at Golden Oaks Spring, which normally runs well into summer so leave Highway 58 well hydrated and with plenty of water.

You may spot the common mourning dove, similar to the collared dove in the UK. With a long, pointed tail and a mournful call, it is the most widespread dove in the US.

## Stage 23 route waypoints – continued

**4** **594.1mi, 12:25hr**
Cross Black Canyon Rd, large tent site nearby

**5** **603.2mi, 16:45hr**
Cross a dirt road leading 0.1mi L to Robin Bird Spring

**6** **605.2mi, 17:05hr**
Cross a seasonal branch of Cottonwood Crk

**7** **608.3mi, 18:55hr**
Cross Landers Crk (early season) and tributaries several times

**8** **609.3mi, 19:20hr**
Cross Piute Mountain Rd

## Stage 24

### Piute Mountain Road to Bird Spring Pass

| | |
|---|---|
| **Start** | **Piute Mountain Road** |
| **Finish** | **Bird Spring Pass** |
| **Distance** | **22.7 miles** |
| **Total ascent** | **2992ft** |
| **Total descent** | **3862ft** |
| **Duration** | **9:40hr** |

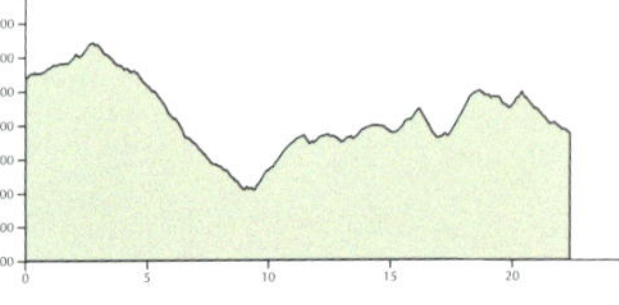


This dry section used to require extra walking to retrieve water from off-trail springs. Trail angels have maintained water caches at key road crossings in recent years, but don't rely on them and treat all water, as it may have been there for some time.

### Stage 24 route waypoints

**1 610.1mi, 0:20hr**
Cross dirt road (L for Landers Camp and piped spring)

**2 612.4mi, 1: 25hr**
Cross Piute Mountain Rd again

**3 617.2mi, 3:10hr**
There may be a water cache at Kelso Valley Rd

**4 619.0mi, 3:50hr**
Cross Butterbredt Canyon Rd (spring 1.2mi NW)

**5 623.1mi, 5:45hr**
Cross Dove Spring Canyon Rd (reliable Willow Spring 1.6mi NW)

**6 632.0mi, 9:40hr**
Bird Spring Pass dirt road junction tent site and water cache

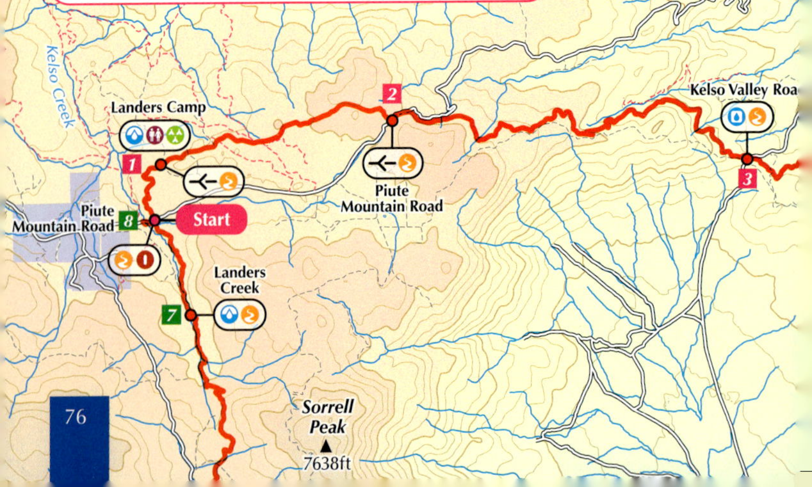

Kelso Peak
5049ft
Kelso Creek
Landers Camp
Piute Mountain Road
Start
Landers Creek
Kelso Valley Roa
Sorrell Peak
7638ft

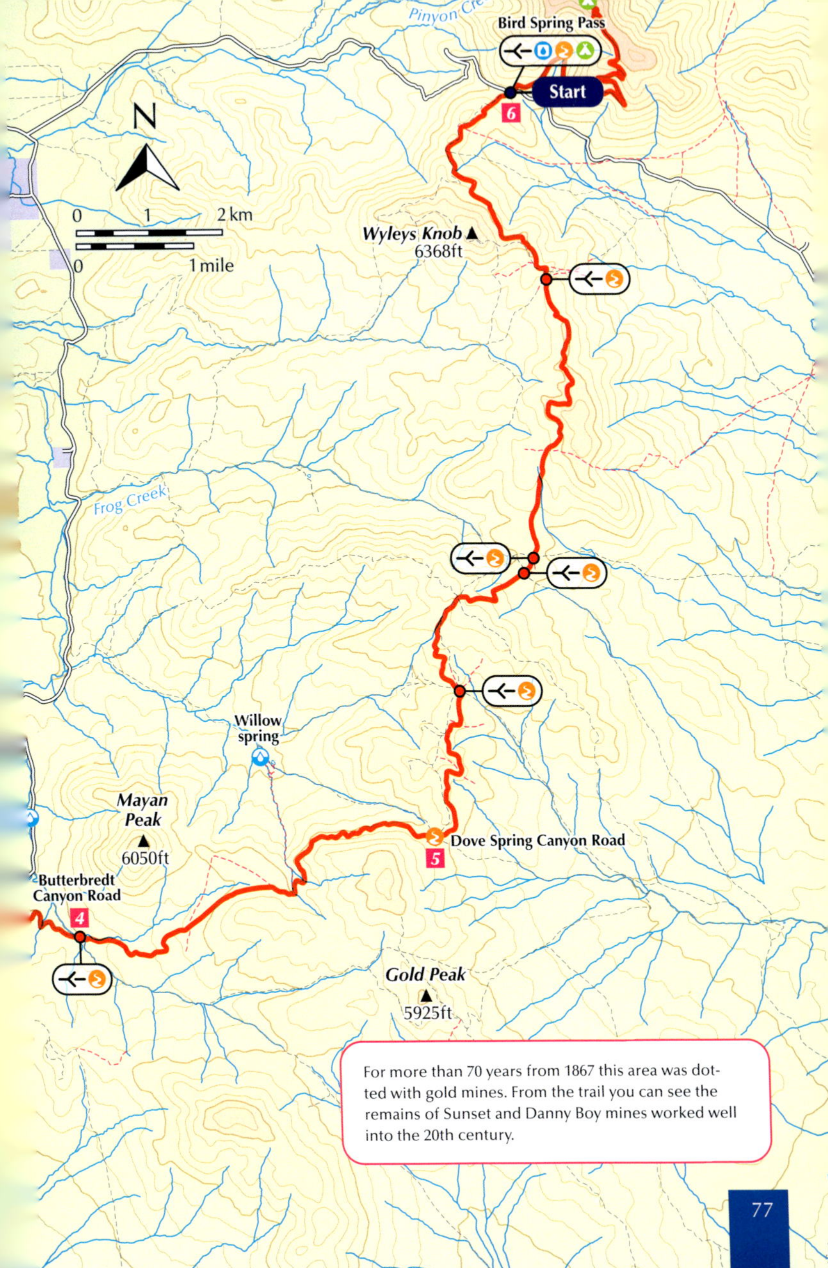


For more than 70 years from 1867 this area was dotted with gold mines. From the trail you can see the remains of Sunset and Danny Boy mines worked well into the 20th century.

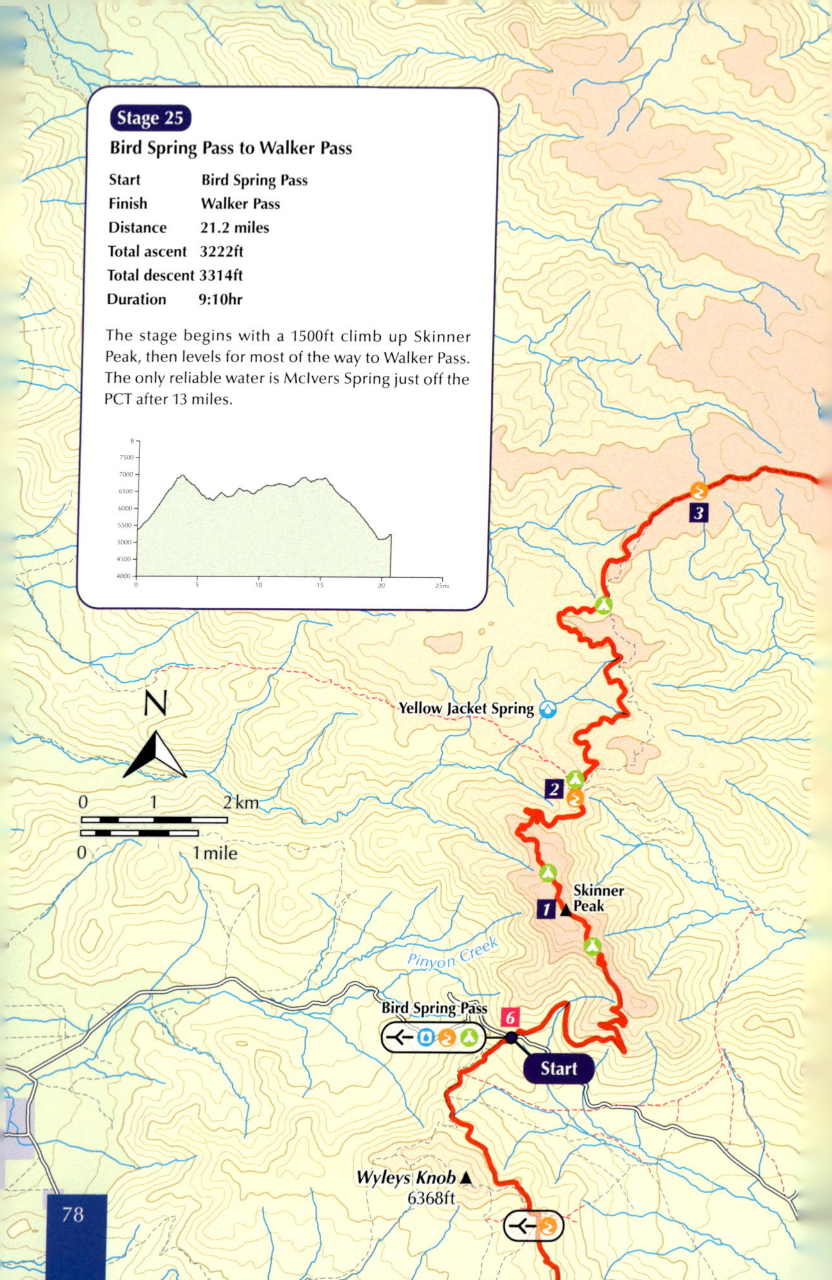
Stage 25
Bird Spring Pass to Walker Pass
Start Bird Spring Pass
Finish Walker Pass
Distance 21.2 miles
Total ascent 3222ft
Total descent 3314ft
Duration 9:10hr
The stage begins with a 1500ft climb up Skinner Peak, then levels for most of the way to Walker Pass. The only reliable water is McIvers Spring just off the PCT after 13 miles.
ft
7500
7000
6500
6000
5500
5000
4500
4000
0
5
10
15
20
25mi
N
0
1
2 km
0
1 mile
3
Yellow Jacket Spring
2
Skinner Peak
1
Pinyon Creek
Bird Spring Pass
6
Start
Wyleys Knob
6368ft

If there is no water at Walker Pass Campground, a piped spring flows into a cow trough just 0.1 miles downhill on the nearside of the highway, alongside a 30mph speed limit sign.

McIver's Hut, a somewhat dilapidated batten-board hut built in 1938 by Murdo McIver, sees regular use by hikers and motorcyclists. With a porch and outhouse, it lies in a shady clearing with a spring.

## Stage 25 route waypoints

**1 635.8mi, 2:35hr**
Cross the stage high point on Skinner Peak

**2 638.2mi, 3:35hr**
Cross a dirt road that leads 0.7mi NW to Yellow Jacket Spring

**3 642.7mi, 5:20hr**
Join dirt McIvers Road heading E for several miles

**4 645.0mi, 6:10hr**
Turn L off dirt road heading N. Continue 0.2mi further E along dirt road to access McIvers Hut and spring

**5 652.5mi, 8:55hr**
Trail junction to Walker Pass campground. Water is not reliable here but a cache is sometimes present

**6 653.2mi, 9:10hr**
Cross Hwy 178 Walker Pass at a historical monument. (Resupply can be undertaken 26mi E at Ridgecrest, or 37mi W at Lake Isabella, Onyx 17.7mi W has a PO)

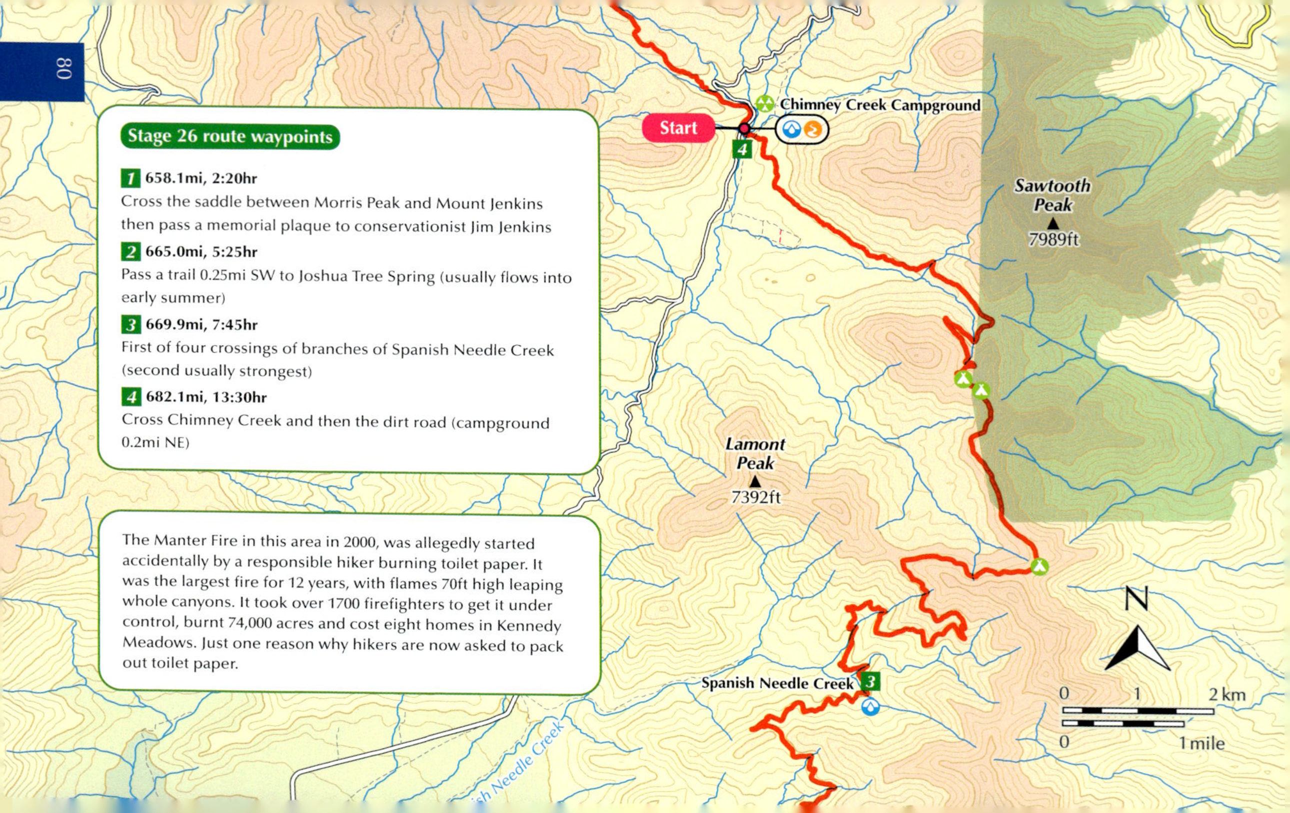


## Stage 26 route waypoints

**1 658.1mi, 2:20hr**
Cross the saddle between Morris Peak and Mount Jenkins then pass a memorial plaque to conservationist Jim Jenkins

**2 665.0mi, 5:25hr**
Pass a trail 0.25mi SW to Joshua Tree Spring (usually flows into early summer)

**3 669.9mi, 7:45hr**
First of four crossings of branches of Spanish Needle Creek (second usually strongest)

**4 682.1mi, 13:30hr**
Cross Chimney Creek and then the dirt road (campground 0.2mi NE)

The Manter Fire in this area in 2000, was allegedly started accidentally by a responsible hiker burning toilet paper. It was the largest fire for 12 years, with flames 70ft high leaping whole canyons. It took over 1700 firefighters to get it under control, burnt 74,000 acres and cost eight homes in Kennedy Meadows. Just one reason why hikers are now asked to pack out toilet paper.

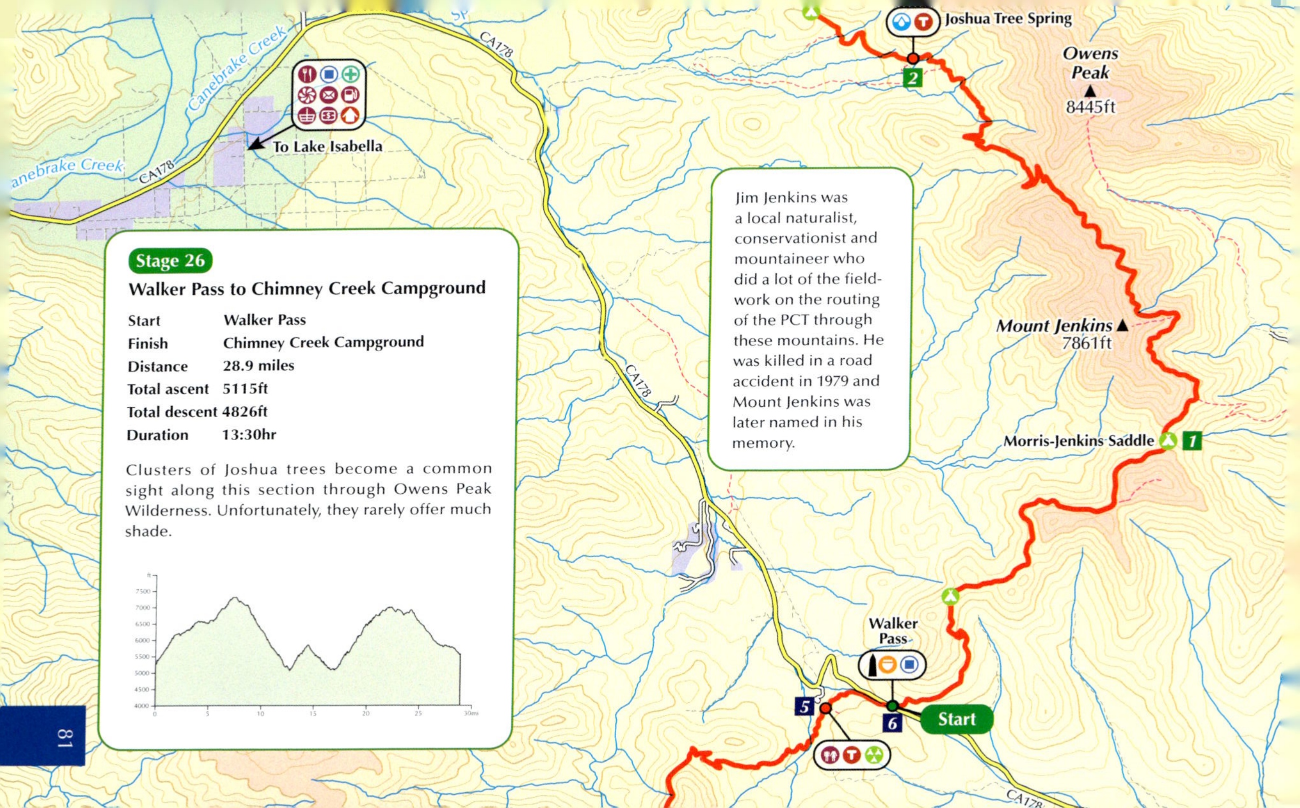


## Stage 26

### Walker Pass to Chimney Creek Campground

| | |
|---|---|
| **Start** | **Walker Pass** |
| **Finish** | **Chimney Creek Campground** |
| **Distance** | **28.9 miles** |
| **Total ascent** | **5115ft** |
| **Total descent** | **4826ft** |
| **Duration** | **13:30hr** |

Clusters of Joshua trees become a common sight along this section through Owens Peak Wilderness. Unfortunately, they rarely offer much shade.

Jim Jenkins was a local naturalist, conservationist and mountaineer who did a lot of the field-work on the routing of the PCT through these mountains. He was killed in a road accident in 1979 and Mount Jenkins was later named in his memory.

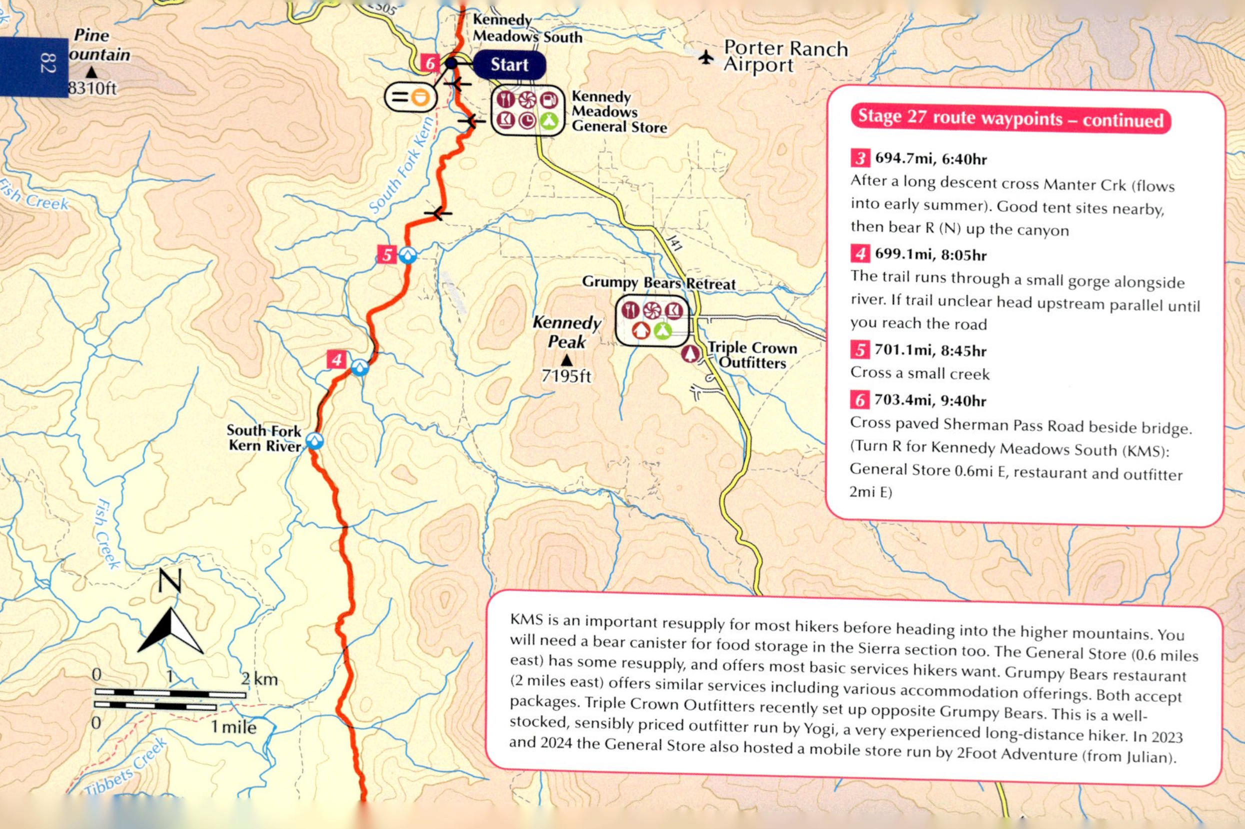


## Stage 27 route waypoints – continued

**3 694.7mi, 6:40hr**
After a long descent cross Manter Crk (flows into early summer). Good tent sites nearby, then bear R (N) up the canyon

**4 699.1mi, 8:05hr**
The trail runs through a small gorge alongside river. If trail unclear head upstream parallel until you reach the road

**5 701.1mi, 8:45hr**
Cross a small creek

**6 703.4mi, 9:40hr**
Cross paved Sherman Pass Road beside bridge. (Turn R for Kennedy Meadows South (KMS): General Store 0.6mi E, restaurant and outfitter 2mi E)

KMS is an important resupply for most hikers before heading into the higher mountains. You will need a bear canister for food storage in the Sierra section too. The General Store (0.6 miles east) has some resupply, and offers most basic services hikers want. Grumpy Bears restaurant (2 miles east) offers similar services including various accommodation offerings. Both accept packages. Triple Crown Outfitters recently set up opposite Grumpy Bears. This is a well-stocked, sensibly priced outfitter run by Yogi, a very experienced long-distance hiker. In 2023 and 2024 the General Store also hosted a mobile store run by 2Foot Adventure (from Julian).

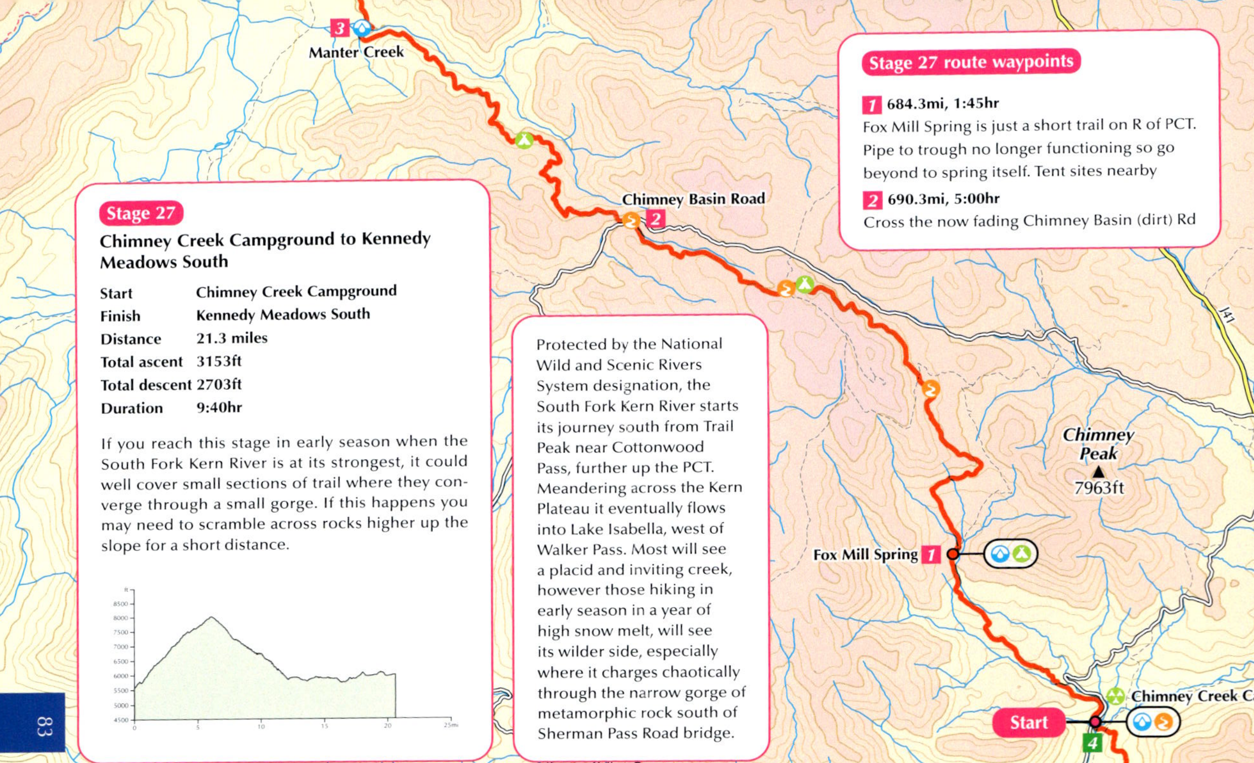


## Stage 27

### Chimney Creek Campground to Kennedy Meadows South

| | |
|---|---|
| **Start** | **Chimney Creek Campground** |
| **Finish** | **Kennedy Meadows South** |
| **Distance** | **21.3 miles** |
| **Total ascent** | **3153ft** |
| **Total descent** | **2703ft** |
| **Duration** | **9:40hr** |

If you reach this stage in early season when the South Fork Kern River is at its strongest, it could well cover small sections of trail where they converge through a small gorge. If this happens you may need to scramble across rocks higher up the slope for a short distance.

Protected by the National Wild and Scenic Rivers System designation, the South Fork Kern River starts its journey south from Trail Peak near Cottonwood Pass, further up the PCT. Meandering across the Kern Plateau it eventually flows into Lake Isabella, west of Walker Pass. Most will see a placid and inviting creek, however those hiking in early season in a year of high snow melt, will see its wilder side, especially where it charges chaotically through the narrow gorge of metamorphic rock south of Sherman Pass Road bridge.

### Stage 27 route waypoints

**1 684.3mi, 1:45hr**
Fox Mill Spring is just a short trail on R of PCT. Pipe to trough no longer functioning so go beyond to spring itself. Tent sites nearby

**2 690.3mi, 5:00hr**
Cross the now fading Chimney Basin (dirt) Rd

# SECTION 4 – KENNEDY MEADOWS SOUTH TO TUOLUMNE MEADOWS

| | Stage | Distance (miles) | Total ascent (feet) | Total descent (feet) | Duration (hr:min) | Page |
|---|---|---|---|---|---|---|
| 28 | Kennedy Meadows – Trail Pass | 43.1 | 7972 | 3494 | 21:45 | 91 |
| 29 | Trail Pass – Crabtree Meadow | 21 | 2756 | 2887 | 9:30 | 95 |
| 30 | Crabtree Meadow – Kearsarge Pass Trail | 22.6 | 5394 | 5016 | 12:50 | 96 |
| 31 | Kearsarge Pass Trail – Taboose Pass Trail | 21.3 | 4780 | 4728 | 13:15 | 101 |
| 32 | Taboose Pass Trail – Bishop Pass Trail | 20.8 | 2759 | 4790 | 10:00 | 103 |
| 33 | Bishop Pass Trail – Piute Pass Trail | 24.9 | 3379 | 4052 | 12:20 | 105 |
| 34 | Piute Pass Trail – Bear Ridge Trail | 18.6 | 4049 | 2231 | 10:10 | 107 |
| 35 | Bear Ridge Trail – Red's Meadow | 32.1 | 5604 | 7792 | 14:45 | 108 |
| 36 | Red's Meadow – Tuolumne Meadows | 35.9 | 4990 | 4094 | 16:25 | 110 |
| **Totals** | | **240.3** | **41,683** | **39,084** | **121:00** | |

## WHAT TO EXPECT

Section 4 marks the transition from Southern into Central California and the Sierra Nevada range. This regional change is also marked by a stark transformation in landscape and climate for the hiker on the PCT. The nature of the trail changes here, leaving behind the hot, dusty and dry desert environment of the south and ascending into a fantastic, roadless, alpine environment of granitic rock, sparkling lakes, snow-covered passes, tumbling creeks and waterfalls.

In early season, especially in a higher snow year, the Sierra section can present some challenges. When significant snowpack remains, tackling the trail requires winter mountaineering experience. The early stages of the melt too can be particularly dangerous. Hidden snowbridges across creeks are hazardous, even before creeks become visible torrents. In an average year thru-hikers will start entering the Sierra section around mid-June. There will still be snow cover on the higher ground,

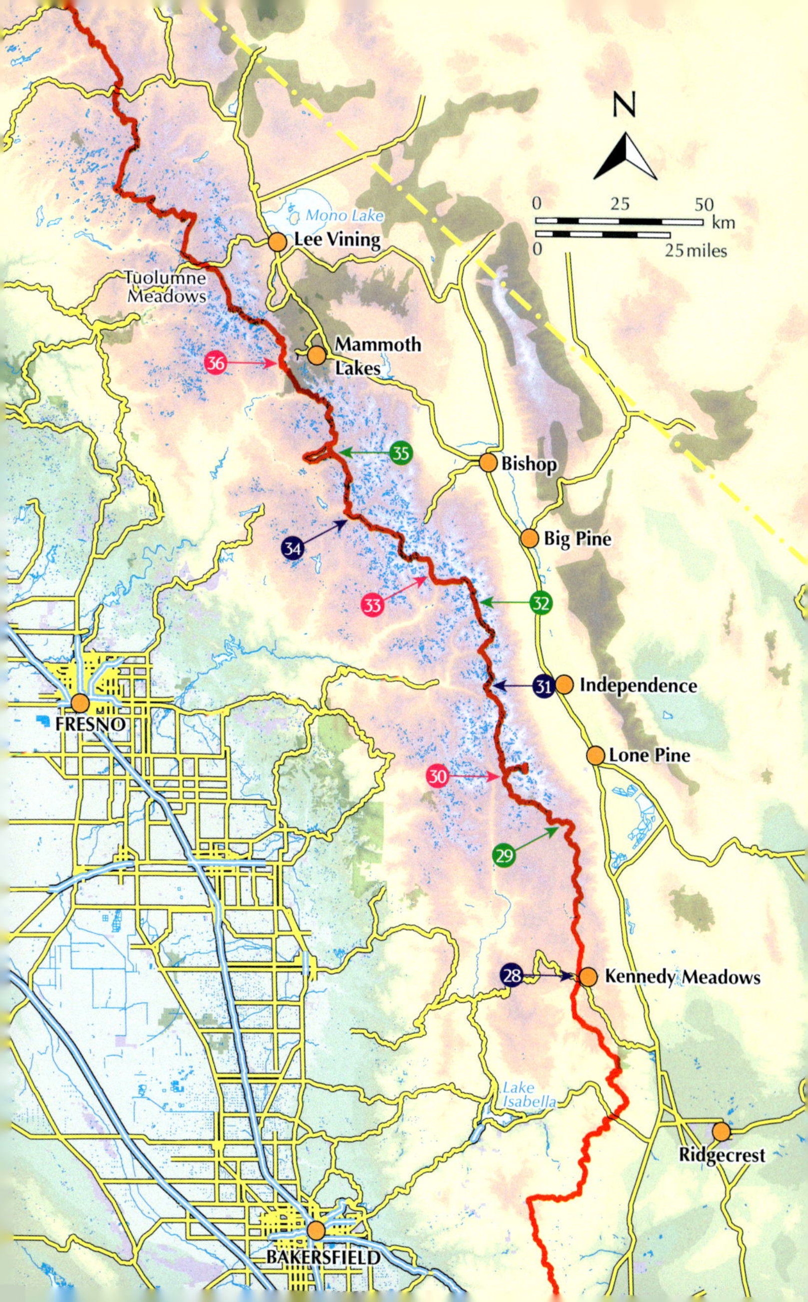
N
0
25
50
km
0
25 miles
Mono Lake
Lee Vining
Tuolumne Meadows
Mammoth Lakes
36
35
Bishop
Big Pine
34
33
32
31
Independence
Lone Pine
30
29
FRESNO
28
Kennedy Meadows
Lake Isabella
Ridgecrest
BAKERSFIELD

Mount Hitchcock and Hitchcock Lakes from Mount Whitney (Stage 29)

especially on the north side of passes, but lower down, most snow will have receded, and creeks should become manageable. The best time to hike in an average year is July to September. However, some of the resorts may close from mid-September.

Altitude sickness is a consideration too, and can occur above 8000ft. While it won't affect many, for some it is a serious and potentially life-threatening issue. There are eight passes over 11,000ft on the PCT, the highest of which is Forester Pass at 13,180ft. Symptoms such as headache, breathlessness, weakness, vomiting, dizziness, or tingling can indicate your body is struggling to adjust to the lower oxygen environment. Symptoms can be exacerbated by cold and fatigue but are usually temporary and should not last longer than 48 hours.

A side trip to summit Mount Whitney, the highest mountain in the contiguous US, is a tempting proposition. It is around a 4000ft climb from Crabtree Meadow and 8 miles each way. A popular approach is an alpine start in the dark with the aim of summiting close to sunrise. It is not technical and does not usually require mountaineering skills with the exception that the upper reaches may remain snow covered in early season and will require some care.

It will be cold at night, but daytime temperatures can be quite pleasant for hiking, especially after the desert heat. The shallower lakes will soon warm up and swimming breaks become increasingly tempting. Marmots and pika will be constant companions, with their whistles and squeaks, and look up and you may spot an eagle or vulture soaring on the thermals.

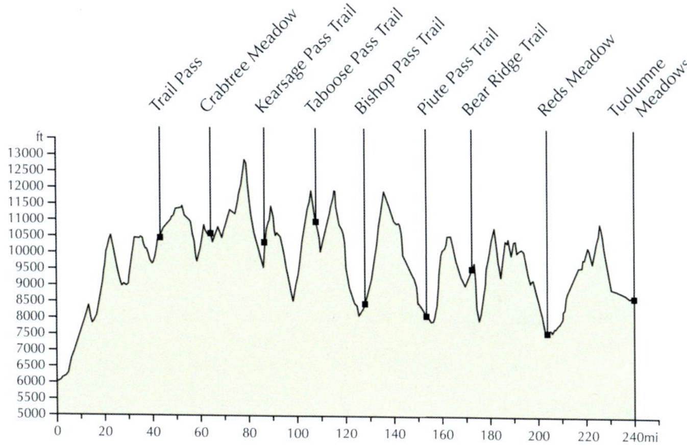


Considerations for the hiker preparing for this stage include the potential need for warmer layers and gloves, and whether micro-spikes or crampons are needed, and possibly an ice-axe. A bear canister will be required for food storage too. Mosquitos may emerge and having some repellent and a head net is recommended.

It can be a long way off trail to resupply in this section so careful planning is required, and it is advisable to carry a little extra food as weather, high creeks and snow can all result in stages taking longer than expected. Your pack will be heavier as a result, and this combined with the greater ascent and descent will likely mean your average daily mileage may be impacted.

If you are uncertain about the conditions in the Sierra section ahead, rather than doing a large resupply at Kennedy Meadows, just pick up enough food to get to Trail Pass. This will give you a good idea of the conditions and snowpack before you reach any tricky passes. Take the side trail from Trail Pass to Horseshoe Meadow and hitch out to Lone Pine to resupply where you also have a good sports shop.

The most common resupply strategy in the Sierra section is to use Kearsage Pass out to Onion Valley Trailhead and hitch to the town of Bishop, then to visit Vermilion Valley Resort having mailed a resupply package in advance, followed by a top-up of snacks from Red's Meadow Resort, then collect a pre-mailed package at Tuolumne Meadows post office.

## RESUPPLY OPTIONS

| Stage | Trail mile | Place | Off trail (miles) | Description | Facilities |
|---|---|---|---|---|---|
| 28 | 745.7 | Lone Pine | 23.4 NE | Friendly small town, mid-size market, two gear/sports shops | |
| 30 | 790.1 | Independence | 20.6 E | Small town with mini-mart at gas station, limited resupply | |
| 30 | 790.1 | Bishop | 62.6 NE | Large town with good resupply and accommodation options | |
| 34 | 858.9 | Muir Trail Ranch | 1.5 NW | Expensive private ranch, accepts packages ($$$) fee | |
| 34 | 875.7 | Vermilion Valley Resort | 6.0 NW | Friendly resort, store, accepts packages ($$), most hiker facilities | |
| 35 | 879.9 | Vermilion Valley Resort | 5.5 W | Friendly resort, store, accepts packages ($$), most hiker facilities | |
| 35 | 907.8 | Red's Meadow Resort | 0.3 NE | Resort accepts packages ($$), most facilities, bus to Mammoth Lakes | |
| 35 | 907.8 | Mammoth Lakes | 16.0 E | Large ski resort town, outfitters, good resupply options | |
| 36 | 943.7 | Tuolumne Meadows | 0.3 W | Seasonal store, campground and facilities | |

### PERMITS

A permit is required for all of Section 4, up to and including stages 37 and 38 of Section 5.

The Inyo National Forest Wilderness Permit is valid for all portions of the PCT from mile 704.5 at the boundary of Inyo National Forest, to mile 1018.1 Sonora Pass at the northern boundary of Yosemite National Park. This is a NON-quota permit from the Kennedy Meadows Trailhead and includes entering the Whitney Zone but a small additional fee is payable.

To obtain a permit visit: www.recreation.gov/permits/233262

For more information call the Inyo National Forest wilderness permit office at (760) 873-2483 or visit: www.fs.usda.gov/main/inyo/passes-permits/recreation

## MAIL DROP INFORMATION

Muir Trail Ranch
'Your Name Here'
c/o Muir Trail Ranch
PO Box 176
Lakeshore, CA 93634
ETA: 'Your ETA'
They are open: seven days a week
Phone them on: (209) 966-3195
Visit them at: www.muirtrailranch.com and read the resupply package information carefully. They have very specific requirements and a considerable pick-up fee.

Vermilion Valley Resort
HOLD FOR HIKER (YOUR NAME)
c/o VVR – General Delivery
Lakeshore, California 93634
ETA: 'Your ETA'
Phone them on: (559) 259-4000 or (preferred) email at: info@vvr.place
Visit them at: www.vvr.place and read the resupply package information carefully. They have a different address for UPS/FedEx deliveries and a significant pick-up fee.

Red's Meadow Resort
'Your Name Here'
c/o Red's Meadow Resort
PO Box 395
Mammoth Lakes, CA 93546
Phone them on: (760) 934-2345 or (preferred) email at: info@redsmeadow.com
Visit them at: www.redsmeadow.com and read the resupply package information carefully. They require submission of a pre-booking and authorisation form and payment.

## POST OFFICE INFORMATION

'Your Name Here'
c\o General Delivery
Lone Pine, CA 93545
Located at: 121 East Bush Street
Phone them on: (760) 876-5681

'Your Name Here'
c\o General Delivery
Independence, CA 93526
Located at: 101 South Edwards Street
Phone them on (760) 878-2210

'Your Name Here'
c\o General Delivery
Bishop, CA 93514
Located at: 585 West Line Street
Phone them on: (760) 873-3526

'Your Name Here'
c\o General Delivery
Mammoth Lakes, CA 93546
Located at: 3330 Main Street
Phone them on: (760) 934-2205

'Your Name Here'
c\o General Delivery
Tuolumne Meadows Post Office
Yosemite National Park, CA 95389
Located at: the seasonal general store
Phone them on: (209) 372-8236.

## Stage 28 route waypoints

Leaving Sherman Pass Rd N cross several dirt roads and through the nearby campground

**1 707.8mi, 1:45hr**
Cross South Fork Kern River on a bridge

**2 713.5mi, 4:10hr**
Keep L past Haiwee Pass Trail junction

**3 717.7mi, 7:05hr**
Cross South Fork Kern River in Monache Meadows then bear L (N)

Leaving KMS you enter the South Sierra Wilderness, established by the California Wilderness Act of 1984. It protected an area of 63,000 acres creating a continuous protected area between Domeland and Golden Trout Wildernesses.

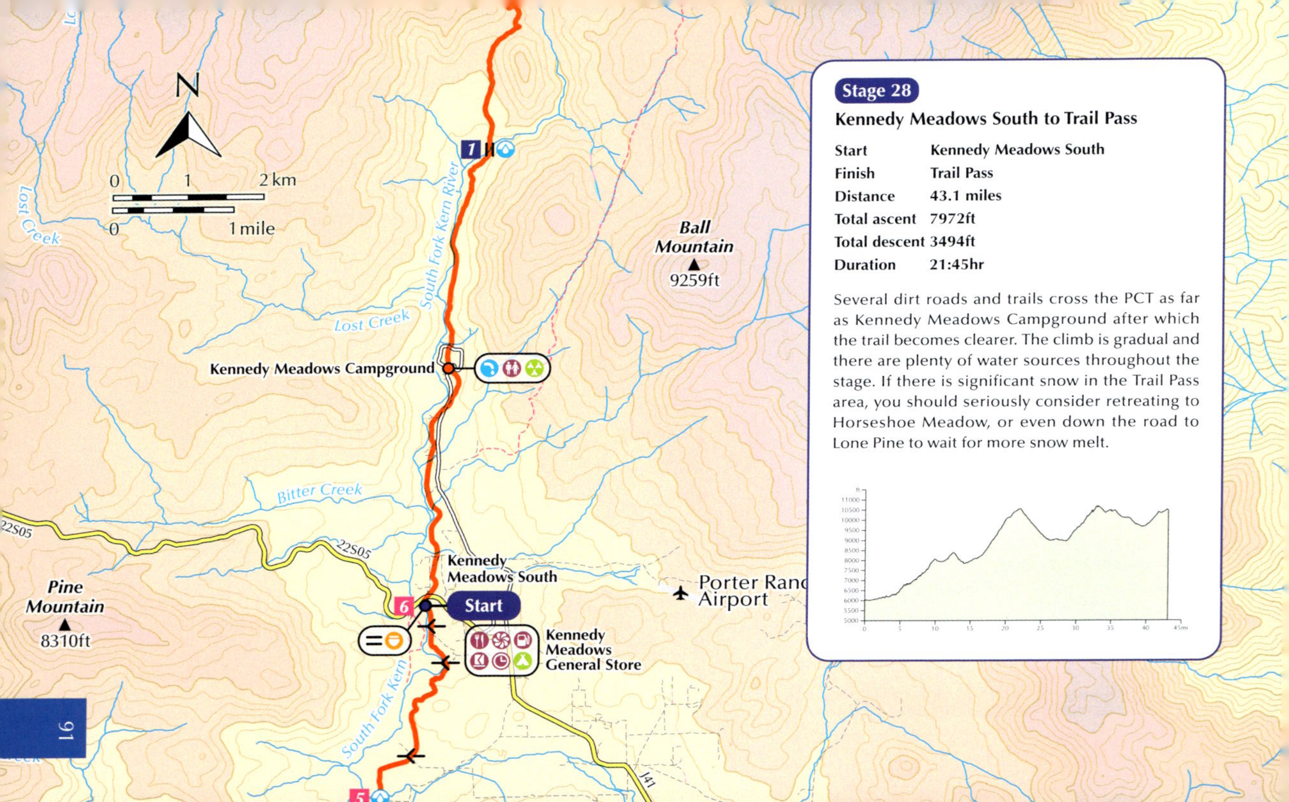


## Stage 28

### Kennedy Meadows South to Trail Pass

| | |
|---|---|
| Start | Kennedy Meadows South |
| Finish | Trail Pass |
| Distance | 43.1 miles |
| Total ascent | 7972ft |
| Total descent | 3494ft |
| Duration | 21:45hr |

Several dirt roads and trails cross the PCT as far as Kennedy Meadows Campground after which the trail becomes clearer. The climb is gradual and there are plenty of water sources throughout the stage. If there is significant snow in the Trail Pass area, you should seriously consider retreating to Horseshoe Meadow, or even down the road to Lone Pine to wait for more snow melt.

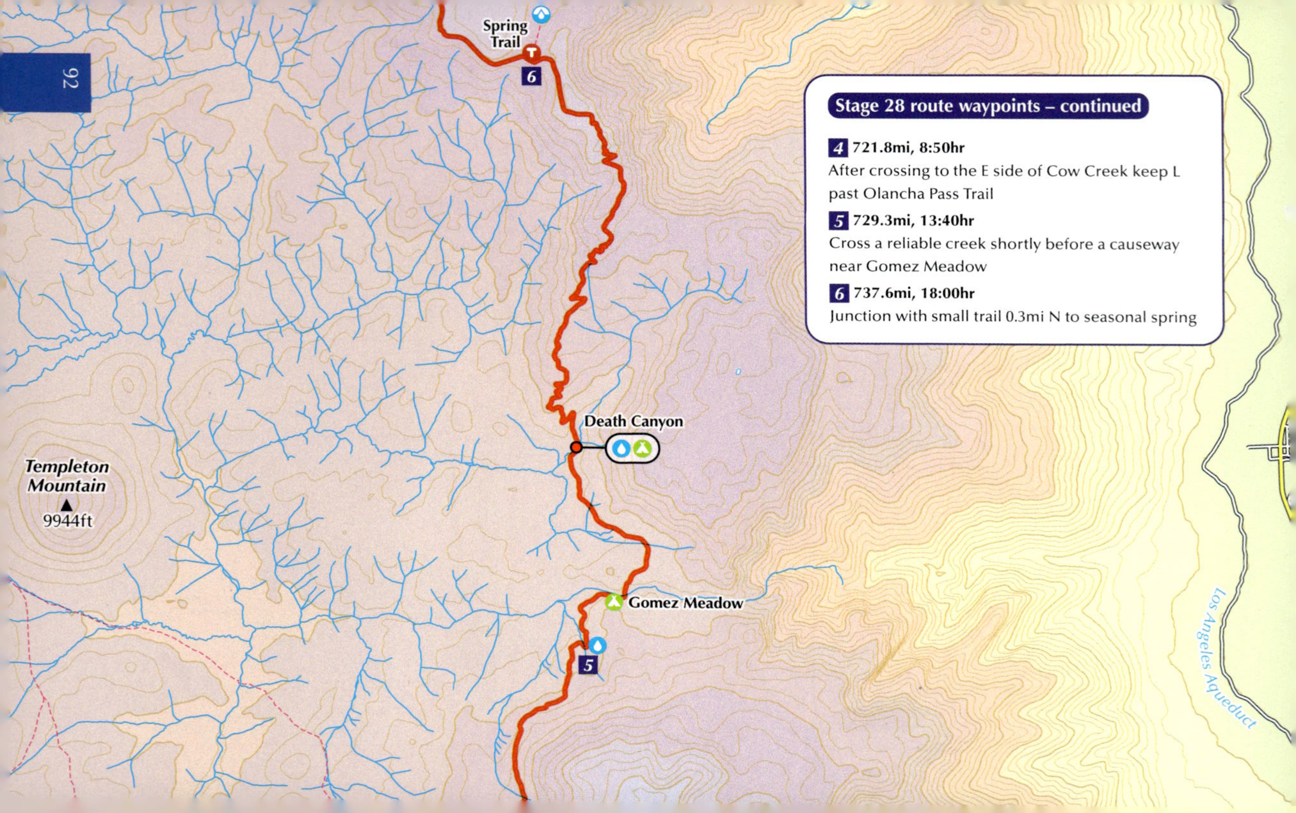


## Stage 28 route waypoints – continued

**4 721.8mi, 8:50hr**
After crossing to the E side of Cow Creek keep L past Olancha Pass Trail

**5 729.3mi, 13:40hr**
Cross a reliable creek shortly before a causeway near Gomez Meadow

**6 737.6mi, 18:00hr**
Junction with small trail 0.3mi N to seasonal spring

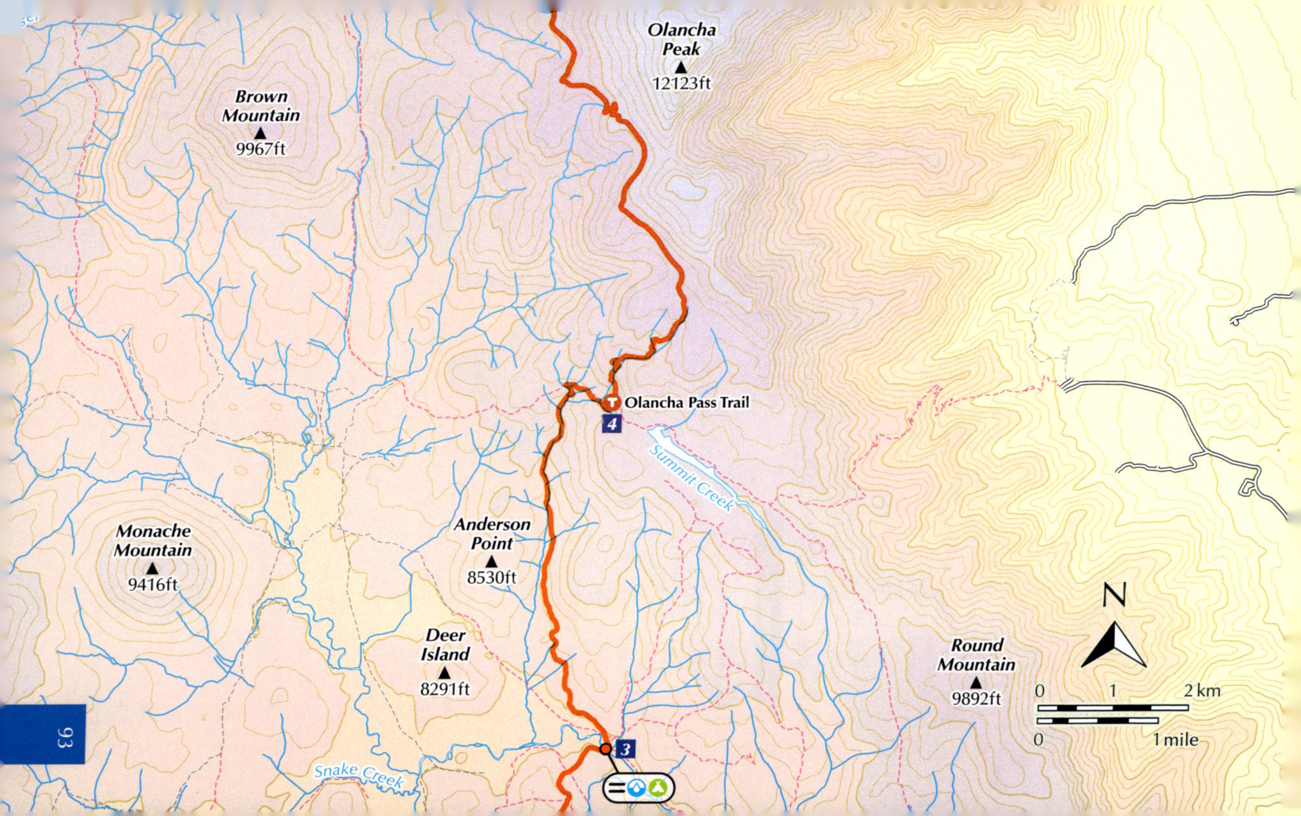
Olancha Peak
12123ft
Brown Mountain
9967ft
Olancha Pass Trail
4
Summit Creek
Monache Mountain
9416ft
Anderson Point
8530ft
Deer Island
8291ft
Round Mountain
9892ft
N
0
1
2 km
0
1 mile
3
Snake Creek

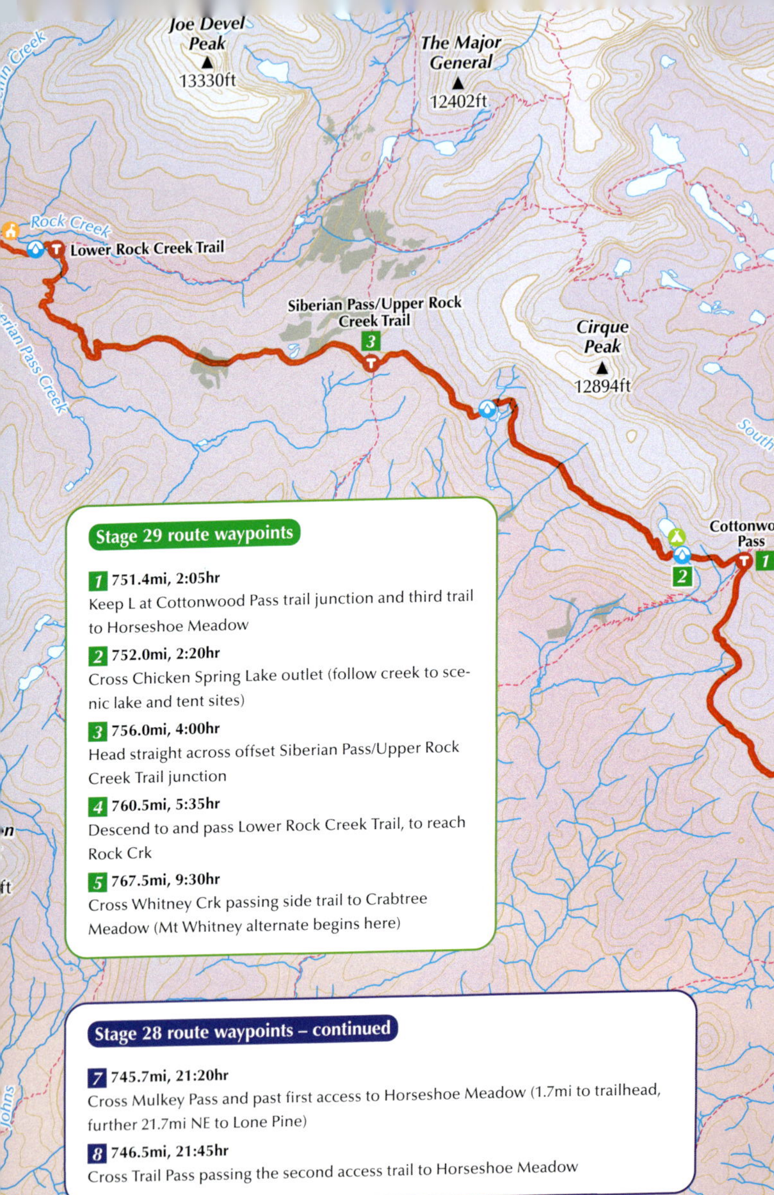


## Stage 29 route waypoints

**1 751.4mi, 2:05hr**
Keep L at Cottonwood Pass trail junction and third trail to Horseshoe Meadow

**2 752.0mi, 2:20hr**
Cross Chicken Spring Lake outlet (follow creek to scenic lake and tent sites)

**3 756.0mi, 4:00hr**
Head straight across offset Siberian Pass/Upper Rock Creek Trail junction

**4 760.5mi, 5:35hr**
Descend to and pass Lower Rock Creek Trail, to reach Rock Crk

**5 767.5mi, 9:30hr**
Cross Whitney Crk passing side trail to Crabtree Meadow (Mt Whitney alternate begins here)

## Stage 28 route waypoints – continued

**7 745.7mi, 21:20hr**
Cross Mulkey Pass and past first access to Horseshoe Meadow (1.7mi to trailhead, further 21.7mi NE to Lone Pine)

**8 746.5mi, 21:45hr**
Cross Trail Pass passing the second access trail to Horseshoe Meadow

## Stage 29

### Trail Pass to Crabtree Meadow

| | |
|---|---|
| Start | Trail Pass |
| Finish | Crabtree Meadow |
| Distance | 21 miles |
| Total ascent | 2756ft |
| Total descent | 2887ft |
| Duration | 9:30hr |

If you are too early, there will be extensive snowpack here, a clue that there will be difficult creek crossings in the next 300 miles. Once winter snows recede the going is fairly easy, and the scenery leaves little doubt you are now in the Sierra Nevada range. However, underfoot the ground remains frustratingly sandy in places, as the desert environment persists, so as the season progresses water can become scarce here.

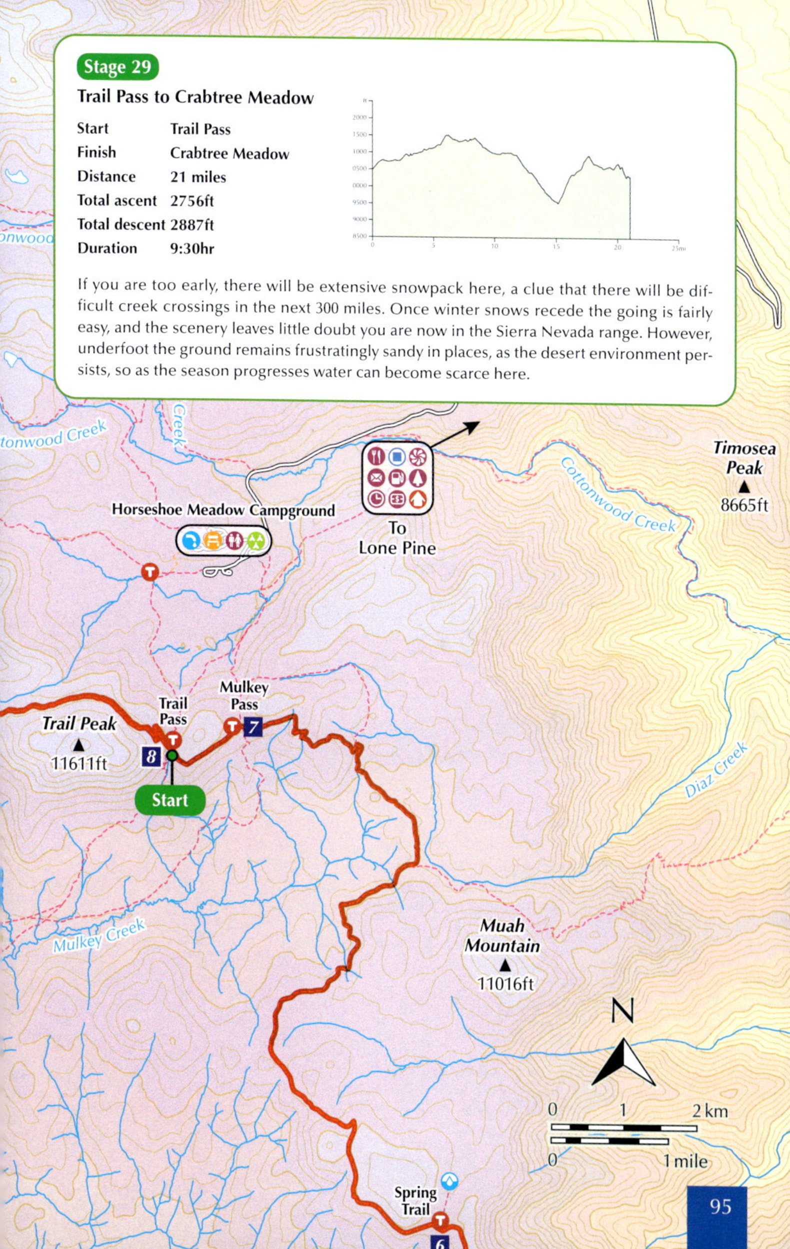

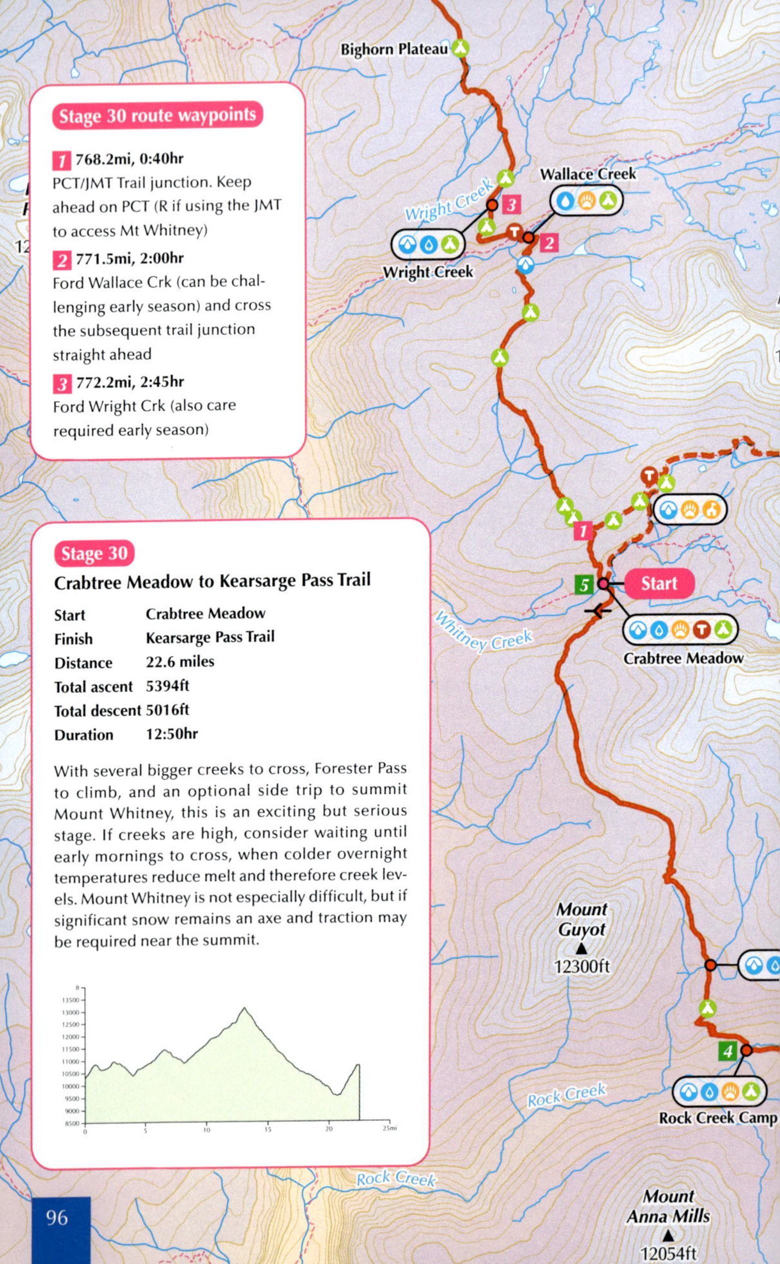


## Stage 30 route waypoints

**1 768.2mi, 0:40hr**
PCT/JMT Trail junction. Keep ahead on PCT (R if using the JMT to access Mt Whitney)

**2 771.5mi, 2:00hr**
Ford Wallace Crk (can be challenging early season) and cross the subsequent trail junction straight ahead

**3 772.2mi, 2:45hr**
Ford Wright Crk (also care required early season)

## Stage 30

### Crabtree Meadow to Kearsarge Pass Trail

| | |
|---|---|
| **Start** | **Crabtree Meadow** |
| **Finish** | **Kearsarge Pass Trail** |
| **Distance** | **22.6 miles** |
| **Total ascent** | **5394ft** |
| **Total descent** | **5016ft** |
| **Duration** | **12:50hr** |

With several bigger creeks to cross, Forester Pass to climb, and an optional side trip to summit Mount Whitney, this is an exciting but serious stage. If creeks are high, consider waiting until early mornings to cross, when colder overnight temperatures reduce melt and therefore creek levels. Mount Whitney is not especially difficult, but if significant snow remains an axe and traction may be required near the summit.

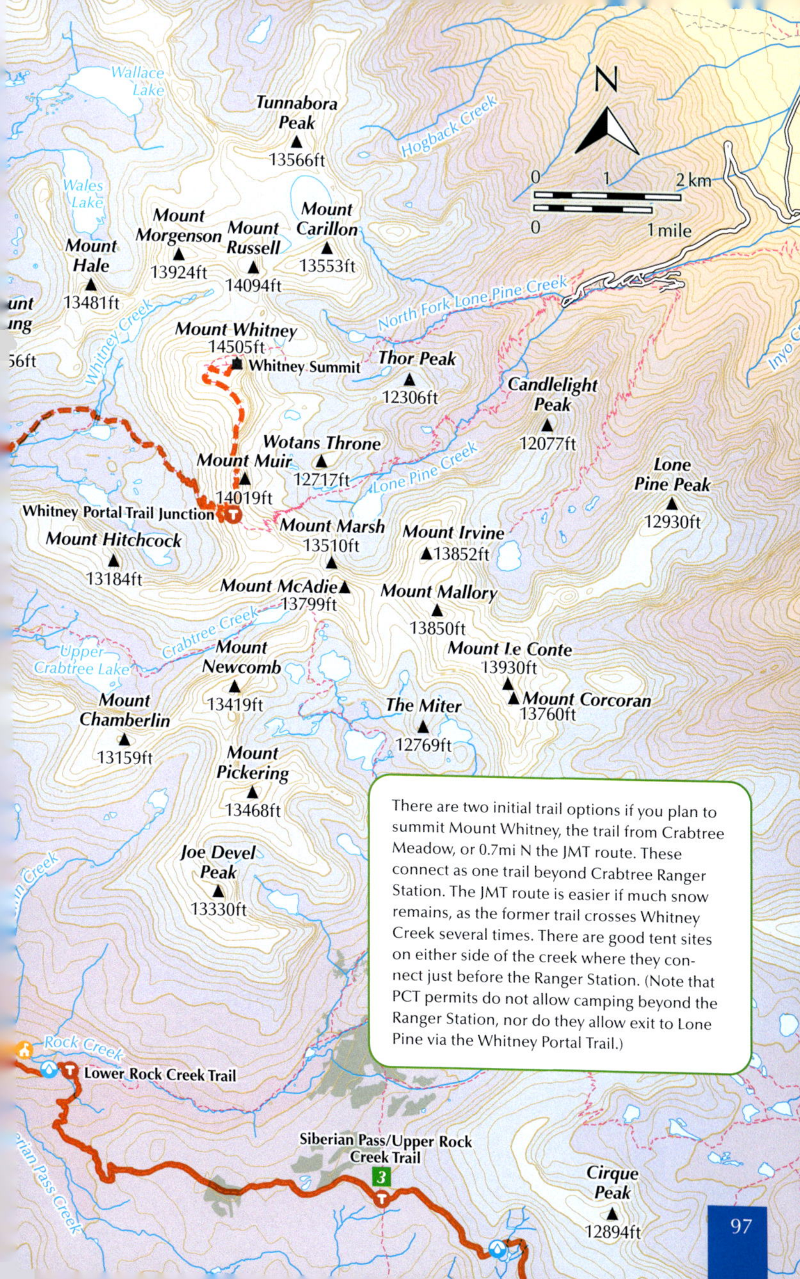
Wallace Lake
Tunnabora Peak 13566ft
Hogback Creek
N
0 1 2 km
0 1 mile
Wales Lake
Mount Carillon 13553ft
Mount Morgenson 13924ft
Mount Russell 14094ft
Mount Hale 13481ft
North Fork Lone Pine Creek
Whitney Creek
Mount Whitney 14505ft
Whitney Summit
Thor Peak 12306ft
Inyo Creek
Candlelight Peak 12077ft
Wotans Throne 12717ft
Mount Muir 14019ft
Lone Pine Creek
Lone Pine Peak 12930ft
Whitney Portal Trail Junction
Mount Marsh 13510ft
Mount Irvine 13852ft
Mount Hitchcock 13184ft
Mount McAdie 13799ft
Mount Mallory 13850ft
Crabtree Creek
Upper Crabtree Lake
Mount Newcomb 13419ft
Mount Le Conte 13930ft
Mount Corcoran 13760ft
Mount Chamberlin 13159ft
The Miter 12769ft
Mount Pickering 13468ft
Joe Devel Peak 13330ft
There are two initial trail options if you plan to summit Mount Whitney, the trail from Crabtree Meadow, or 0.7mi N the JMT route. These connect as one trail beyond Crabtree Ranger Station. The JMT route is easier if much snow remains, as the former trail crosses Whitney Creek several times. There are good tent sites on either side of the creek where they connect just before the Ranger Station. (Note that PCT permits do not allow camping beyond the Ranger Station, nor do they allow exit to Lone Pine via the Whitney Portal Trail.)
Rock Creek
Lower Rock Creek Trail
Siberian Pass/Upper Rock Creek Trail
3
Cirque Peak 12894ft

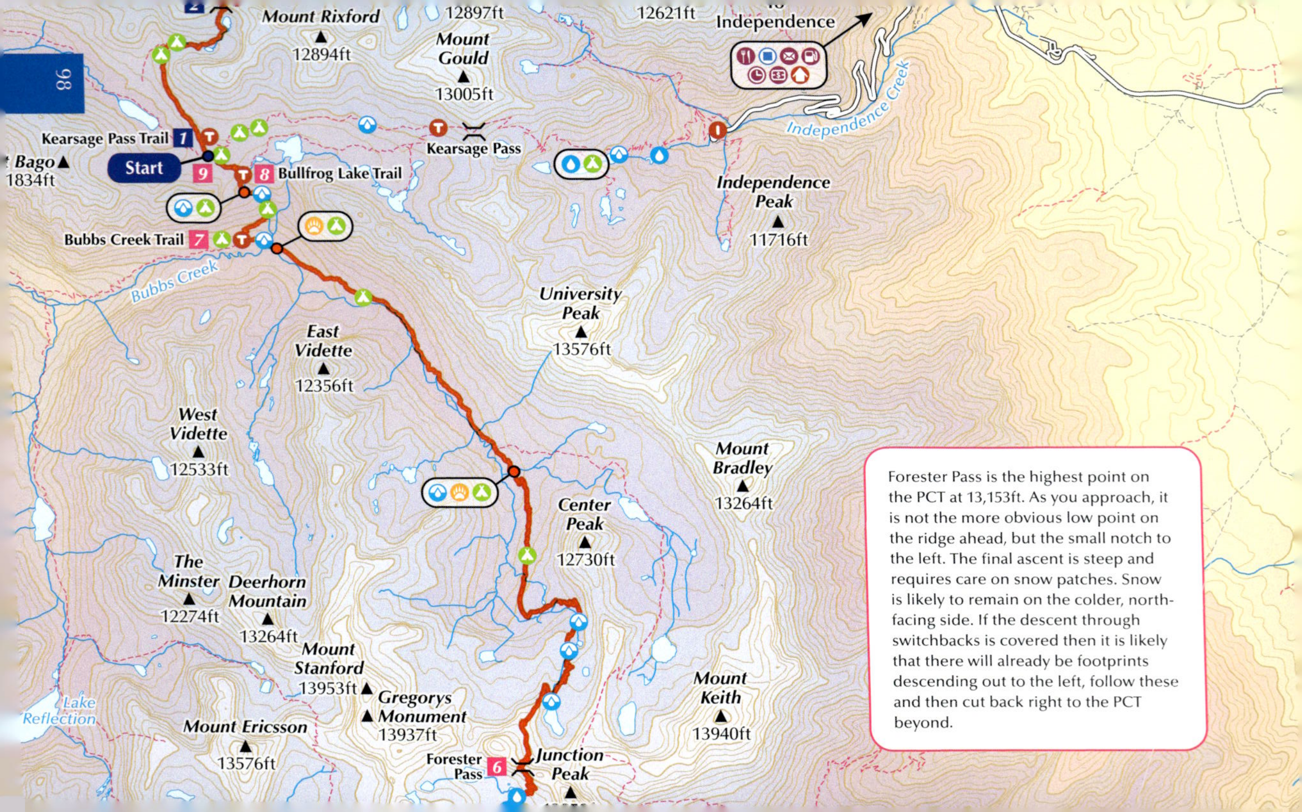


Forester Pass is the highest point on the PCT at 13,153ft. As you approach, it is not the more obvious low point on the ridge ahead, but the small notch to the left. The final ascent is steep and requires care on snow patches. Snow is likely to remain on the colder, north-facing side. If the descent through switchbacks is covered then it is likely that there will already be footprints descending out to the left, follow these and then cut back right to the PCT beyond.

**Stage 30 route waypoints – continued**

**4 775.3mi, 4:15hr**
Cross the seasonal outflow at Tyndall Frog Ponds

**5 775.9mi, 4:30hr**
Just beyond Shephard Pass Trail and junction to ranger station, ford Tyndall Crk (can be challenging early season)

**6 780.7mi, 8:00hr**
Ascend Forester Pass with care and descend NW of PCT initially if snowbound

**7 788.5mi, 11:55hr**
Keep R and ascend NE from Bubbs Crk Trail junction

**8 789.7mi, 12:25hr**
Pass Bullfrog Lake Trail (an option out to Kearsarge Pass but steep)

**9 790.1mi, 12:50hr**
Kearsarge Pass Trail (main route out to Onion Valley Trailhead, 7.6mi E over Kearsarge Pass, further 13mi E to Independence, or 42mi further to Bishop, a larger town, for resupply)

## Stage 31 route waypoints

**1 790.3mi, 0:10hr**
Second junction to Kearsarge Pass Trail

**2 792.3mi, 2:00hr**
Ascend Glen Pass by steep switchbacks. To descend, head R initially across boulders to avoid steep convex slope. Take care here, especially in snow

**3 794.1mi, 3:00hr**
Keep R at Sixty Lakes Trail junction to cross between Rae Lakes

**4 797.1mi, 4:10hr**
After crossing flow between Arrowhead and Dollar Lakes, keep L at junction with Baxter Pass Trail

**5 801.0mi, 6:00hr**
Cross Woods Crk suspension bridge, then turn R at junction heading NE

**6 801.3mi, 6:10hr**
Pass Woods Crk 'waterslide'. Slippery rocks make this dangerous so best avoided. Subsequent White Fork also requires care if flowing well

**7 804.6mi, 9:00hr**
Keep L at Sawmill Pass Trail junction

**8 808.3mi, 12:00hr**
Cross Pinchot Pass

**9 811.4mi, 13:15hr**
Taboose Pass Trail (exit possible 9.4mi NE over pass to Taboose Creek Rd, then 5.8mi out to Hwy 395, 12mi S of Big Pine)

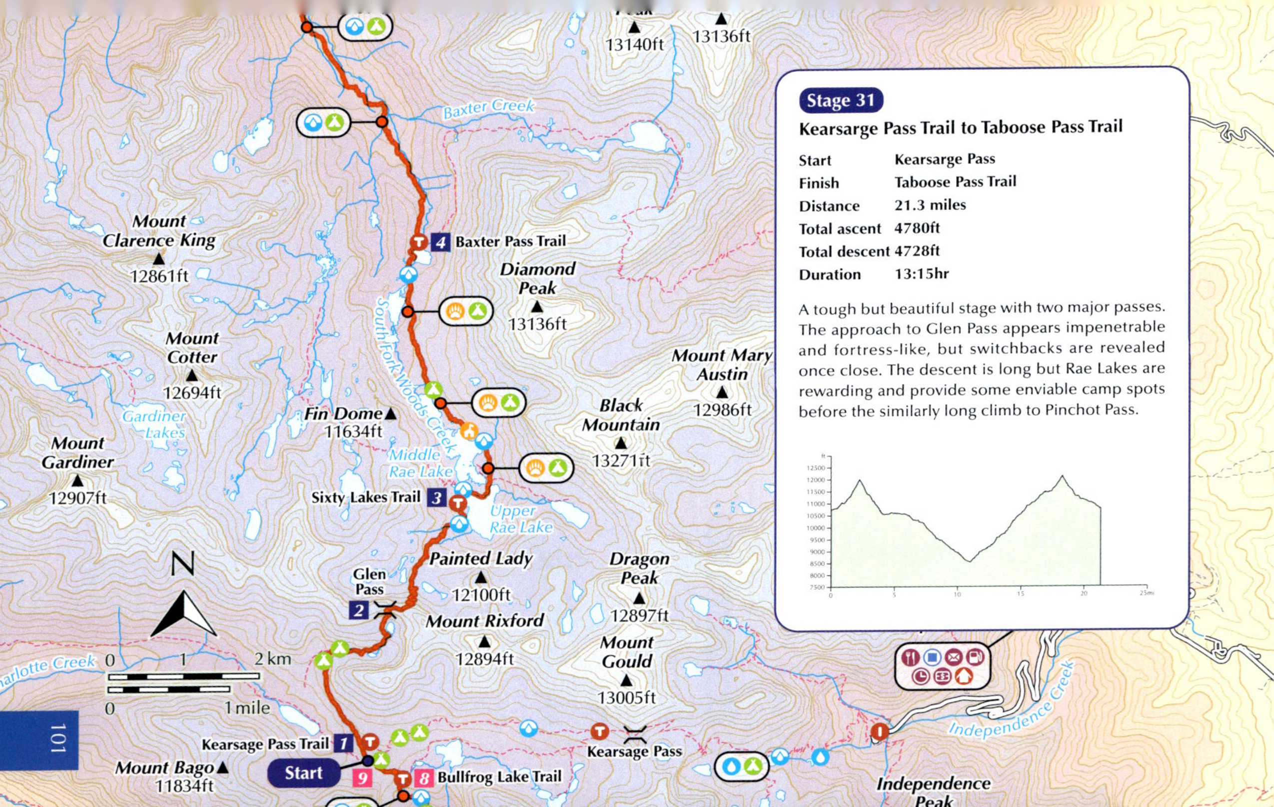


## Stage 31

### Kearsarge Pass Trail to Taboose Pass Trail

| | |
|---|---|
| Start | Kearsarge Pass |
| Finish | Taboose Pass Trail |
| Distance | 21.3 miles |
| Total ascent | 4780ft |
| Total descent | 4728ft |
| Duration | 13:15hr |

A tough but beautiful stage with two major passes. The approach to Glen Pass appears impenetrable and fortress-like, but switchbacks are revealed once close. The descent is long but Rae Lakes are rewarding and provide some enviable camp spots before the similarly long climb to Pinchot Pass.

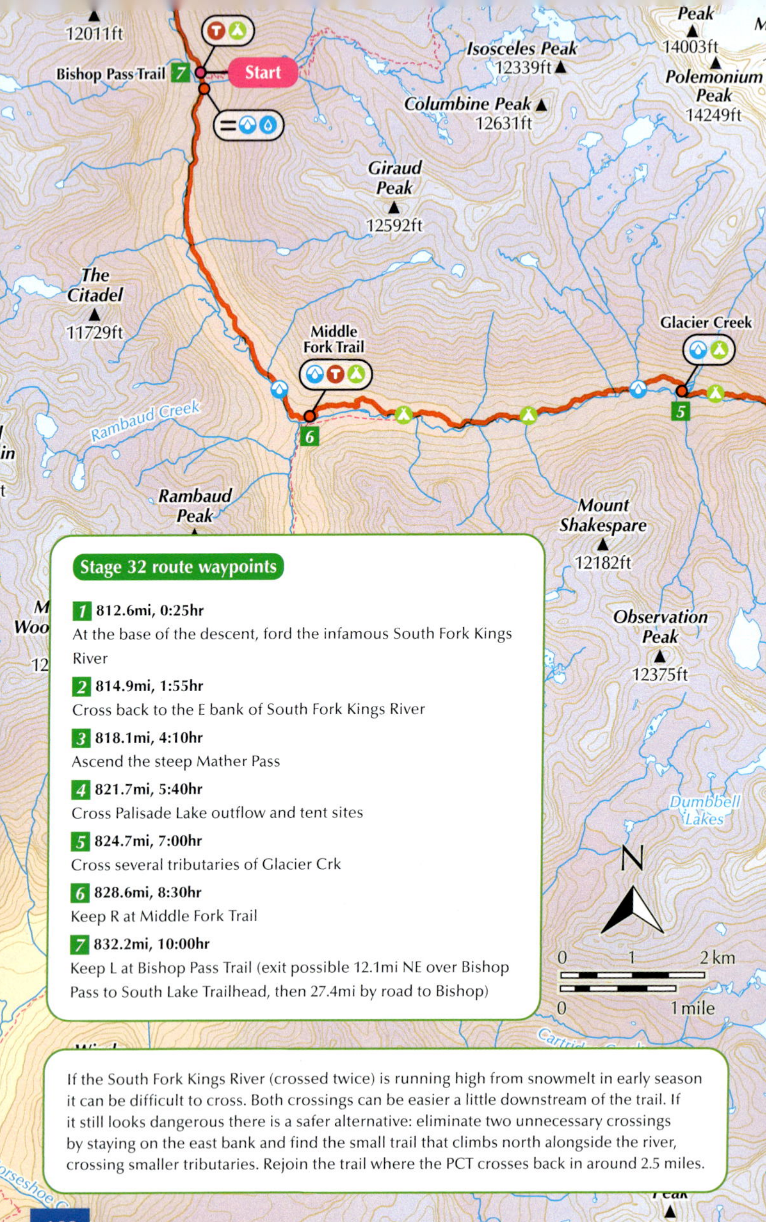


## Stage 32 route waypoints

**1 812.6mi, 0:25hr**
At the base of the descent, ford the infamous South Fork Kings River

**2 814.9mi, 1:55hr**
Cross back to the E bank of South Fork Kings River

**3 818.1mi, 4:10hr**
Ascend the steep Mather Pass

**4 821.7mi, 5:40hr**
Cross Palisade Lake outflow and tent sites

**5 824.7mi, 7:00hr**
Cross several tributaries of Glacier Crk

**6 828.6mi, 8:30hr**
Keep R at Middle Fork Trail

**7 832.2mi, 10:00hr**
Keep L at Bishop Pass Trail (exit possible 12.1mi NE over Bishop Pass to South Lake Trailhead, then 27.4mi by road to Bishop)

If the South Fork Kings River (crossed twice) is running high from snowmelt in early season it can be difficult to cross. Both crossings can be easier a little downstream of the trail. If it still looks dangerous there is a safer alternative: eliminate two unnecessary crossings by staying on the east bank and find the small trail that climbs north alongside the river, crossing smaller tributaries. Rejoin the trail where the PCT crosses back in around 2.5 miles.

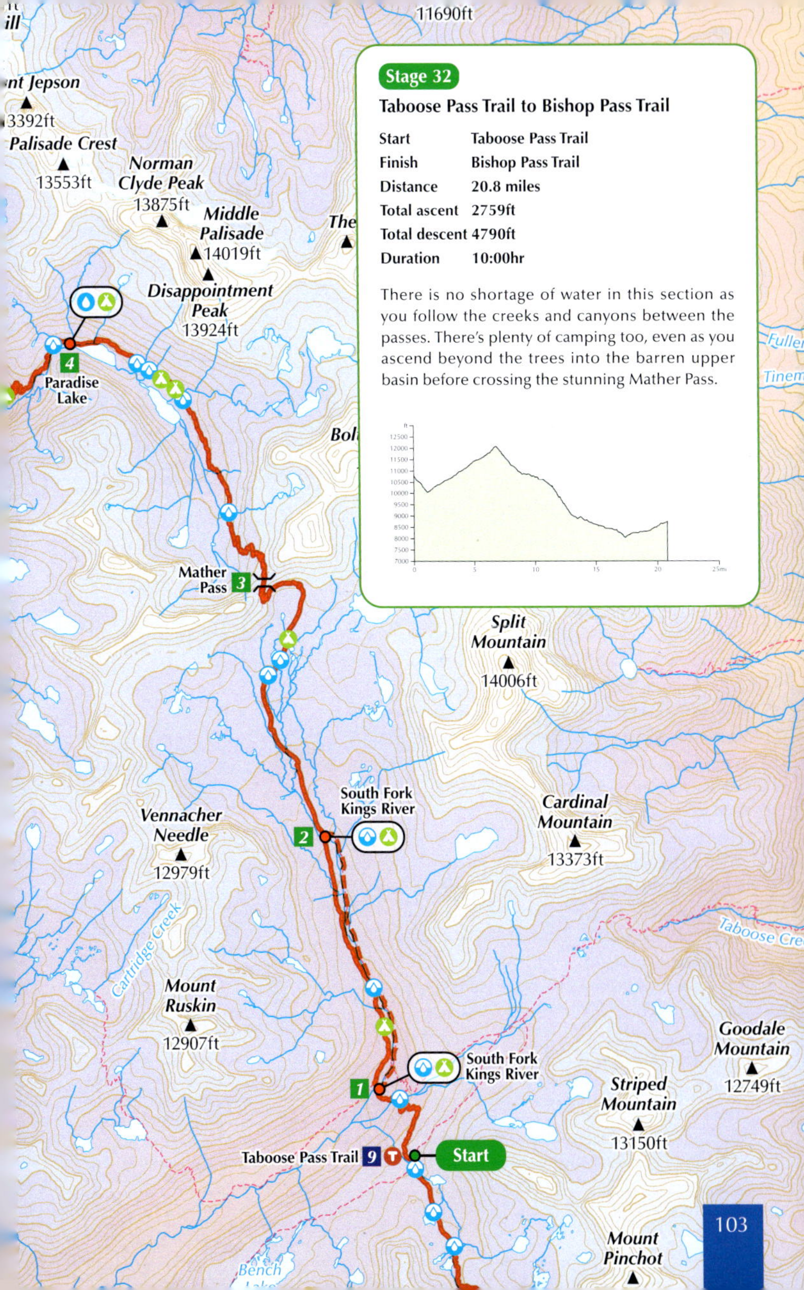


## Stage 32

### Taboose Pass Trail to Bishop Pass Trail

| | |
|---|---|
| Start | Taboose Pass Trail |
| Finish | Bishop Pass Trail |
| Distance | 20.8 miles |
| Total ascent | 2759ft |
| Total descent | 4790ft |
| Duration | 10:00hr |

There is no shortage of water in this section as you follow the creeks and canyons between the passes. There's plenty of camping too, even as you ascend beyond the trees into the barren upper basin before crossing the stunning Mather Pass.

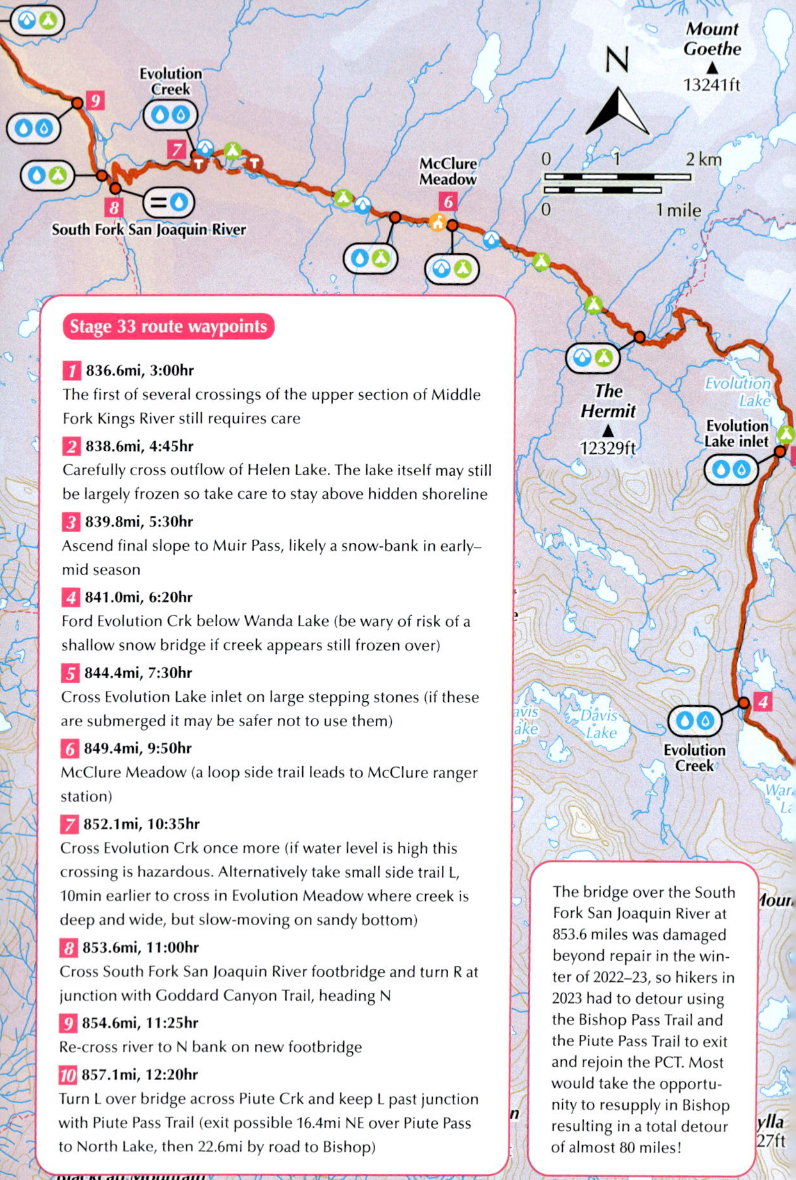


## Stage 33 route waypoints

**1 836.6mi, 3:00hr**
The first of several crossings of the upper section of Middle Fork Kings River still requires care

**2 838.6mi, 4:45hr**
Carefully cross outflow of Helen Lake. The lake itself may still be largely frozen so take care to stay above hidden shoreline

**3 839.8mi, 5:30hr**
Ascend final slope to Muir Pass, likely a snow-bank in early–mid season

**4 841.0mi, 6:20hr**
Ford Evolution Crk below Wanda Lake (be wary of risk of a shallow snow bridge if creek appears still frozen over)

**5 844.4mi, 7:30hr**
Cross Evolution Lake inlet on large stepping stones (if these are submerged it may be safer not to use them)

**6 849.4mi, 9:50hr**
McClure Meadow (a loop side trail leads to McClure ranger station)

**7 852.1mi, 10:35hr**
Cross Evolution Crk once more (if water level is high this crossing is hazardous. Alternatively take small side trail L, 10min earlier to cross in Evolution Meadow where creek is deep and wide, but slow-moving on sandy bottom)

**8 853.6mi, 11:00hr**
Cross South Fork San Joaquin River footbridge and turn R at junction with Goddard Canyon Trail, heading N

**9 854.6mi, 11:25hr**
Re-cross river to N bank on new footbridge

**10 857.1mi, 12:20hr**
Turn L over bridge across Piute Crk and keep L past junction with Piute Pass Trail (exit possible 16.4mi NE over Piute Pass to North Lake, then 22.6mi by road to Bishop)

The bridge over the South Fork San Joaquin River at 853.6 miles was damaged beyond repair in the winter of 2022–23, so hikers in 2023 had to detour using the Bishop Pass Trail and the Piute Pass Trail to exit and rejoin the PCT. Most would take the opportunity to resupply in Bishop resulting in a total detour of almost 80 miles!

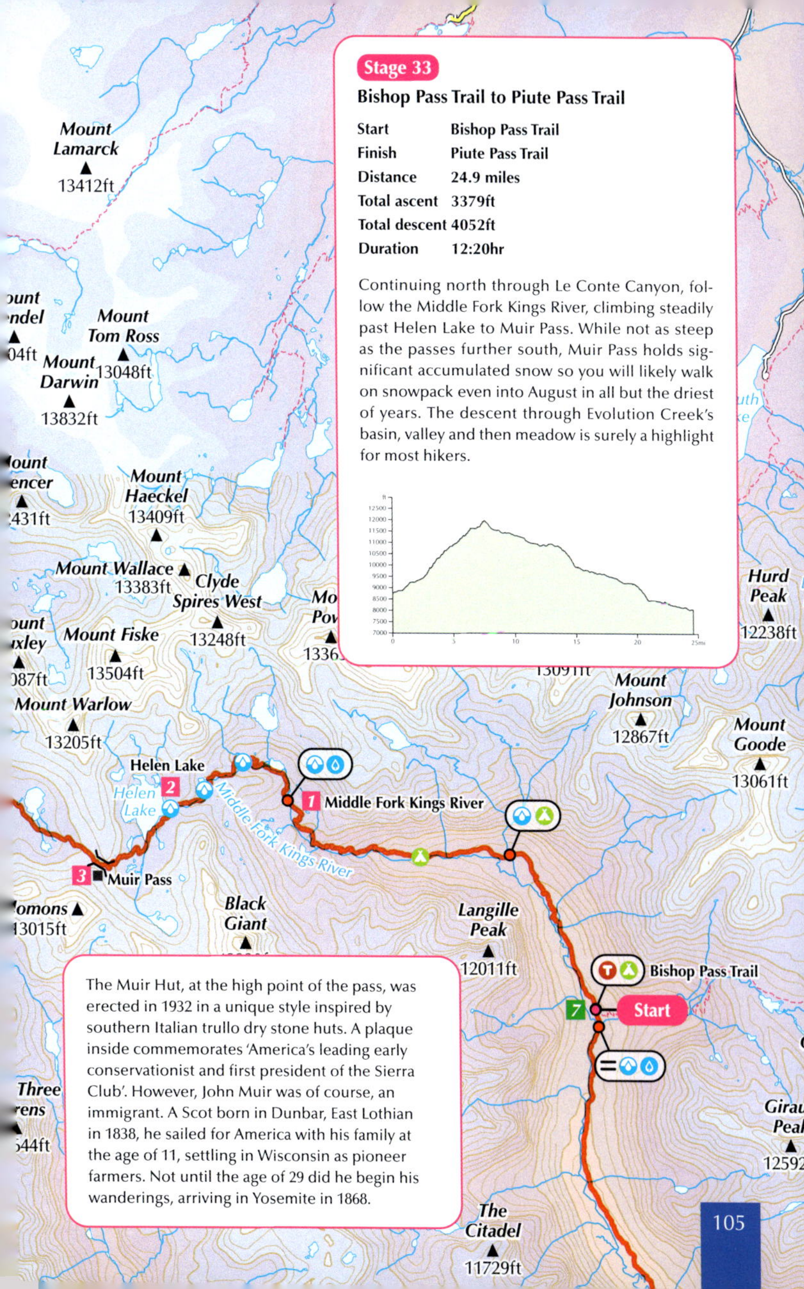


## Stage 33

### Bishop Pass Trail to Piute Pass Trail

| | |
|---|---|
| Start | Bishop Pass Trail |
| Finish | Piute Pass Trail |
| Distance | 24.9 miles |
| Total ascent | 3379ft |
| Total descent | 4052ft |
| Duration | 12:20hr |

Continuing north through Le Conte Canyon, follow the Middle Fork Kings River, climbing steadily past Helen Lake to Muir Pass. While not as steep as the passes further south, Muir Pass holds significant accumulated snow so you will likely walk on snowpack even into August in all but the driest of years. The descent through Evolution Creek's basin, valley and then meadow is surely a highlight for most hikers.

The Muir Hut, at the high point of the pass, was erected in 1932 in a unique style inspired by southern Italian trullo dry stone huts. A plaque inside commemorates 'America's leading early conservationist and first president of the Sierra Club'. However, John Muir was of course, an immigrant. A Scot born in Dunbar, East Lothian in 1838, he sailed for America with his family at the age of 11, settling in Wisconsin as pioneer farmers. Not until the age of 29 did he begin his wanderings, arriving in Yosemite in 1868.

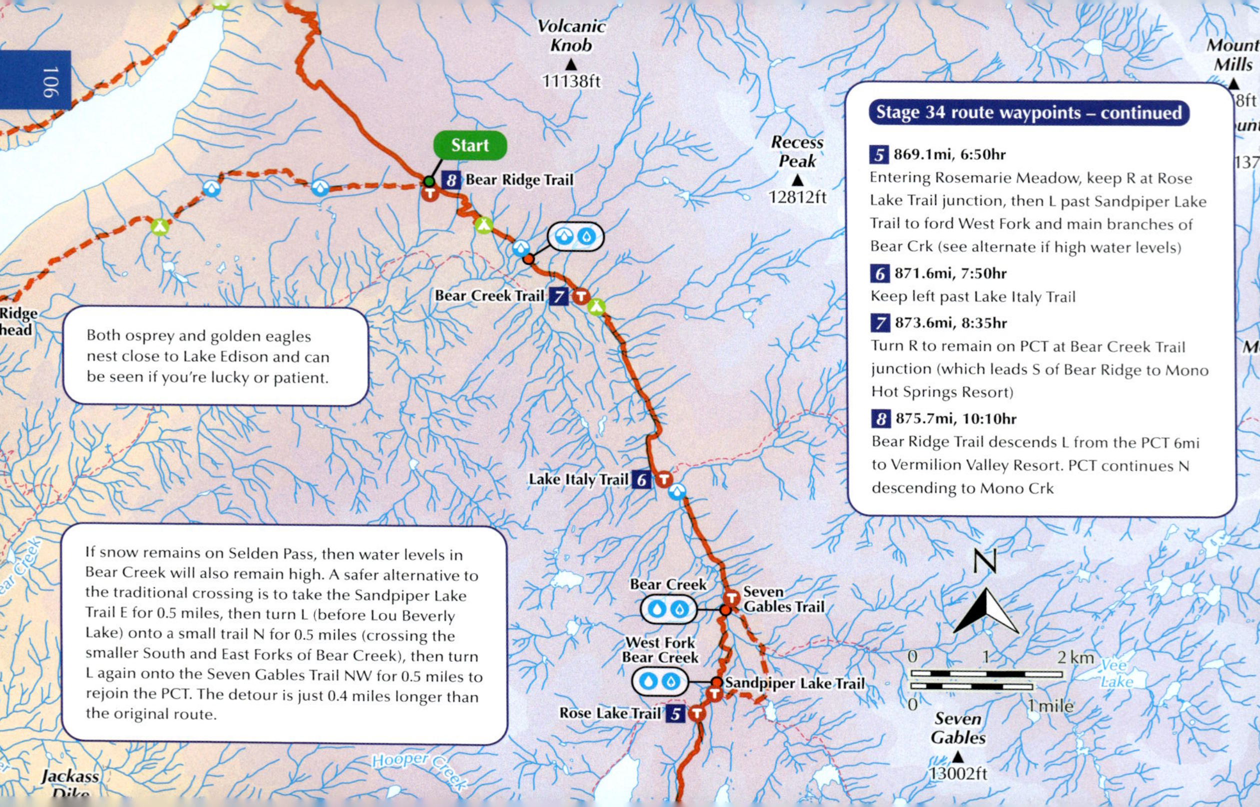


## Stage 34 route waypoints – continued

**5 869.1mi, 6:50hr**
Entering Rosemarie Meadow, keep R at Rose Lake Trail junction, then L past Sandpiper Lake Trail to ford West Fork and main branches of Bear Crk (see alternate if high water levels)

**6 871.6mi, 7:50hr**
Keep left past Lake Italy Trail

**7 873.6mi, 8:35hr**
Turn R to remain on PCT at Bear Creek Trail junction (which leads S of Bear Ridge to Mono Hot Springs Resort)

**8 875.7mi, 10:10hr**
Bear Ridge Trail descends L from the PCT 6mi to Vermilion Valley Resort. PCT continues N descending to Mono Crk

Both osprey and golden eagles nest close to Lake Edison and can be seen if you're lucky or patient.

If snow remains on Selden Pass, then water levels in Bear Creek will also remain high. A safer alternative to the traditional crossing is to take the Sandpiper Lake Trail E for 0.5 miles, then turn L (before Lou Beverly Lake) onto a small trail N for 0.5 miles (crossing the smaller South and East Forks of Bear Creek), then turn L again onto the Seven Gables Trail NW for 0.5 miles to rejoin the PCT. The detour is just 0.4 miles longer than the original route.

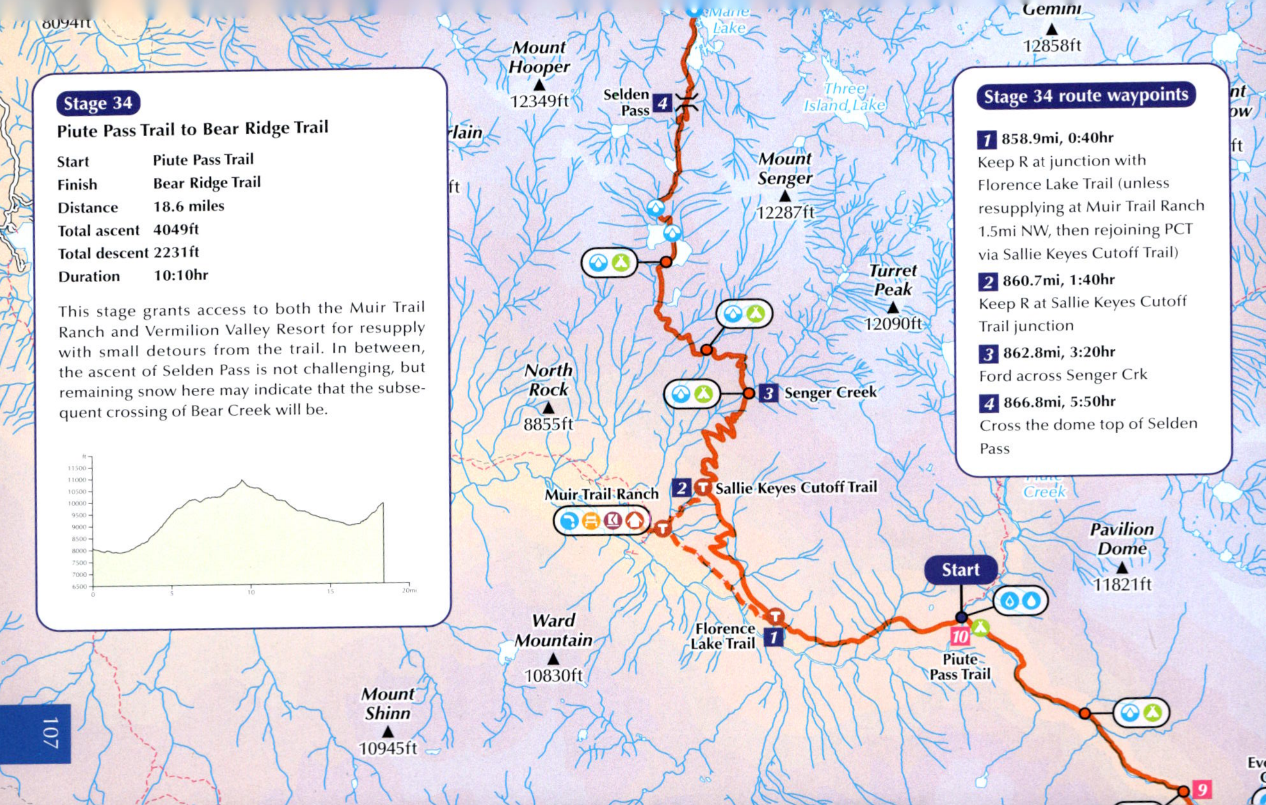


## Stage 34

### Piute Pass Trail to Bear Ridge Trail

| | |
|---|---|
| **Start** | **Piute Pass Trail** |
| **Finish** | **Bear Ridge Trail** |
| **Distance** | **18.6 miles** |
| **Total ascent** | **4049ft** |
| **Total descent** | **2231ft** |
| **Duration** | **10:10hr** |

This stage grants access to both the Muir Trail Ranch and Vermilion Valley Resort for resupply with small detours from the trail. In between, the ascent of Selden Pass is not challenging, but remaining snow here may indicate that the subsequent crossing of Bear Creek will be.



### Stage 34 route waypoints

**1 858.9mi, 0:40hr**
Keep R at junction with Florence Lake Trail (unless resupplying at Muir Trail Ranch 1.5mi NW, then rejoining PCT via Sallie Keyes Cutoff Trail)

**2 860.7mi, 1:40hr**
Keep R at Sallie Keyes Cutoff Trail junction

**3 862.8mi, 3:20hr**
Ford across Senger Crk

**4 866.8mi, 5:50hr**
Cross the dome top of Selden Pass

## Stage 35 route waypoints

**1 879.9mi, 1:40hr**
Cross Mono Crk on a footbridge into Quail Meadow. Turn R at trail junction (1mi W to ferry landing, then 4.5m W to VVR,) then cross North Fork Mono Crk (difficult in early season)

**2 881.3mi, 2:30hr**
Keep L past Mono Pass Trail

**3 882.7mi, 3:20hr**
Turn L at Mott Lake Trail junction, across North Fork Mono Creek again (deep, cold and dangerous in early season), climb alongside Silver Pass Crk

**4 886.1mi, 5:25hr**
Cross Silver Pass and climb to viewpoint

**5 887.2mi, 5:50hr**
Bear R at Goodale Pass Trail junction (alternate route 11.3mi to/from VVR)

**6 889.7mi, 7:00hr**
Keep R at Cascade Valley Trail junction

**7 890.7mi, 7:40hr**
Keep L past McGee Pass Trail at Tully Hole

**8 896.9mi, 10:40hr**
Keep L past Duck Pass Trail

**9 907.8mi, 14:45hr**
Spur to Red's Meadow Pack Station and Resort (0.3mi NE)

## Stage 35

### Bear Ridge Trail to Red's Meadow

| | |
|---|---|
| **Start** | **Bear Ridge Trail** |
| **Finish** | **Red's Meadow** |
| **Distance** | **32.1 miles** |
| **Total ascent** | **5604ft** |
| **Total descent** | **7792ft** |
| **Duration** | **14:45hr** |

As most hikers will visit Vermilion Valley Resort (VVR), the stage will start there for many. The morning boat across the lake is popular, but the trail around the north shore of the lake is a good option if you wish to leave earlier, either way, rejoining the PCT at the junction by Mono Creek. An interesting alternative is to use the Goodale Pass Trail to rejoin the PCT beyond Silver Pass. Red's Meadow is conveniently just off trail, and a regular bus runs down the mountain to the town of Mammoth Lakes.

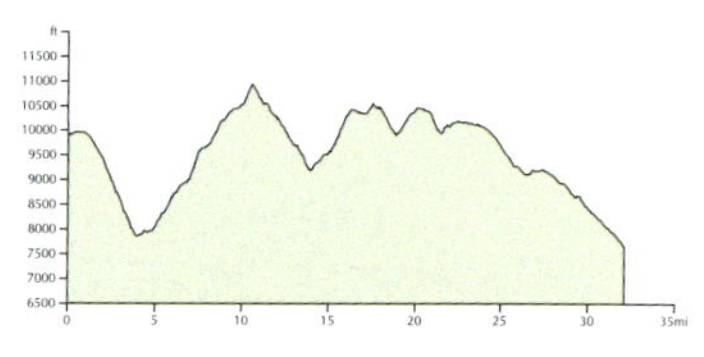


VVR Ferry: operates June–September (incl.)
VVR Dock: 9am–4pm
Mono Creek: 9:45am–4.45pm
$20/head (2024), max 8 persons/boat
No operation in thunder/lightning/high wind

13140ft
7 McGee Pass Trail
Fish Creek
6 Cascade Valley Trail
Red and White Mountain
12822ft
Goodale Pass Trail 5
Mount Izaak Walton
12051ft
Silver Pass 4
Grinnell Lake
3 Mott Lake Trail
0 1 2 km
0 1 mile
Mono Pass Trail 2
North Fork Mono Creek
1
VVR ferry
Quail Meadow
Volcanic Knob
11138ft
Start
8 Bear Ridge Trail
Recess Peak
12812ft
Bear Creek Trail 7

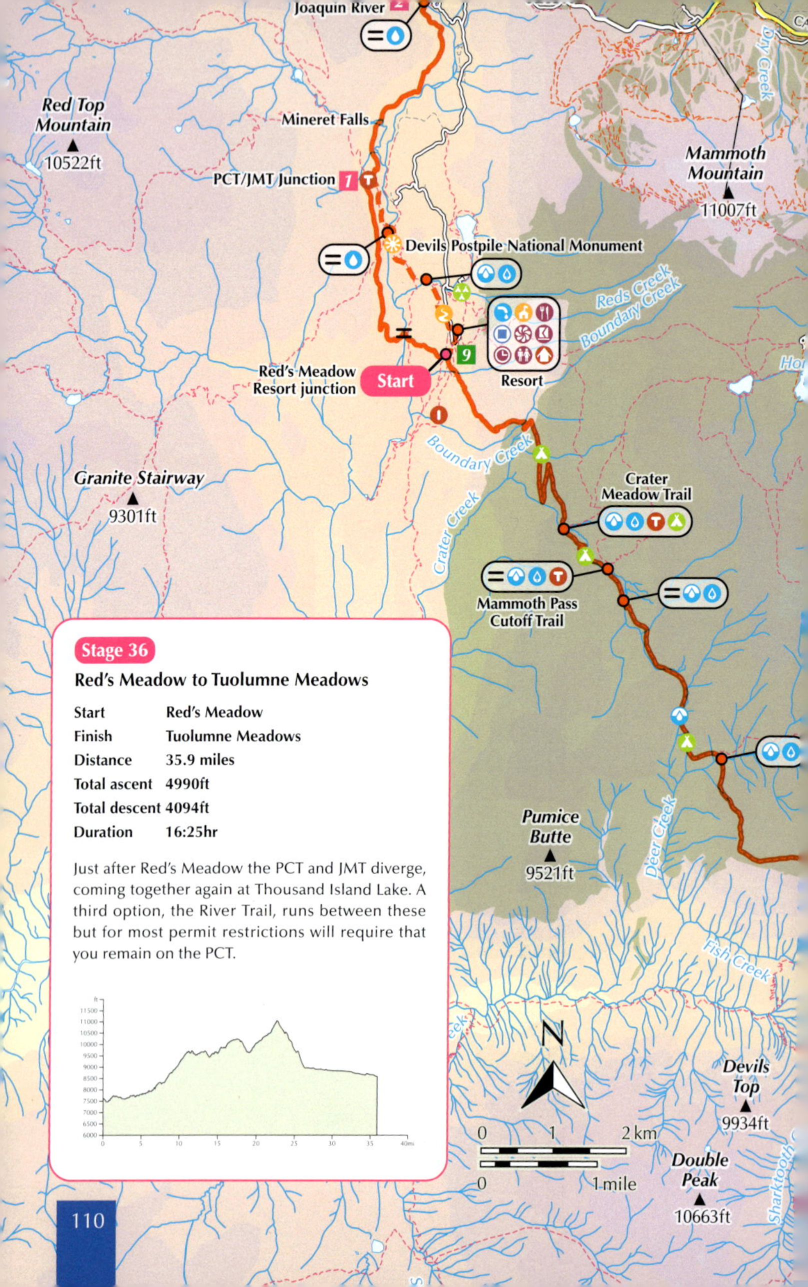


## Stage 36

### Red's Meadow to Tuolumne Meadows

| | |
|---|---|
| Start | Red's Meadow |
| Finish | Tuolumne Meadows |
| Distance | 35.9 miles |
| Total ascent | 4990ft |
| Total descent | 4094ft |
| Duration | 16:25hr |

Just after Red's Meadow the PCT and JMT diverge, coming together again at Thousand Island Lake. A third option, the River Trail, runs between these but for most permit restrictions will require that you remain on the PCT.

**Stage 36 route waypoints**

**1 910.2mi, 0:40hr**
Keep R at junction as PCT and JMT diverge just before Minaret Falls

**2 912.2mi, 1:30hr**
Bridge over Middle Fork San Joaquin River

Thru-hikers passing through before mid-July should not send ice axes or spikes home yet. The north-facing descent from Sonora Pass can hold dangerous, icy snow slopes well into summer. Bear canisters are still required also.

Few hikers will pass up the opportunity to take a brief side trip to see the Devils Postpile National Monument. Formed around 900,000 years ago by the slow cooling and cracking of hot lava, the result is the polygonal basaltic columns that remain today. A signed trail from Red's Meadow Resort leads past the Devils Postpile then over a bridge across Middle Fork San Joaquin River to a junction with the PCT and JMT.

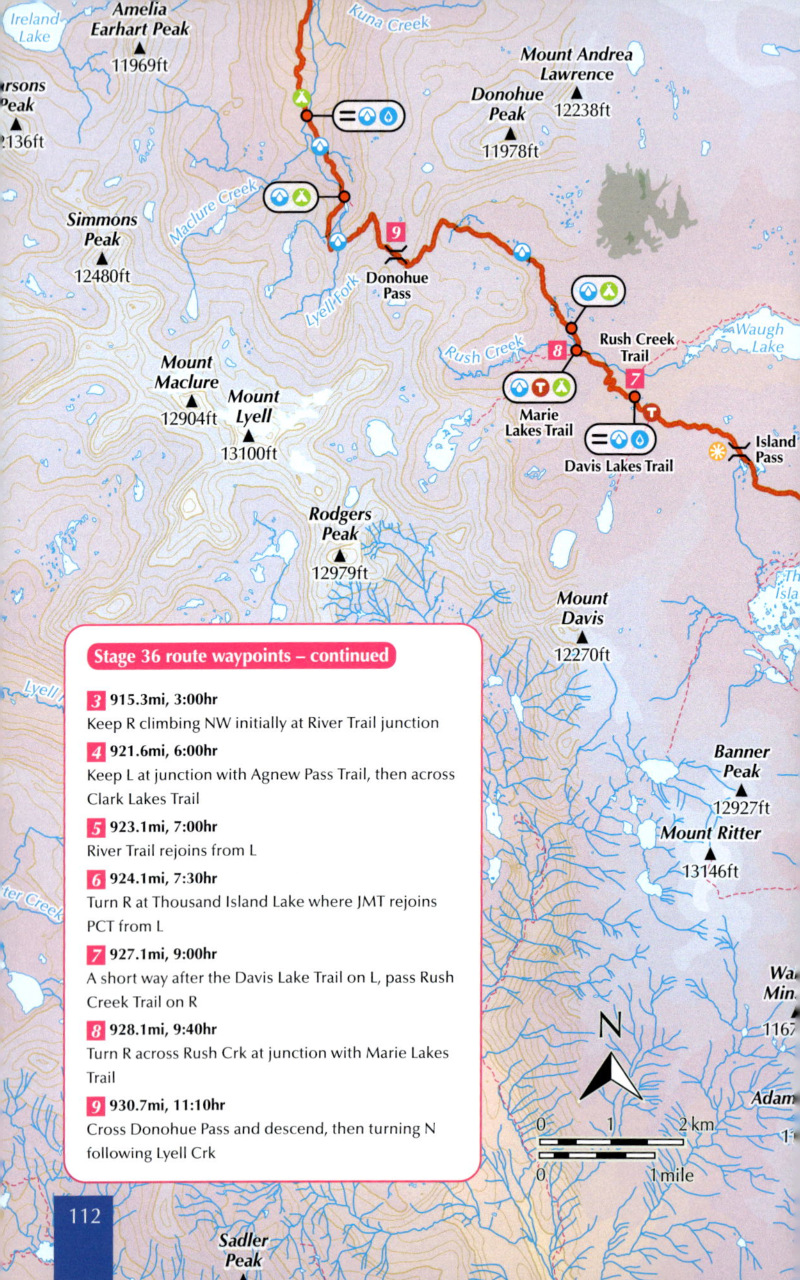


## Stage 36 route waypoints – continued

**3** **915.3mi, 3:00hr**
Keep R climbing NW initially at River Trail junction

**4** **921.6mi, 6:00hr**
Keep L at junction with Agnew Pass Trail, then across Clark Lakes Trail

**5** **923.1mi, 7:00hr**
River Trail rejoins from L

**6** **924.1mi, 7:30hr**
Turn R at Thousand Island Lake where JMT rejoins PCT from L

**7** **927.1mi, 9:00hr**
A short way after the Davis Lake Trail on L, pass Rush Creek Trail on R

**8** **928.1mi, 9:40hr**
Turn R across Rush Crk at junction with Marie Lakes Trail

**9** **930.7mi, 11:10hr**
Cross Donohue Pass and descend, then turning N following Lyell Crk

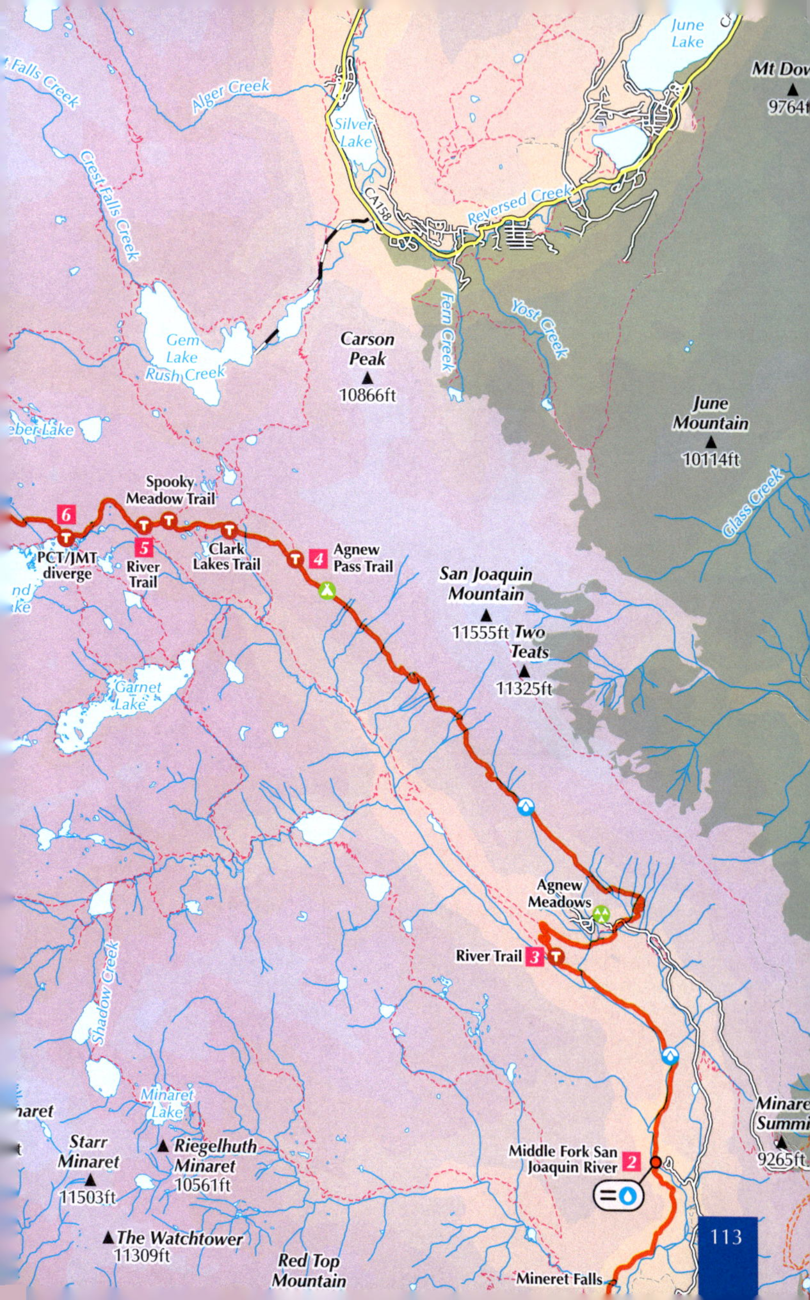
June Lake
Mt Dov
9764ft
Falls Creek
Alger Creek
Silver Lake
Crest Falls Creek
CA158
Reversed Creek
Fern Creek
Yost Creek
Gem Lake
Rush Creek
Carson Peak
10866ft
June Mountain
10114ft
Glass Creek
Spooky Meadow Trail
6
PCT/JMT diverge
5
River Trail
Clark Lakes Trail
4
Agnew Pass Trail
San Joaquin Mountain
11555ft
Two Teats
11325ft
Garnet Lake
Agnew Meadows
River Trail
3
Shadow Creek
Minaret Lake
Starr Minaret
11503ft
Riegelhuth Minaret
10561ft
Minaret Summit
9265ft
Middle Fork San Joaquin River
2
The Watchtower
11309ft
Red Top Mountain
Mineret Falls

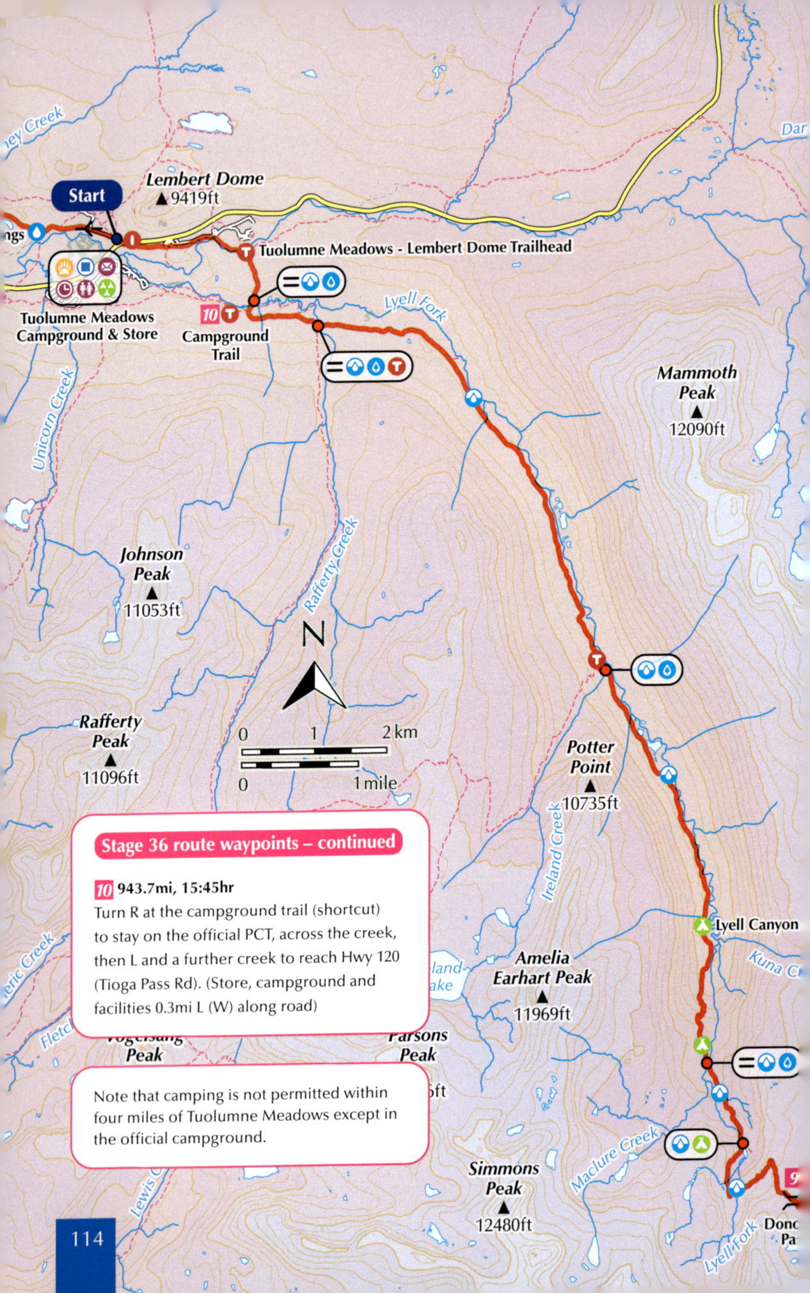


## Stage 36 route waypoints – continued

**10 943.7mi, 15:45hr**
Turn R at the campground trail (shortcut) to stay on the official PCT, across the creek, then L and a further creek to reach Hwy 120 (Tioga Pass Rd). (Store, campground and facilities 0.3mi L (W) along road)

Note that camping is not permitted within four miles of Tuolumne Meadows except in the official campground.

# SECTION 5 – TUOLUMNE MEADOWS TO INTERSTATE 80

| | Stage | Distance (miles) | Total ascent (feet) | Total descent (feet) | Average duration (hr:min) | Page |
|---|---|---|---|---|---|---|
| 37 | Tuolumne Meadows – Bear Valley Trail | 37.2 | 6775 | 7372 | 19:00 | 119 |
| 38 | Bear Valley Trail – Sonora Pass | 37.2 | 6348 | 4689 | 18:50 | 123 |
| 39 | Sonora Pass – Ebbetts Pass | 31.5 | 5384 | 6335 | 14:45 | 124 |
| 40 | Ebbetts Pass – Carson Pass | 28.3 | 4285 | 4432 | 12:10 | 129 |
| 41 | Carson Pass – Echo Lake | 15.5 | 2018 | 3150 | 6:45 | 131 |
| 42 | Echo Lake – Barker Pass | 32.6 | 4908 | 4485 | 14:50 | 133 |
| 43 | Barker Pass – Interstate 80 | 32.2 | 5236 | 5659 | 14:50 | 134 |
| **Totals** | | **214.5** | **34,954** | **36,122** | **101:10** | |

## WHAT TO EXPECT

The first two stages of this section, as far as Sonora Pass, are perhaps the most challenging of the whole trail when undertaken at the typical time for thru-hikers, in early July. Most hikers would be better to wait until mid–late July when the creeks have subsided, and most of the snow is gone. While the overall altitudes are slightly lower, you cross a succession of ridges and face some of the most difficult creek crossings yet. This section is more difficult to hike under snowpack than the previous one because of the time spent traversing, rather than ascending or descending, steep slopes. A particularly exposed alpine pass leads to a descent to Sonora Pass on a steep north-facing slope that holds snow and ice until late in the year. This descent catches out unprepared hikers each year. Microspikes or crampons and possibly an axe may be required to undertake this safely in early season. Beyond Sonora Pass the trail does become a little gentler and there are no more difficult creek crossings south of Washington.

It is hard not to notice the changes around you at Sonora Pass. The granite that has dominated the Sierra Crest so far, has given way to an increasingly and obviously volcanic landscape, and for a while there is an absence of lakes due to the porous nature of the underlying rock. Where small lakes do occur, it is generally because they have an underlying granitic bowl. This changes north of Highway 50 when you enter Desolation Wilderness. This is a wonderfully colorful section among the headwaters of the Truckee

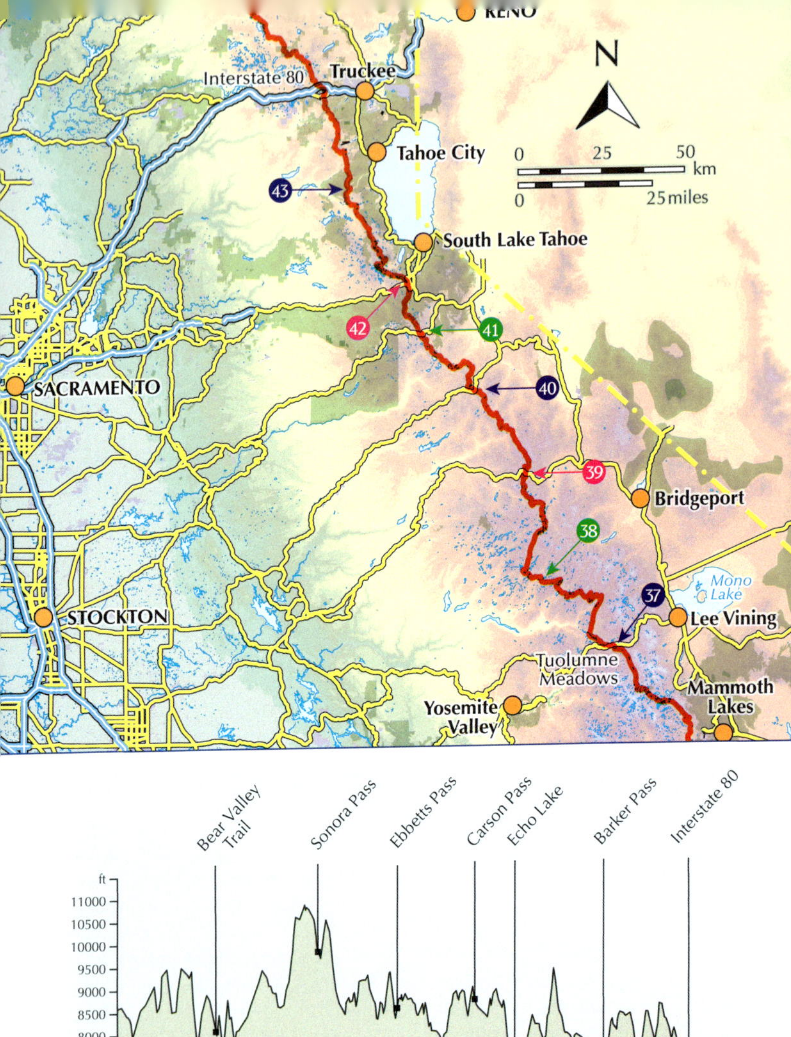

RENO
Interstate 80
Truckee
N
Tahoe City
0
25
50
km
0
25 miles
43
South Lake Tahoe
42
41
SACRAMENTO
40
39
Bridgeport
38
Mono Lake
37
STOCKTON
Lee Vining
Tuolumne Meadows
Mammoth Lakes
Yosemite Valley
Bear Valley Trail
Sonora Pass
Ebbetts Pass
Carson Pass
Echo Lake
Barker Pass
Interstate 80
ft
11000
10500
10000
9500
9000
8500
8000
7500
7000
6500
6000
5500
0
20
40
60
80
100
120
140
160
180
200
220mi

River, after the long sections of snow and rock that preceded. The contrasting purples and reds of lupines and paintbrush commonly found together, are a sight bound to delight.

Resupply continues to be more challenging with the route generally staying away from settlements. Most will want to head west at Sonora Pass, 9 miles to Kennedy Meadows Road, then 1.4 miles south to Kennedy Meadows (North) pack station and resort. In recent years the resort here has increased its offering to hikers with a range of affordable accommodation options and a store where you could certainly resupply. Beyond this, Caples Lake Resort has a small store, 5 miles west of Carson Pass, but most will wait until Echo Summit at Highway 50 and hitch into South Lake Tahoe for a full resupply to take them as far as Donner Pass and possibly into Truckee.

## RESUPPLY OPTIONS

| Stage | Trail mile | Place | Off trail (miles) | Description | Facilities |
|---|---|---|---|---|---|
| 38 | 1018.1 | Kennedy Meadows North | 10.2 W | Packstation with most hiker services and shuttle, accepts packages ($$) | |
| 38 | 1018.1 | Bridgeport | 32.0 E | Small town, most facilities but a long/challenging hitch | |
| 40 | 1077.9 | Caples Lake Resort | 5.0 W | Resort with rooms and cabins, restaurant and small store | |
| 41 | 1091.2 | South Lake Tahoe | 12.0 NE | Large but sprawling casino town, takes time to get around | |
| 41 | 1093.4 | Echo Lake Resort | On trail | Small summer resort with deli and limited/snack store | |
| 43 | 1154.6 | Donner Ski Ranch | 0.3 W | Bar/restaurant with some bunks, laundry | |
| 43 | 1154.6 | Soda Springs | 3.4 W | Small community with hiker-focused store and nearby PO | |
| 43 | 1154.6 | Truckee | 9.0 E | Small town with good facilities and expensive accommodation | |

## PERMITS

If you have not secured a PCT long-distance permit starting from either the southern terminus or Sonora Pass, then local permits are required for overnight trips in Carson Iceberg Wilderness, PCT miles 1022.2 to 1042.9, overnight trips in Mokelumne Wilderness, PCT miles 1053.0 to 1077.3, and overnight trips in Desolation Wilderness, PCT miles 1096.6 to 1118.3.

Sonora Pass is within the boundary of the Stanislaus National Forest, Summit Ranger District. The Stanislaus National Forest is authorized to issue wilderness permits for trips as far north as Echo Summit.

To obtain a permit, visit Sonora Pass Summit Ranger Station on Highway 108 where permits can be obtained on a self-service basis from a kiosk at the front of the ranger station.

For more information call the Stanislaus National Forest office on (209) 532-3671 or visit: www.fs.usda.gov/detailfull/stanislaus/specialplaces/?cid=stelprdb5361242

Desolation Wilderness permits are subject to a daily quota and 70% of these can be reserved up to six months in advance online. The remaining 30% are available on a walk-in/same day basis at Placerville Ranger Station in Camino, seven days a week.

Note that a hard-sided bear canister is now a requirement in Desolation Wilderness.

To obtain a permit visit: www.recreation.gov/permits/233261

## MAIL DROP INFORMATION

Kennedy Meadows (North) resort and Pack Station
'Your Name Here'
c\o Kennedy Meadows Resort & Pack Station
57 Miles East of Sonora on Hwy 108
Sonora, CA 95370
ETA: 'Your ETA'
They are open: seven days a week
Phone them on: (209) 965-3900
Visit them at: www.kennedymeadows.com. Note that packages must be sent UPS only.

## POST OFFICE INFORMATION

'Your Name Here'
c\o General Delivery
Bridgeport, CA 93517
Located at: 29 Kingsley Street
Phone them on: (760) 932-7991

'Your Name Here'
c\o General Delivery
South Lake Tahoe, CA 96150
Located at: 950 Emerald Bay Road
Phone them on: (530) 541-4365

'Your Name Here'
c\o General Delivery
Soda Springs, CA 95728
Located at: 21719 Donner Pass Road
Phone them on: (530) 426-3082.

'Your Name Here'
c\o General Delivery
Truckee, CA 96161
Located at: 10050 Bridge Street
Phone them on: (530) 587-7158.

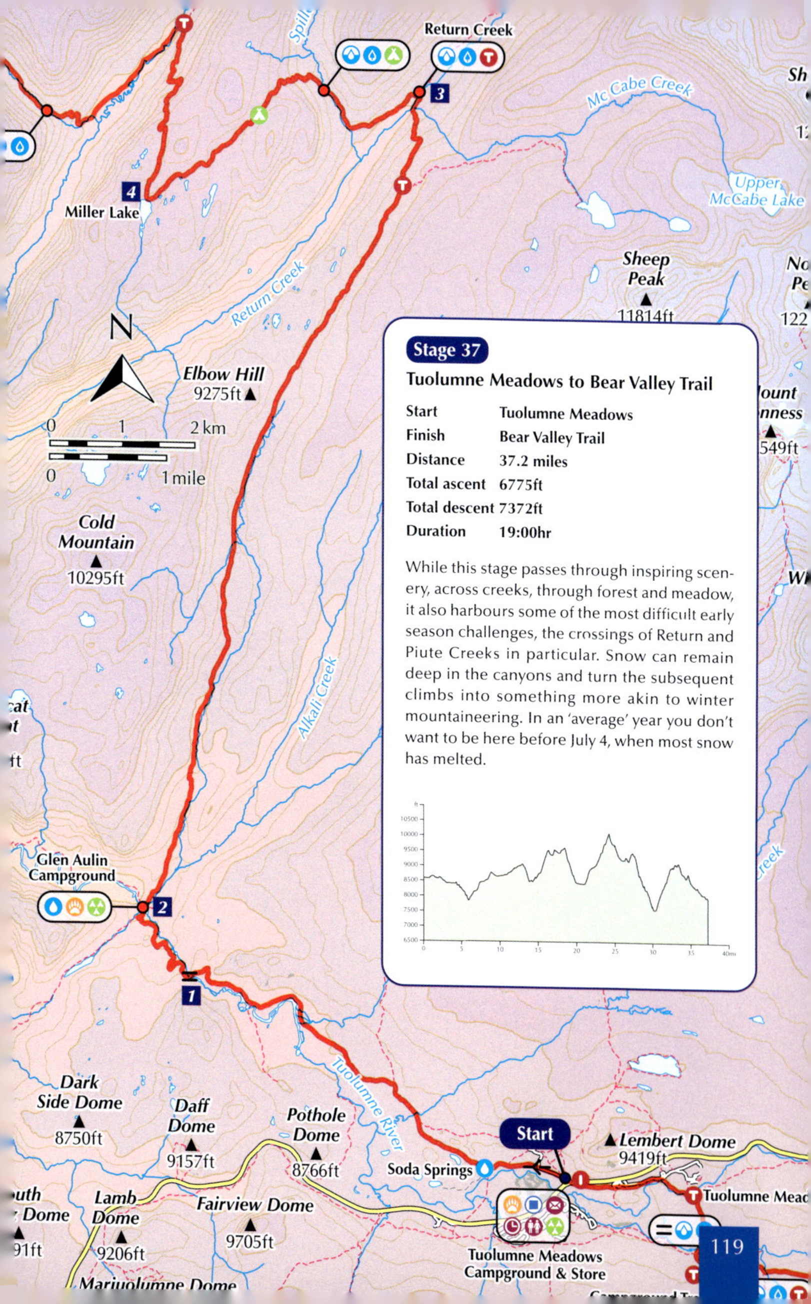


**Stage 37**

## Tuolumne Meadows to Bear Valley Trail

| | |
|---|---|
| **Start** | Tuolumne Meadows |
| **Finish** | Bear Valley Trail |
| **Distance** | 37.2 miles |
| **Total ascent** | 6775ft |
| **Total descent** | 7372ft |
| **Duration** | 19:00hr |

While this stage passes through inspiring scenery, across creeks, through forest and meadow, it also harbours some of the most difficult early season challenges, the crossings of Return and Piute Creeks in particular. Snow can remain deep in the canyons and turn the subsequent climbs into something more akin to winter mountaineering. In an 'average' year you don't want to be here before July 4, when most snow has melted.

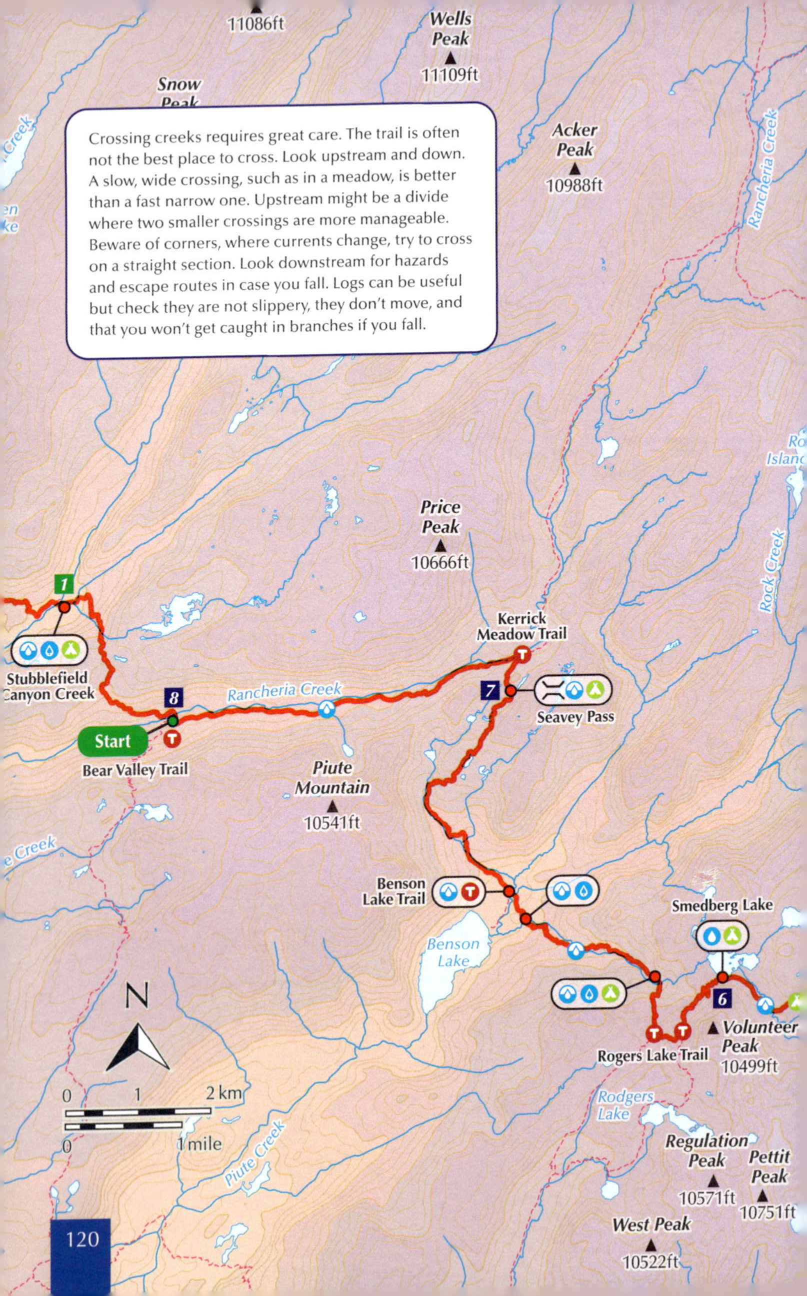


Crossing creeks requires great care. The trail is often not the best place to cross. Look upstream and down. A slow, wide crossing, such as in a meadow, is better than a fast narrow one. Upstream might be a divide where two smaller crossings are more manageable. Beware of corners, where currents change, try to cross on a straight section. Look downstream for hazards and escape routes in case you fall. Logs can be useful but check they are not slippery, they don't move, and that you won't get caught in branches if you fall.

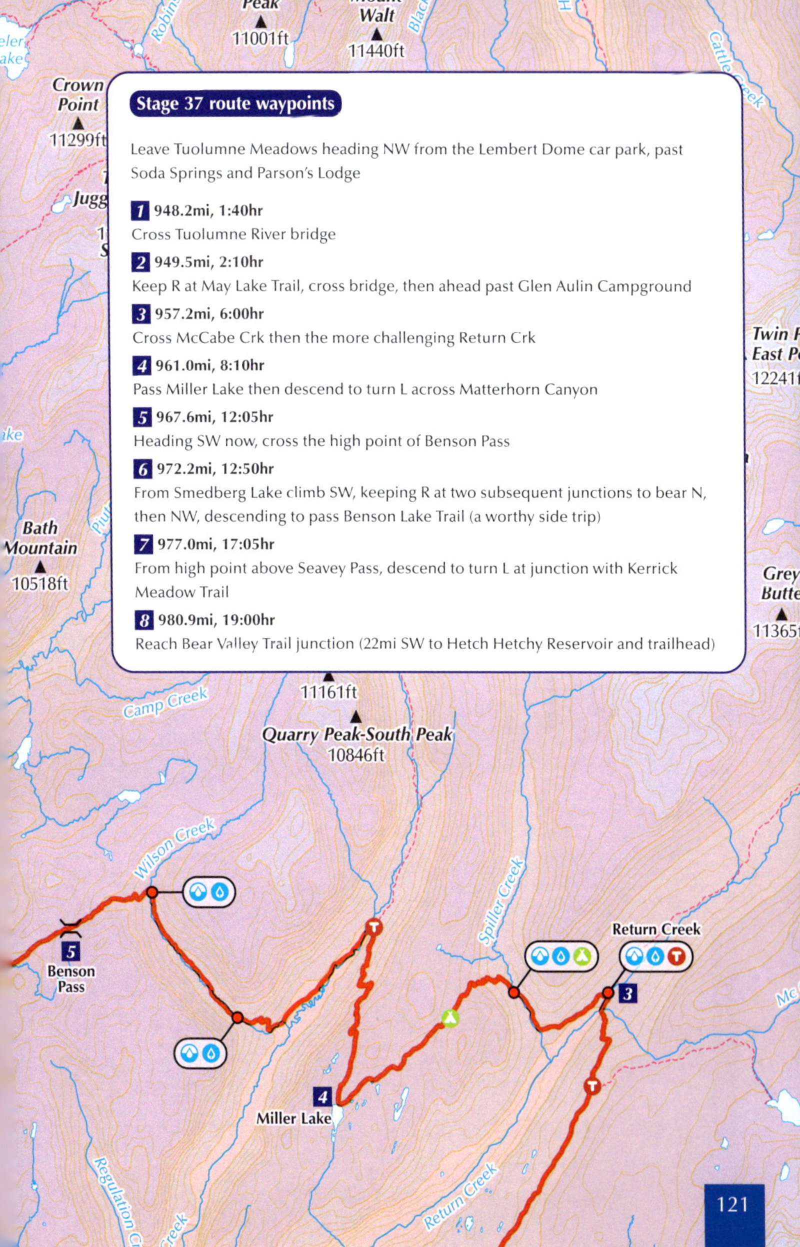


## Stage 37 route waypoints

Leave Tuolumne Meadows heading NW from the Lembert Dome car park, past Soda Springs and Parson's Lodge

**1 948.2mi, 1:40hr**
Cross Tuolumne River bridge

**2 949.5mi, 2:10hr**
Keep R at May Lake Trail, cross bridge, then ahead past Glen Aulin Campground

**3 957.2mi, 6:00hr**
Cross McCabe Crk then the more challenging Return Crk

**4 961.0mi, 8:10hr**
Pass Miller Lake then descend to turn L across Matterhorn Canyon

**5 967.6mi, 12:05hr**
Heading SW now, cross the high point of Benson Pass

**6 972.2mi, 12:50hr**
From Smedberg Lake climb SW, keeping R at two subsequent junctions to bear N, then NW, descending to pass Benson Lake Trail (a worthy side trip)

**7 977.0mi, 17:05hr**
From high point above Seavey Pass, descend to turn L at junction with Kerrick Meadow Trail

**8 980.9mi, 19:00hr**
Reach Bear Valley Trail junction (22mi SW to Hetch Hetchy Reservoir and trailhead)

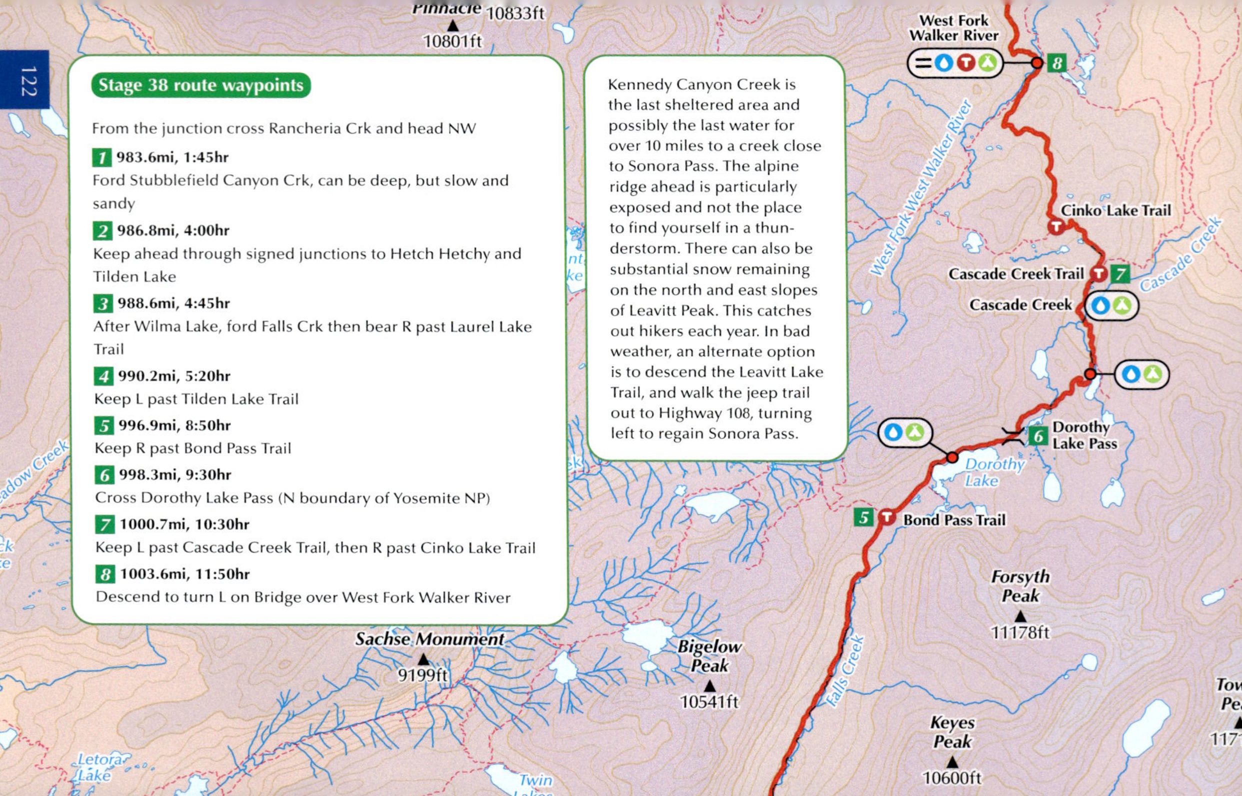


## Stage 38 route waypoints

From the junction cross Rancheria Crk and head NW

**1 983.6mi, 1:45hr**
Ford Stubblefield Canyon Crk, can be deep, but slow and sandy

**2 986.8mi, 4:00hr**
Keep ahead through signed junctions to Hetch Hetchy and Tilden Lake

**3 988.6mi, 4:45hr**
After Wilma Lake, ford Falls Crk then bear R past Laurel Lake Trail

**4 990.2mi, 5:20hr**
Keep L past Tilden Lake Trail

**5 996.9mi, 8:50hr**
Keep R past Bond Pass Trail

**6 998.3mi, 9:30hr**
Cross Dorothy Lake Pass (N boundary of Yosemite NP)

**7 1000.7mi, 10:30hr**
Keep L past Cascade Creek Trail, then R past Cinko Lake Trail

**8 1003.6mi, 11:50hr**
Descend to turn L on Bridge over West Fork Walker River

Kennedy Canyon Creek is the last sheltered area and possibly the last water for over 10 miles to a creek close to Sonora Pass. The alpine ridge ahead is particularly exposed and not the place to find yourself in a thunderstorm. There can also be substantial snow remaining on the north and east slopes of Leavitt Peak. This catches out hikers each year. In bad weather, an alternate option is to descend the Leavitt Lake Trail, and walk the jeep trail out to Highway 108, turning left to regain Sonora Pass.

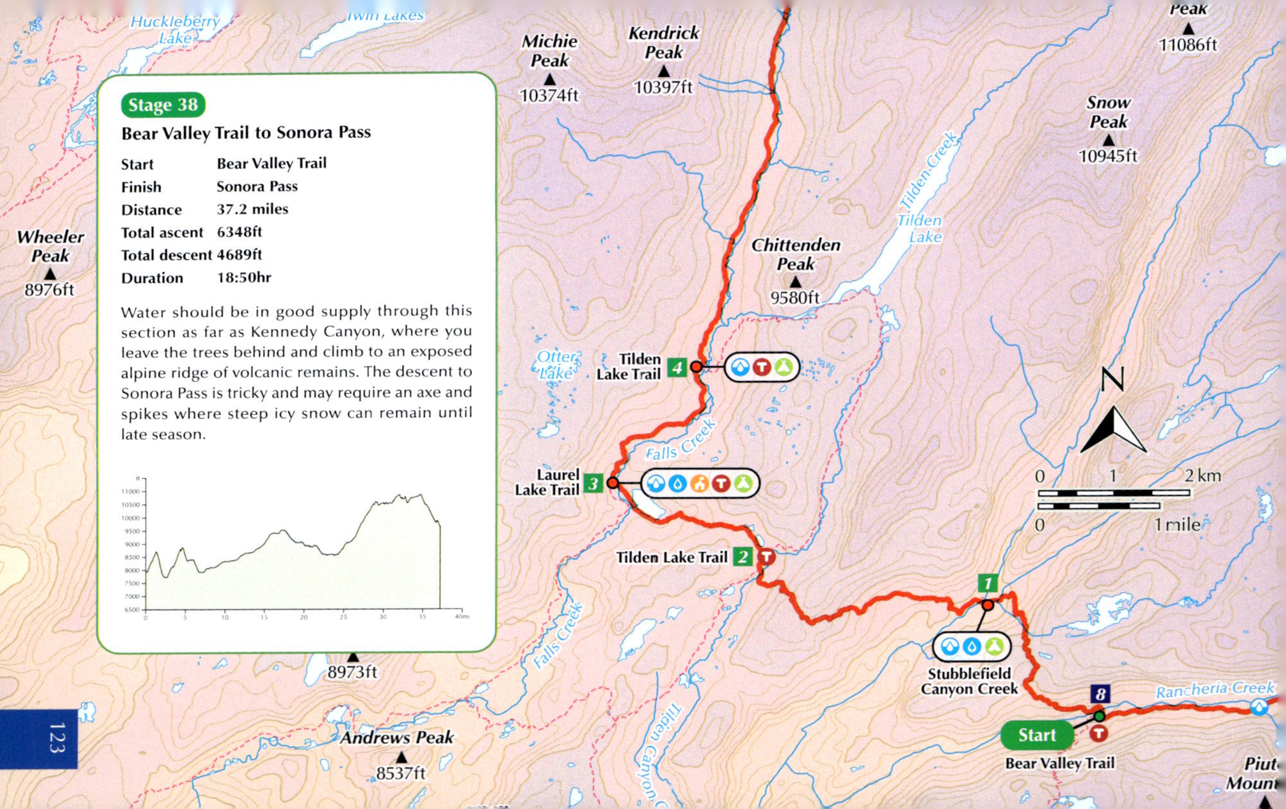


## Stage 38

### Bear Valley Trail to Sonora Pass

| | |
|---|---|
| **Start** | **Bear Valley Trail** |
| **Finish** | **Sonora Pass** |
| **Distance** | **37.2 miles** |
| **Total ascent** | **6348ft** |
| **Total descent** | **4689ft** |
| **Duration** | **18:50hr** |

Water should be in good supply through this section as far as Kennedy Canyon, where you leave the trees behind and climb to an exposed alpine ridge of volcanic remains. The descent to Sonora Pass is tricky and may require an axe and spikes where steep icy snow can remain until late season.

## Stage 39

### Sonora Pass to Ebbetts Pass

| | |
|---|---|
| **Start** | Sonora Pass |
| **Finish** | Ebbetts Pass |
| **Distance** | 31.5 miles |
| **Total ascent** | 5384ft |
| **Total descent** | 6335ft |
| **Duration** | 14:45hr |

Leaving Sonora Pass there is no doubt that you are still in the big mountains but be reassured that the most challenging creek crossings south of Washington are now behind you. Just take care as you descend the north side of Sierra Crest where snow can linger into late season.

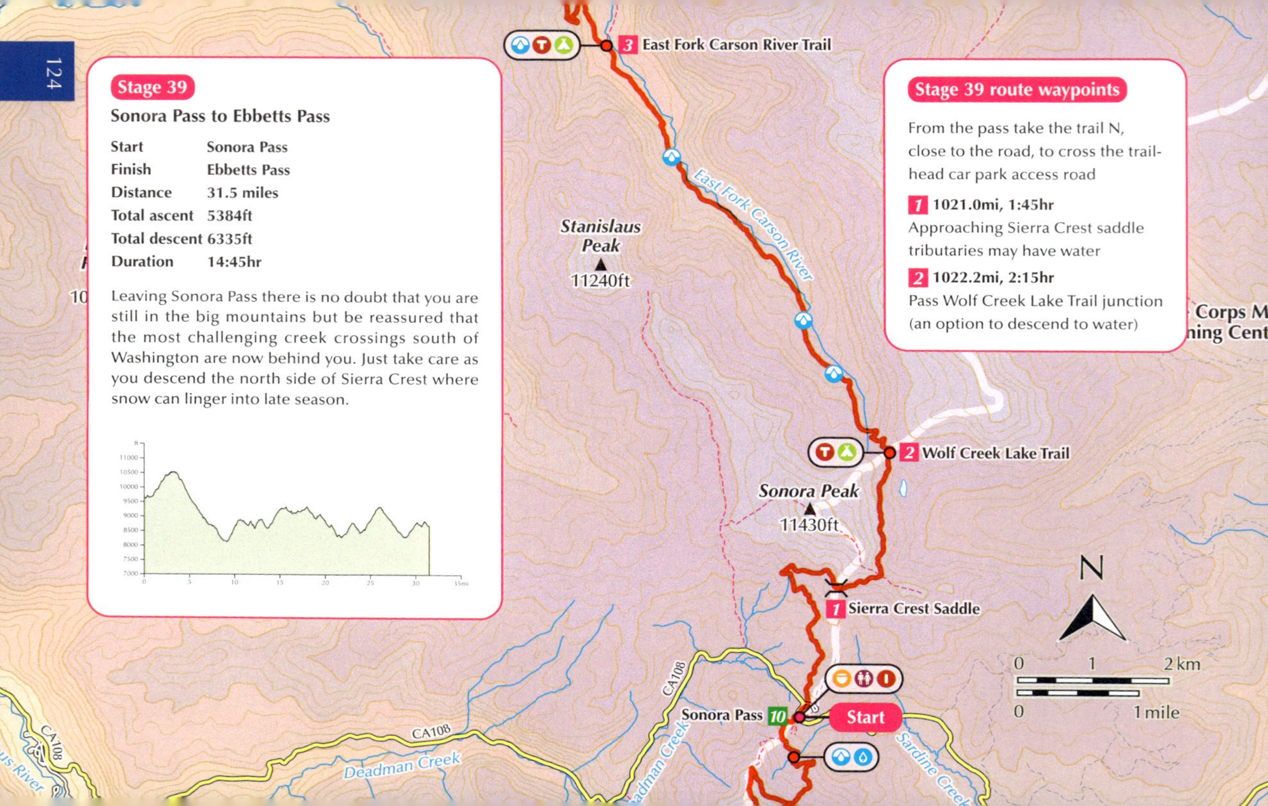


## Stage 39 route waypoints

From the pass take the trail N, close to the road, to cross the trail-head car park access road

**1 1021.0mi, 1:45hr**
Approaching Sierra Crest saddle tributaries may have water

**2 1022.2mi, 2:15hr**
Pass Wolf Creek Lake Trail junction (an option to descend to water)

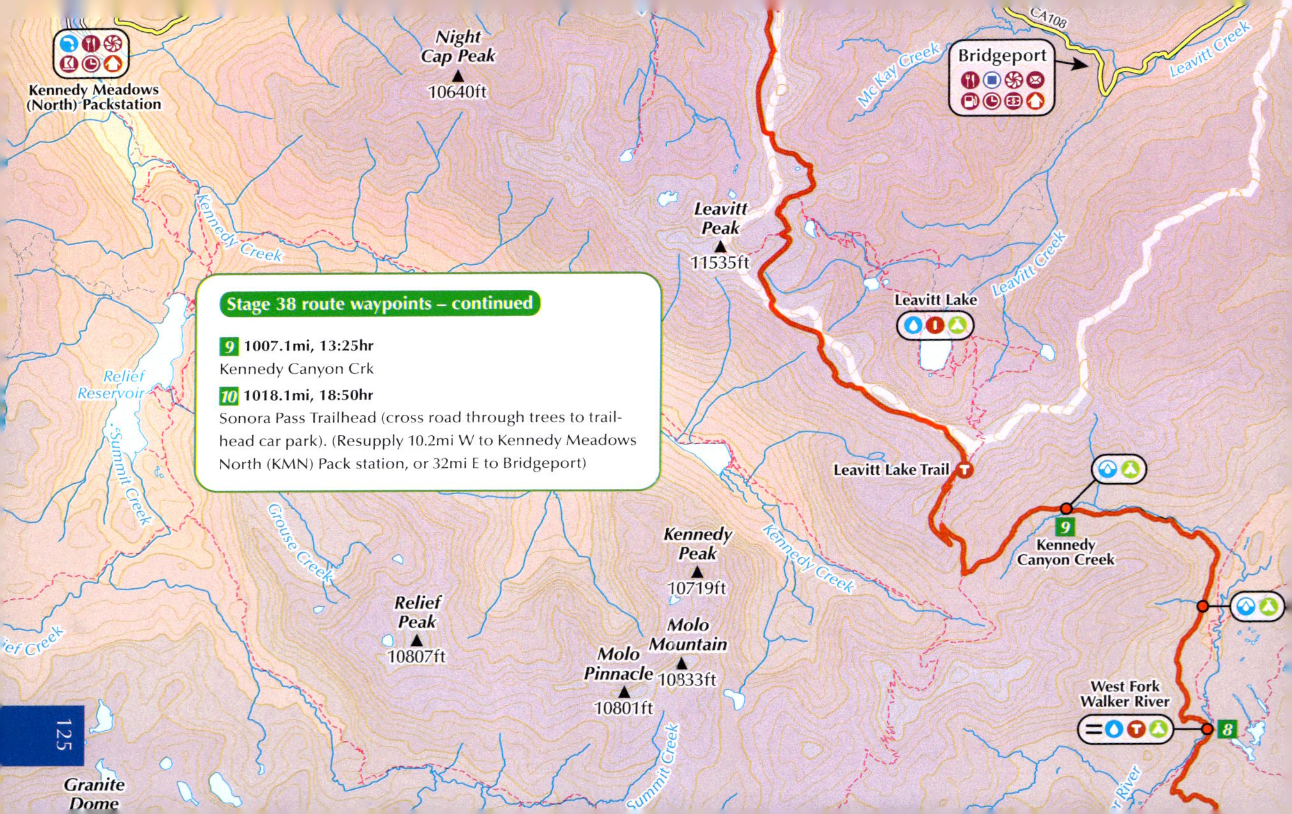


## Stage 38 route waypoints – continued

**9** **1007.1mi, 13:25hr**
Kennedy Canyon Crk

**10** **1018.1mi, 18:50hr**
Sonora Pass Trailhead (cross road through trees to trail-head car park). (Resupply 10.2mi W to Kennedy Meadows North (KMN) Pack station, or 32mi E to Bridgeport)

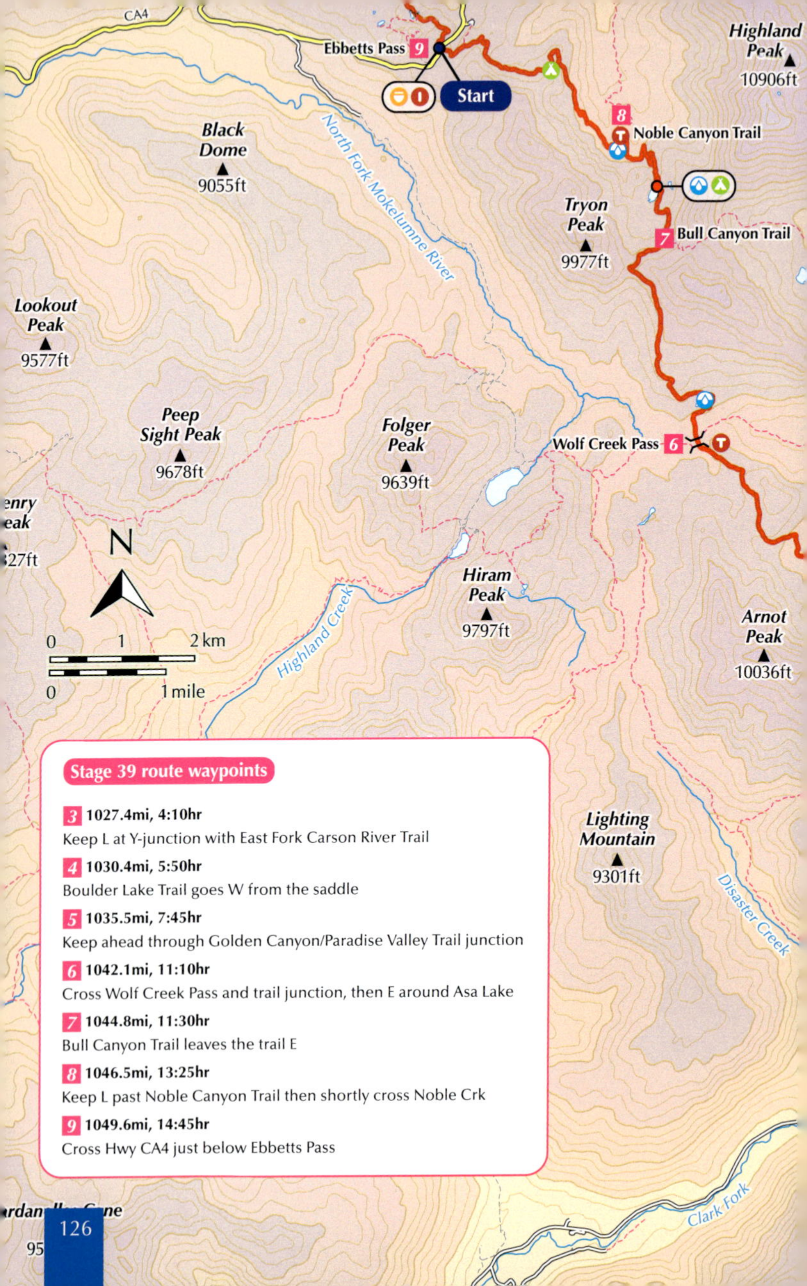


## Stage 39 route waypoints

**3** **1027.4mi, 4:10hr**
Keep L at Y-junction with East Fork Carson River Trail

**4** **1030.4mi, 5:50hr**
Boulder Lake Trail goes W from the saddle

**5** **1035.5mi, 7:45hr**
Keep ahead through Golden Canyon/Paradise Valley Trail junction

**6** **1042.1mi, 11:10hr**
Cross Wolf Creek Pass and trail junction, then E around Asa Lake

**7** **1044.8mi, 11:30hr**
Bull Canyon Trail leaves the trail E

**8** **1046.5mi, 13:25hr**
Keep L past Noble Canyon Trail then shortly cross Noble Crk

**9** **1049.6mi, 14:45hr**
Cross Hwy CA4 just below Ebbetts Pass

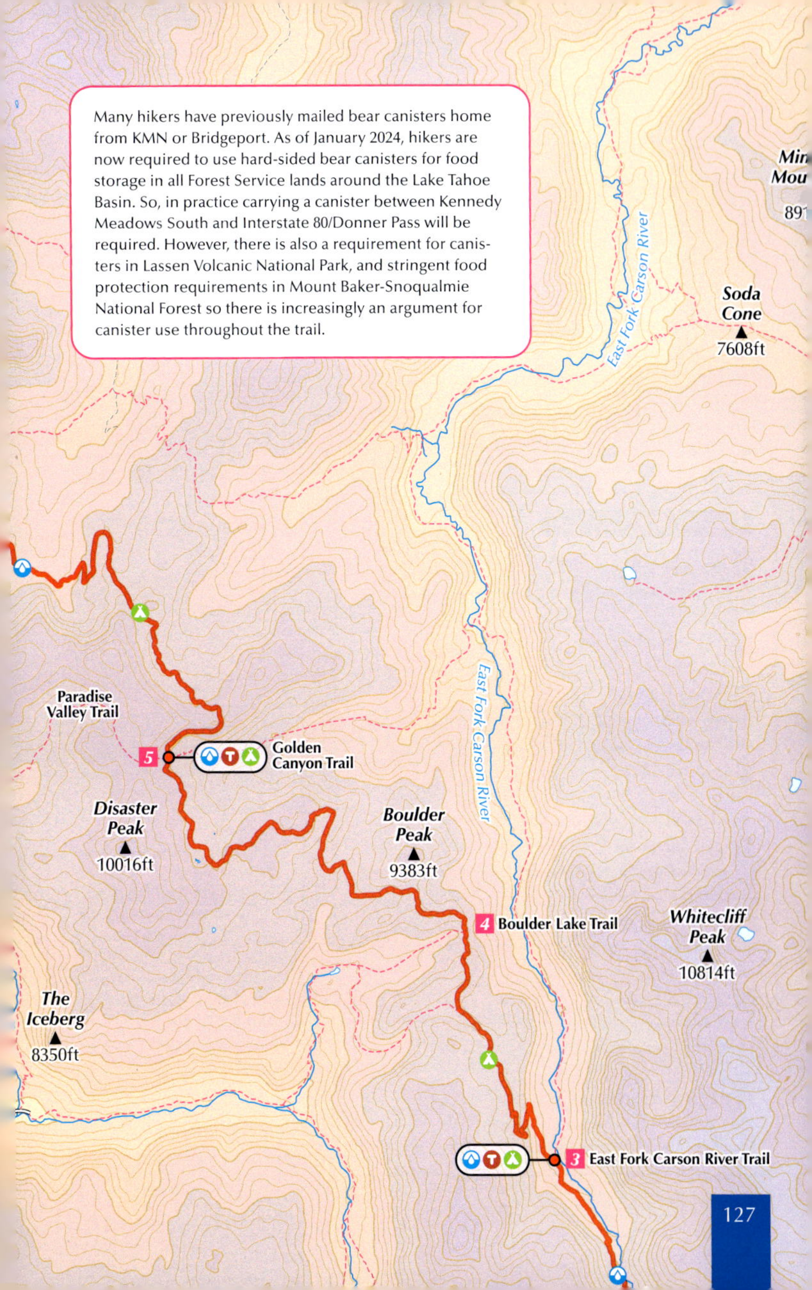


Many hikers have previously mailed bear canisters home from KMN or Bridgeport. As of January 2024, hikers are now required to use hard-sided bear canisters for food storage in all Forest Service lands around the Lake Tahoe Basin. So, in practice carrying a canister between Kennedy Meadows South and Interstate 80/Donner Pass will be required. However, there is also a requirement for canisters in Lassen Volcanic National Park, and stringent food protection requirements in Mount Baker-Snoqualmie National Forest so there is increasingly an argument for canister use throughout the trail.

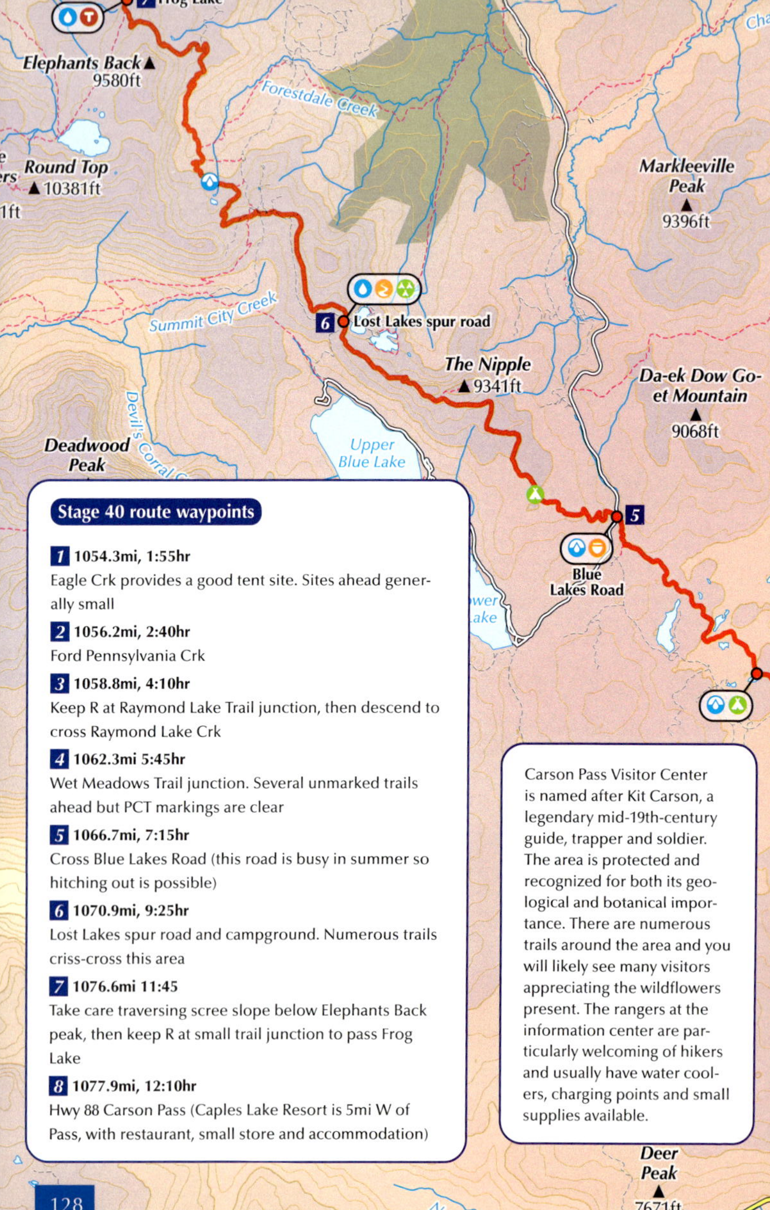


## Stage 40 route waypoints

**1 1054.3mi, 1:55hr**
Eagle Crk provides a good tent site. Sites ahead generally small

**2 1056.2mi, 2:40hr**
Ford Pennsylvania Crk

**3 1058.8mi, 4:10hr**
Keep R at Raymond Lake Trail junction, then descend to cross Raymond Lake Crk

**4 1062.3mi 5:45hr**
Wet Meadows Trail junction. Several unmarked trails ahead but PCT markings are clear

**5 1066.7mi, 7:15hr**
Cross Blue Lakes Road (this road is busy in summer so hitching out is possible)

**6 1070.9mi, 9:25hr**
Lost Lakes spur road and campground. Numerous trails criss-cross this area

**7 1076.6mi 11:45**
Take care traversing scree slope below Elephants Back peak, then keep R at small trail junction to pass Frog Lake

**8 1077.9mi, 12:10hr**
Hwy 88 Carson Pass (Caples Lake Resort is 5mi W of Pass, with restaurant, small store and accommodation)

Carson Pass Visitor Center is named after Kit Carson, a legendary mid-19th-century guide, trapper and soldier. The area is protected and recognized for both its geological and botanical importance. There are numerous trails around the area and you will likely see many visitors appreciating the wildflowers present. The rangers at the information center are particularly welcoming of hikers and usually have water coolers, charging points and small supplies available.

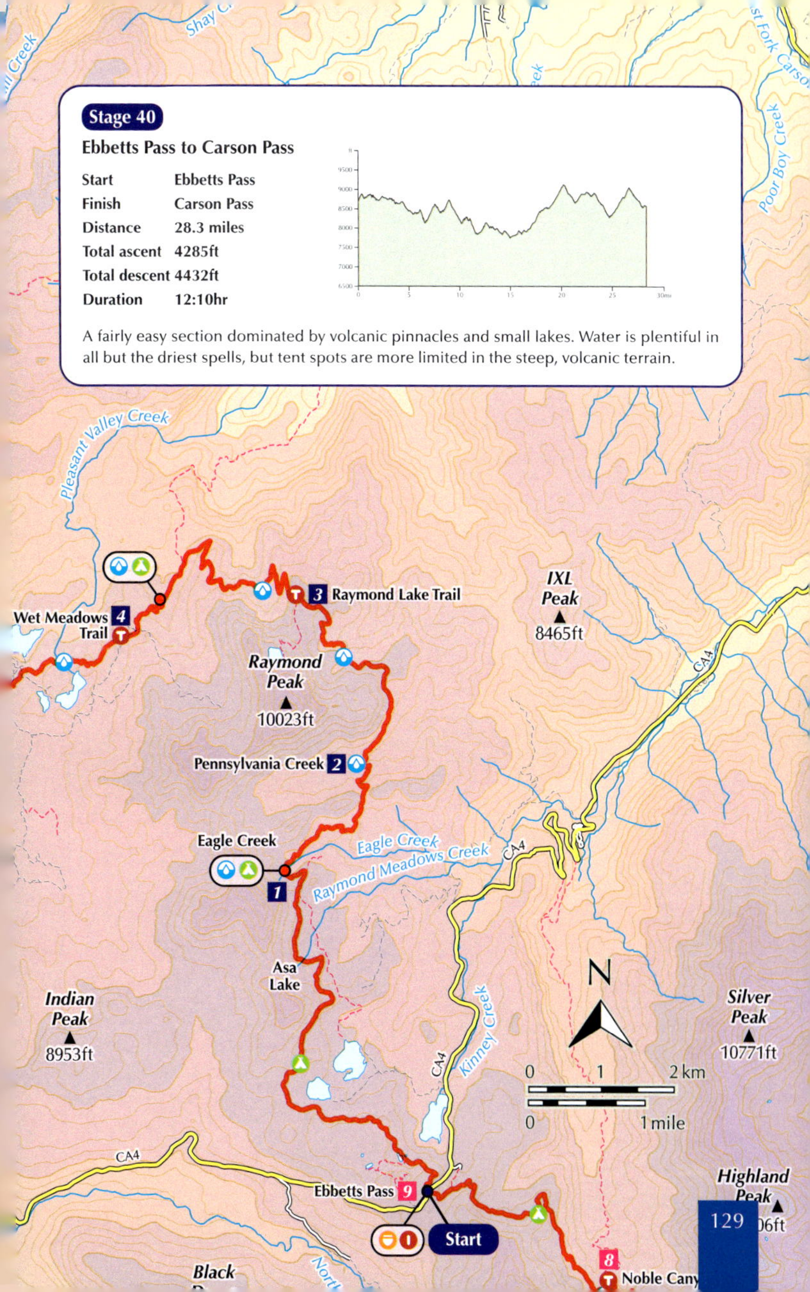
Stage 40
Ebbetts Pass to Carson Pass
Start Ebbetts Pass
Finish Carson Pass
Distance 28.3 miles
Total ascent 4285ft
Total descent 4432ft
Duration 12:10hr
A fairly easy section dominated by volcanic pinnacles and small lakes. Water is plentiful in all but the driest spells, but tent spots are more limited in the steep, volcanic terrain.
Shay Cr
Poor Boy Creek
Pleasant Valley Creek
Wet Meadows Trail 4
3 Raymond Lake Trail
IXL Peak 8465ft
Raymond Peak 10023ft
CA4
Pennsylvania Creek 2
Eagle Creek
Eagle Creek
Raymond Meadows Creek
1
Asa Lake
Kinney Creek
Indian Peak 8953ft
Silver Peak 10771ft
N
0 1 2 km
0 1 mile
Highland Peak
Ebbetts Pass 9
Start
Black
8 Noble Cany

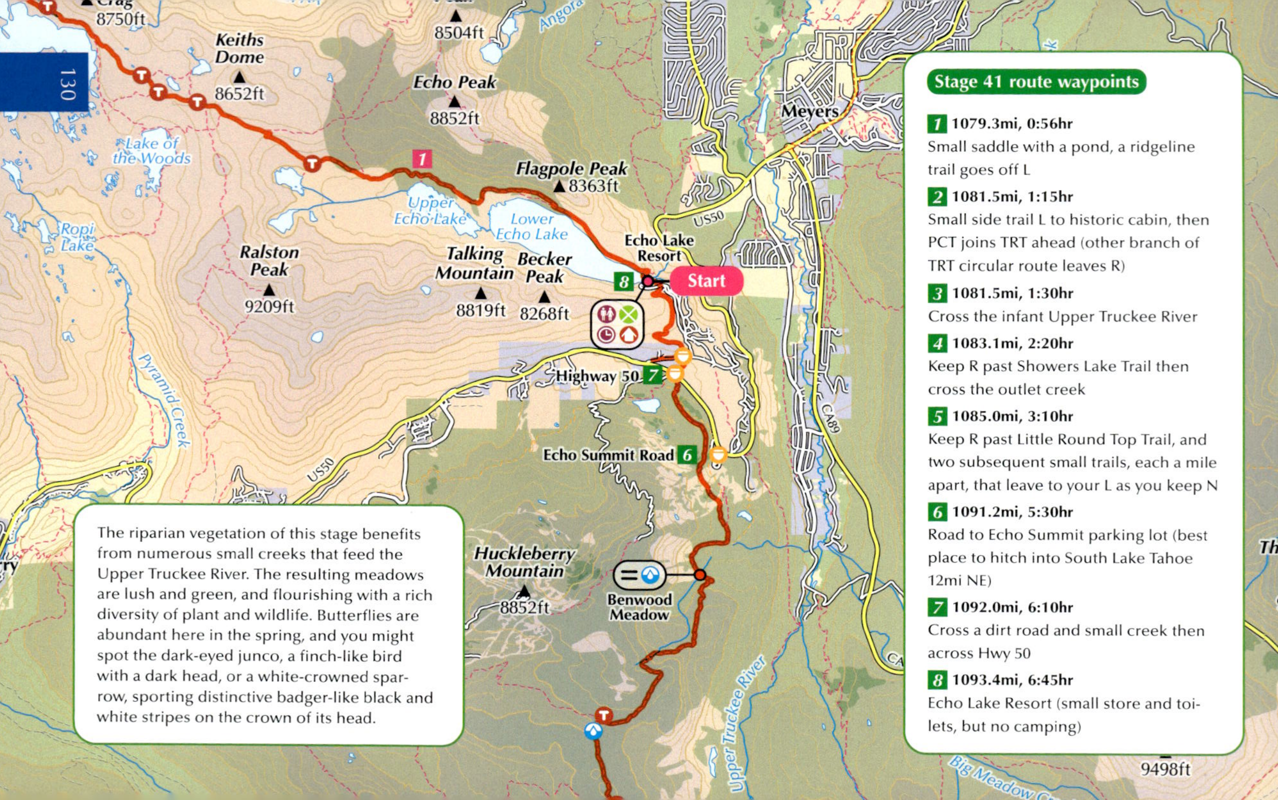


## Stage 41 route waypoints

**1** **1079.3mi, 0:56hr**
Small saddle with a pond, a ridgeline trail goes off L

**2** **1081.5mi, 1:15hr**
Small side trail L to historic cabin, then PCT joins TRT ahead (other branch of TRT circular route leaves R)

**3** **1081.5mi, 1:30hr**
Cross the infant Upper Truckee River

**4** **1083.1mi, 2:20hr**
Keep R past Showers Lake Trail then cross the outlet creek

**5** **1085.0mi, 3:10hr**
Keep R past Little Round Top Trail, and two subsequent small trails, each a mile apart, that leave to your L as you keep N

**6** **1091.2mi, 5:30hr**
Road to Echo Summit parking lot (best place to hitch into South Lake Tahoe 12mi NE)

**7** **1092.0mi, 6:10hr**
Cross a dirt road and small creek then across Hwy 50

**8** **1093.4mi, 6:45hr**
Echo Lake Resort (small store and toilets, but no camping)

The riparian vegetation of this stage benefits from numerous small creeks that feed the Upper Truckee River. The resulting meadows are lush and green, and flourishing with a rich diversity of plant and wildlife. Butterflies are abundant here in the spring, and you might spot the dark-eyed junco, a finch-like bird with a dark head, or a white-crowned sparrow, sporting distinctive badger-like black and white stripes on the crown of its head.

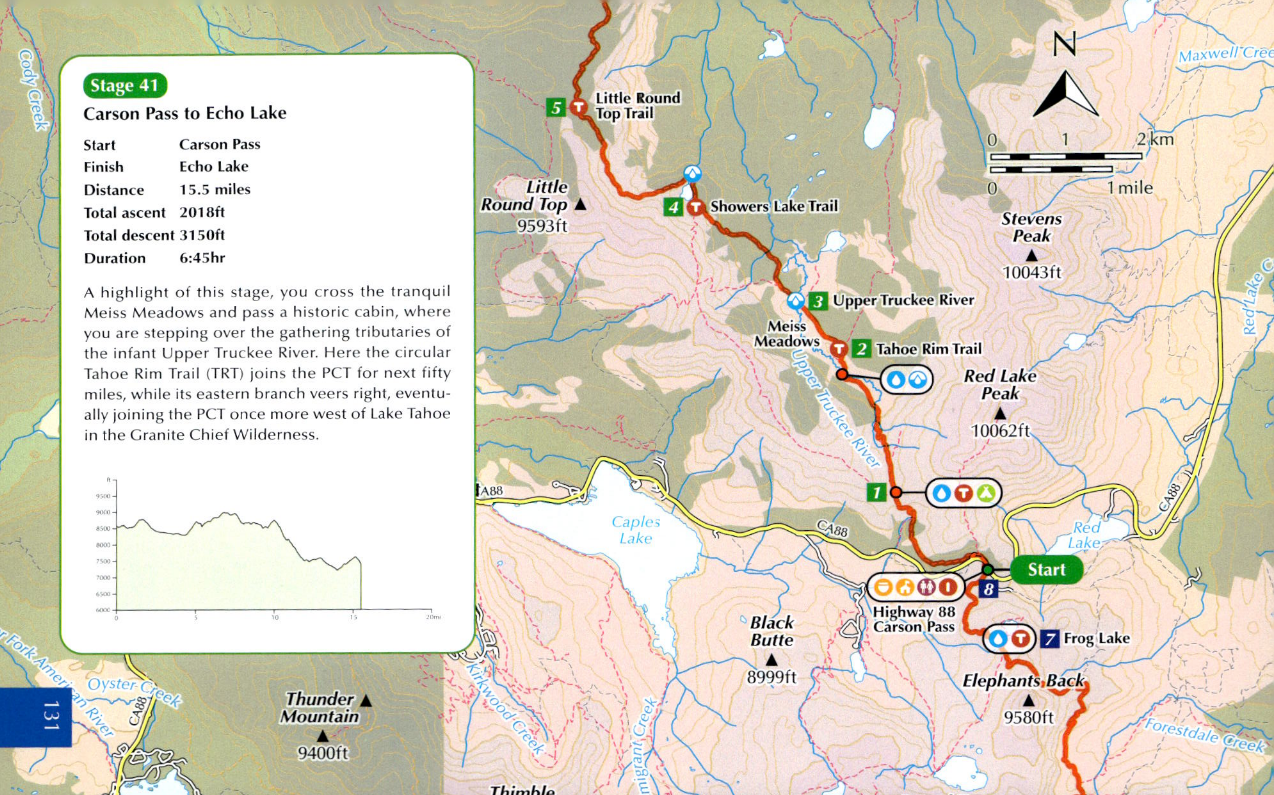



## Stage 41

### Carson Pass to Echo Lake

| | |
|---|---|
| **Start** | Carson Pass |
| **Finish** | Echo Lake |
| **Distance** | 15.5 miles |
| **Total ascent** | 2018ft |
| **Total descent** | 3150ft |
| **Duration** | 6:45hr |

A highlight of this stage, you cross the tranquil Meiss Meadows and pass a historic cabin, where you are stepping over the gathering tributaries of the infant Upper Truckee River. Here the circular Tahoe Rim Trail (TRT) joins the PCT for next fifty miles, while its eastern branch veers right, eventually joining the PCT once more west of Lake Tahoe in the Granite Chief Wilderness.

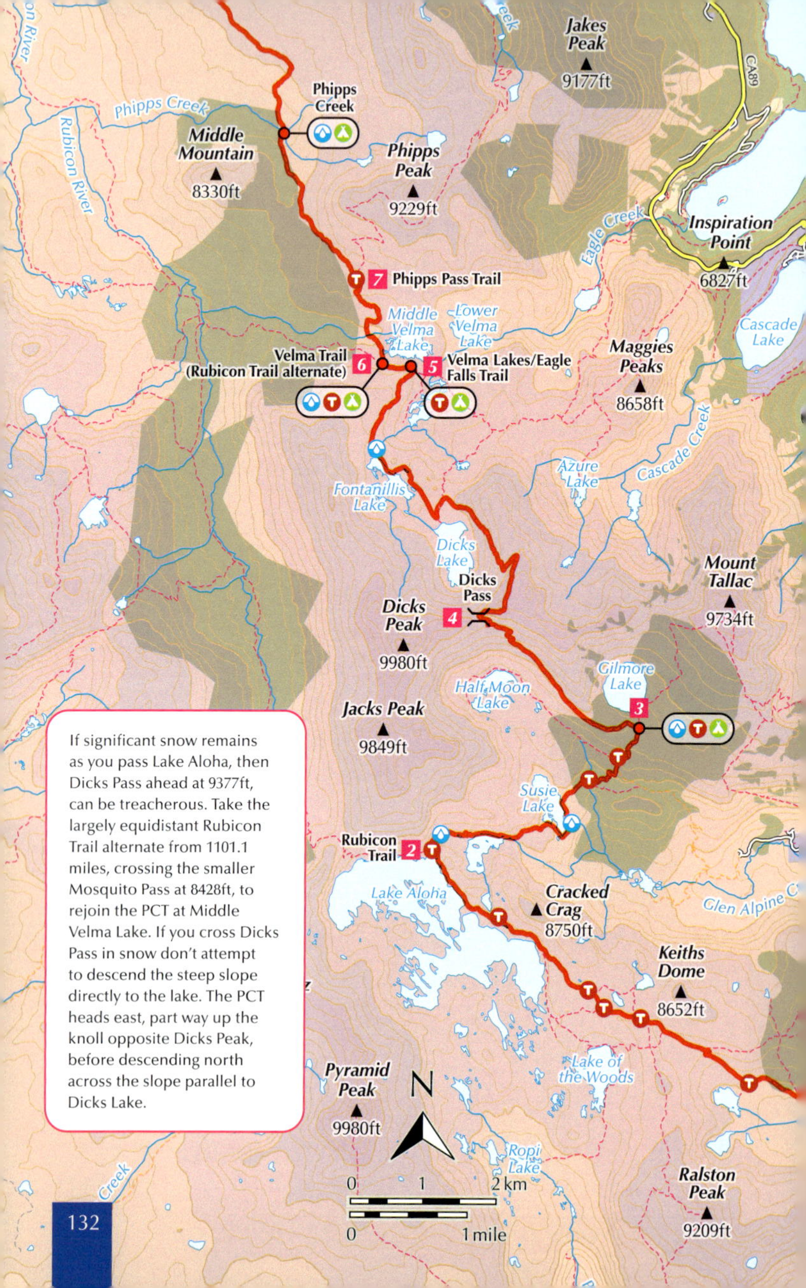


If significant snow remains as you pass Lake Aloha, then Dicks Pass ahead at 9377ft, can be treacherous. Take the largely equidistant Rubicon Trail alternate from 1101.1 miles, crossing the smaller Mosquito Pass at 8428ft, to rejoin the PCT at Middle Velma Lake. If you cross Dicks Pass in snow don't attempt to descend the steep slope directly to the lake. The PCT heads east, part way up the knoll opposite Dicks Peak, before descending north across the slope parallel to Dicks Lake.

## Stage 42

### Echo Lake to Barker Pass

| | |
|---|---|
| Start | Echo Lake |
| Finish | Barker Pass |
| Distance | 32.6 miles |
| Total ascent | 4908ft |
| Total descent | 4485ft |
| Duration | 14:50hr |

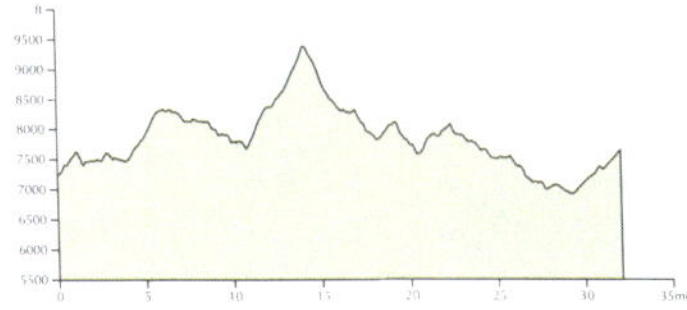

Hiking north from Echo Lake you enter the glacier-scoured rocks of Desolation Wilderness. Initially among the myriad lakes, trees are scarce, but the same can't be said for hikers. The natural beauty of the region, its proximity to several cities, and the ease of access afforded by major highways, mean it is justifiably popular with hikers. The resort runs a regular water taxi to the head of Upper Echo Lake. This can be a pleasant start to the stage, especially on a hot day.

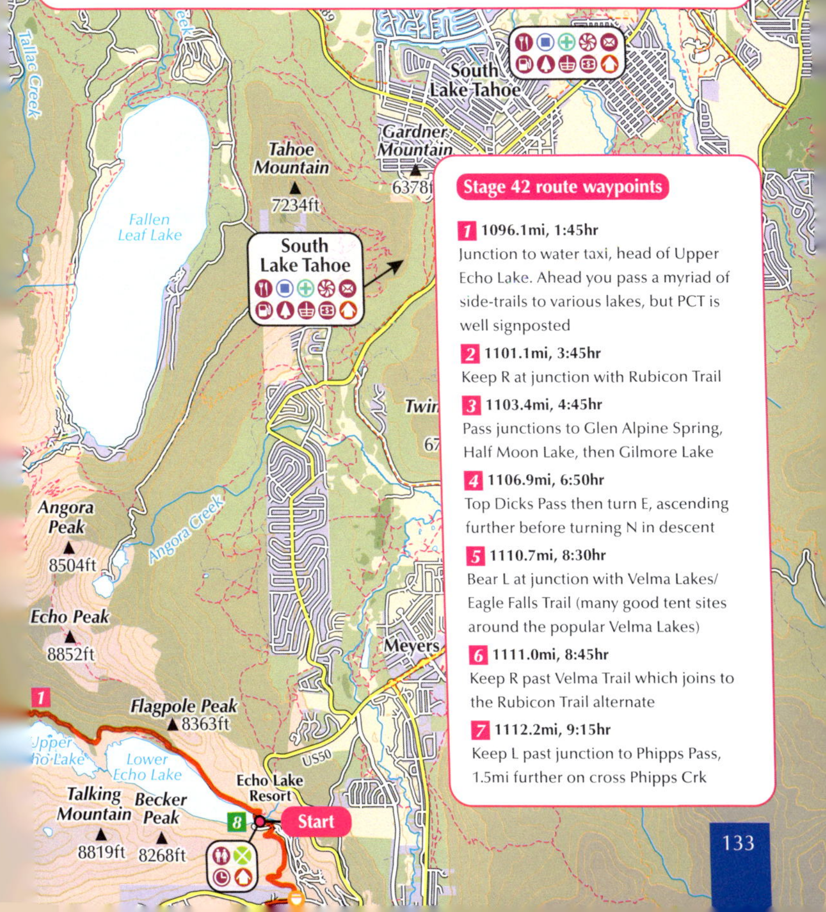

### Stage 42 route waypoints

**1 1096.1mi, 1:45hr**
Junction to water taxi, head of Upper Echo Lake. Ahead you pass a myriad of side-trails to various lakes, but PCT is well signposted

**2 1101.1mi, 3:45hr**
Keep R at junction with Rubicon Trail

**3 1103.4mi, 4:45hr**
Pass junctions to Glen Alpine Spring, Half Moon Lake, then Gilmore Lake

**4 1106.9mi, 6:50hr**
Top Dicks Pass then turn E, ascending further before turning N in descent

**5 1110.7mi, 8:30hr**
Bear L at junction with Velma Lakes/ Eagle Falls Trail (many good tent sites around the popular Velma Lakes)

**6 1111.0mi, 8:45hr**
Keep R past Velma Trail which joins to the Rubicon Trail alternate

**7 1112.2mi, 9:15hr**
Keep L past junction to Phipps Pass, 1.5mi further on cross Phipps Crk

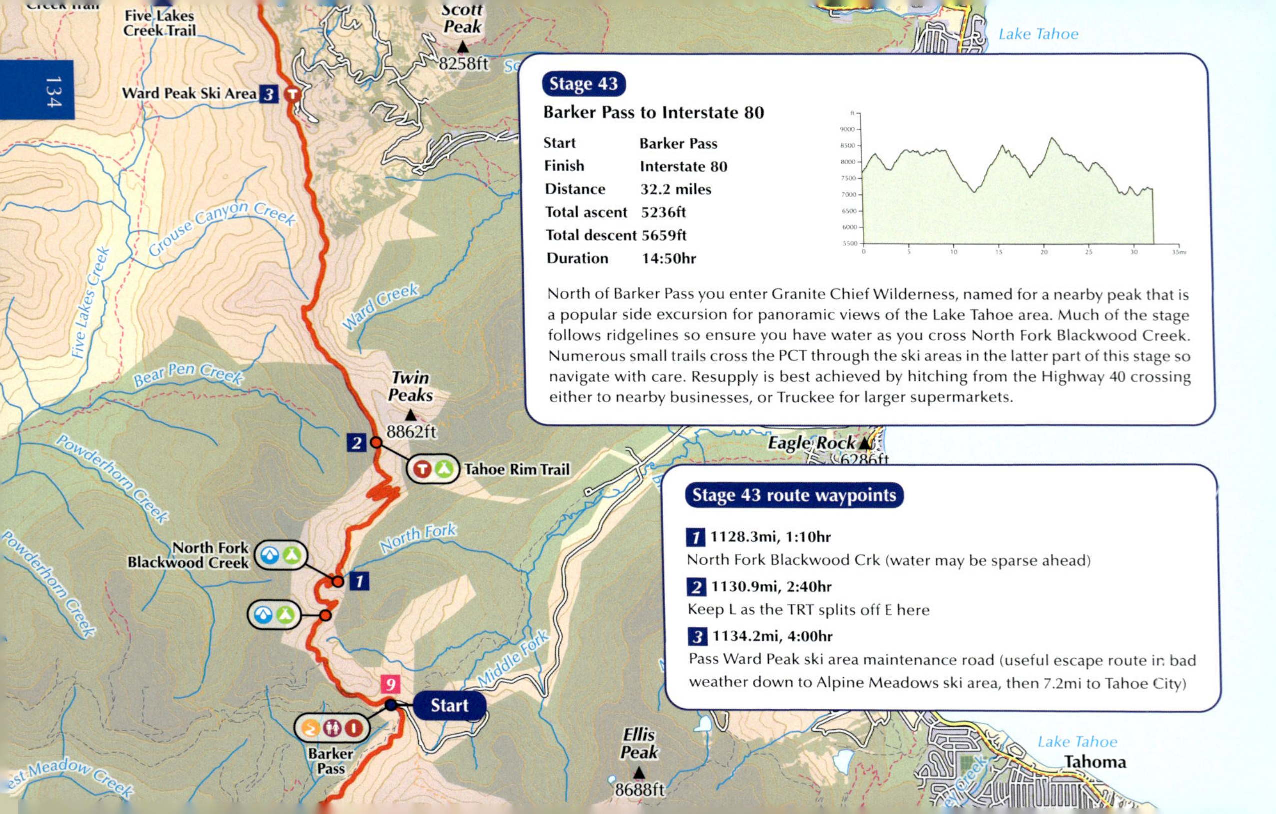


## Stage 43

### Barker Pass to Interstate 80

| | |
|---|---|
| Start | Barker Pass |
| Finish | Interstate 80 |
| Distance | 32.2 miles |
| Total ascent | 5236ft |
| Total descent | 5659ft |
| Duration | 14:50hr |



North of Barker Pass you enter Granite Chief Wilderness, named for a nearby peak that is a popular side excursion for panoramic views of the Lake Tahoe area. Much of the stage follows ridgelines so ensure you have water as you cross North Fork Blackwood Creek. Numerous small trails cross the PCT through the ski areas in the latter part of this stage so navigate with care. Resupply is best achieved by hitching from the Highway 40 crossing either to nearby businesses, or Truckee for larger supermarkets.

## Stage 43 route waypoints

**1 1128.3mi, 1:10hr**
North Fork Blackwood Crk (water may be sparse ahead)

**2 1130.9mi, 2:40hr**
Keep L as the TRT splits off E here

**3 1134.2mi, 4:00hr**
Pass Ward Peak ski area maintenance road (useful escape route in bad weather down to Alpine Meadows ski area, then 7.2mi to Tahoe City)

## Stage 42 route waypoints – continued

**8 1121.6mi, 13:00hr**

Cross a minor dirt road, then Miller Crk, then a bigger dirt road. (If you follow this E, with one R at a junction, it is 4.2mi to a trailhead then 2.5mi into Tahoma, which has a good market and deli, on the W shore of Lake Tahoe)

**9 1126.0mi, 14:50hr**

Cross Forest Rd 3 at Barker Pass Trailhead

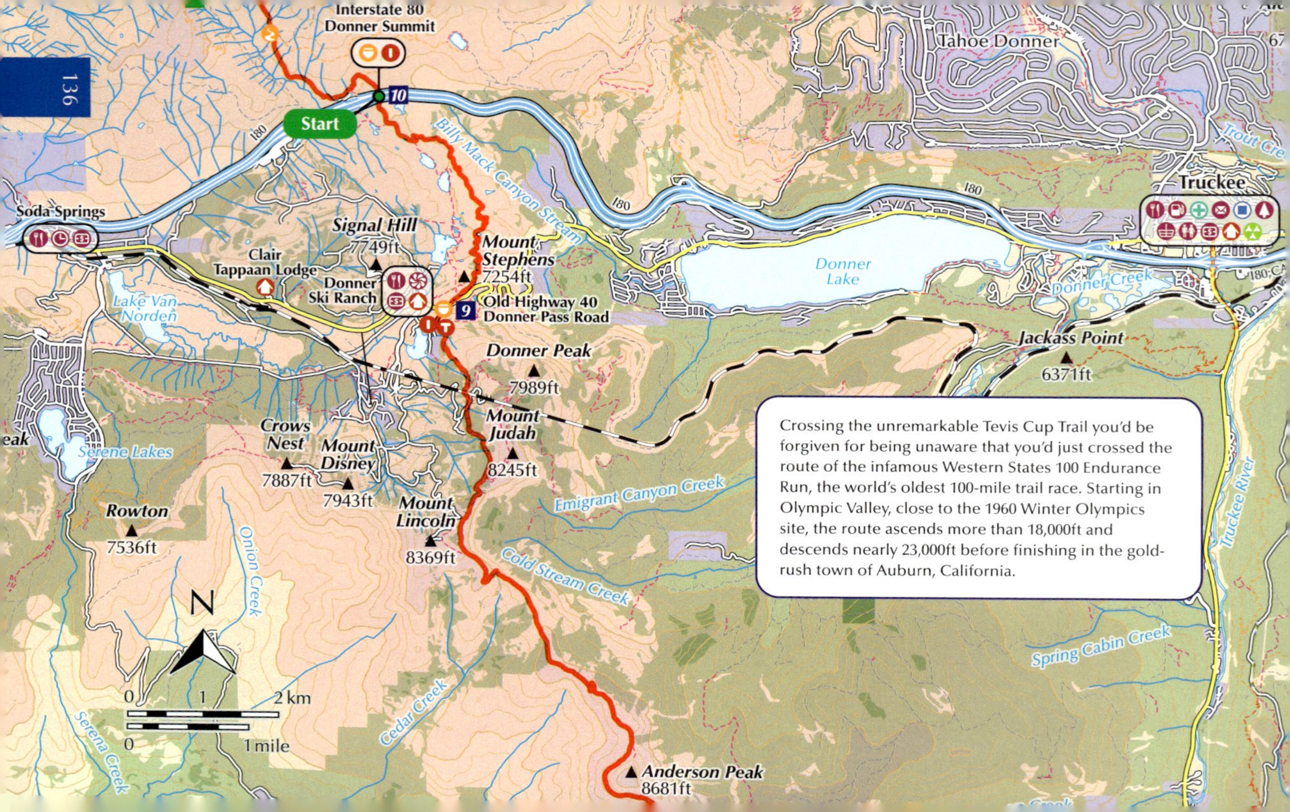


Crossing the unremarkable Tevis Cup Trail you'd be forgiven for being unaware that you'd just crossed the route of the infamous Western States 100 Endurance Run, the world's oldest 100-mile trail race. Starting in Olympic Valley, close to the 1960 Winter Olympics site, the route ascends more than 18,000ft and descends nearly 23,000ft before finishing in the gold-rush town of Auburn, California.

## Stage 43 route waypoints – continued

**4** **1137.1mi, 5:20hr**
Ford creek, then keep L at Five Lakes Creek Trail junction

**5** **1138.1mi, 5:45hr**
Keep R at fork with Whiskey Creek Trail

**6** **1140.3mi, 6:40hr**
Cross the Tevis Cup Trail

**7** **1144.6mi, 9:10hr**
Keep R past Painted Rock Trail and cross creek (usually flows into summer)

**8** **1146.9mi, 10:30hr**
From saddle below Tinker Knob, keep L past Coldstream Trail junction

**9** **1154.6mi, 13:30hr**
Cross Hwy 40 Donner Pass (Donner Ski Ranch 0.3mi W, Clair Tappaan Lodge 1.4mi W, Soda Springs Store 3.4mi W, or hitch 9mi E into Truckee)

**10** **1158.2mi, 14:50hr**
Use tunnels to pass underneath Hwy I-80 (junction to parking lot 0.25mi S of tunnels)

# SECTION 6 – INTERSTATE 80 TO INTERSTATE 5 (CASTELLA)

| | Stage | Distance (miles) | Total ascent (feet) | Total descent (feet) | Average duration (hr:min) | Page |
|---|---|---|---|---|---|---|
| 44 | Interstate 80 – Hwy 49 Sierra City | 38.4 | 4547 | 7205 | 16:20 | 145 |
| 45 | Hwy 49 Sierra City – Quincy/ LaPorte Road | 39.4 | 7664 | 5712 | 18:35 | 146 |
| 46 | Quincy/LaPorte Road – Big Creek Road | 28.7 | 5023 | 5984 | 12:40 | 151 |
| 47 | Big Creek Road – Hwy 70 Belden | 23.4 | 2300 | 5627 | 9:45 | 153 |
| 48 | Hwy 70 Belden – Humboldt Summit | 24.7 | 6811 | 2356 | 13:45 | 152 |
| 49 | Humboldt Summit – Hwy 36 nr Chester | 19.5 | 2218 | 3819 | 8:20 | 157 |
| 50 | Hwy 36 nr Chester – Hat Creek Resort | 42.1 | 4455 | 4961 | 18:15 | 156 |
| 51 | Hat Creek Resort – Road 22 | 20.1 | 1112 | 1066 | 8:00 | 163 |
| 52 | Road 22 – Burney Falls | 25.5 | 669 | 2323 | 9:50 | 165 |
| 53 | Burney Falls – Bartle Gap | 27 | 4678 | 2510 | 13:00 | 167 |
| 54 | Bartle Gap – McCloud River | 25 | 2612 | 5302 | 10:20 | 169 |
| 55 | McCloud River – Interstate 5 | 30.2 | 5039 | 5335 | 13:35 | 171 |
| **Totals** | | **344** | **47,128** | **52,200** | **152.25** | |

## *WHAT TO EXPECT*

The changing region is again quite noticeable in the landscape. Thickly forested hills in this section provide welcome shade. Although not as much as once was the case. Stages 48 and 49 in particular suffered extensively in the devastating Dixie Fire of 2021, the largest single source wildfire in California history, and the first to burn across the Sierra Crest (followed by the Caldor Fire later the same season). Of course, fire is part of a natural cycle, but these fires burned particularly hot, and it will be some years before the landscape begins to recover. By contrast, at the start of Hat Creek Rim, where a lightning strike caused a big fire in 2009, the landscape is now recovering well, and it is not hard to imagine that in a few more years these trees will become a welcome source of shade.

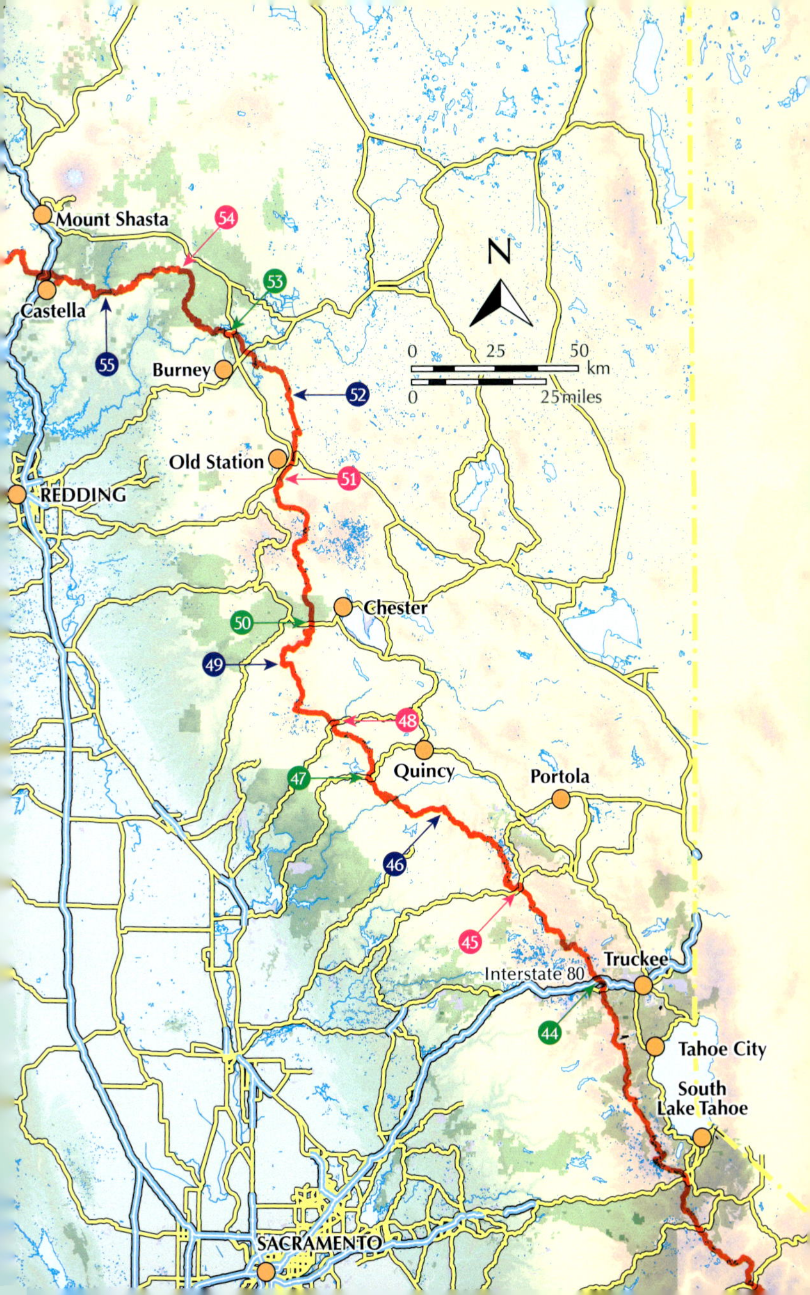

Mount Shasta
Castella
Burney
Old Station
REDDING
Chester
Quincy
Portola
Truckee
Interstate 80
Tahoe City
South
Lake Tahoe
SACRAMENTO
N
0
25
50
km
0
25 miles
54
53
55
52
51
50
49
48
47
46
45
44

While much of the trail is best described as undulating, there are big descents and subsequent climbs where the trail drops to crossings of the Middle Fork and North Fork Feather Rivers and McCloud River, as well as some long flattish sections. Water is an issue across much of the section and you will need to take care to ensure you have enough. Local water reports will be critical to this. The section across Hat Creek Rim is famed for being dry and for many years a small unreliable water cache was maintained at Road 22. This was recently replaced with a proper water tank that is filled regularly. It is still a cache that is volunteer maintained but so far it seems to be more reliable. In contrast to the relative scarcity of water so far, at the far side of Hat Creek Rim you reach Burney Falls, an enormous and spectacular waterfall 129ft high.

The section sees you enter the Cascade Range passing Lassen Peak, the first in a long line of volcanos and volcanic features that will be with you from here to the border. It is best hiked from July to October when it is free of snow.

Resupply in the first half of this section can seem rather sparse if you are to avoid the 12mi hitch into Quincy on a quiet road. If you can stretch supplies as far as Chester, perhaps with a pleasant detour to the facilities at Bucks Lake, then a local bus service now caters to hikers looking to get into town where there are a good range of stores and a post office. Similarly, Burney has everything you are likely to need, including a sports

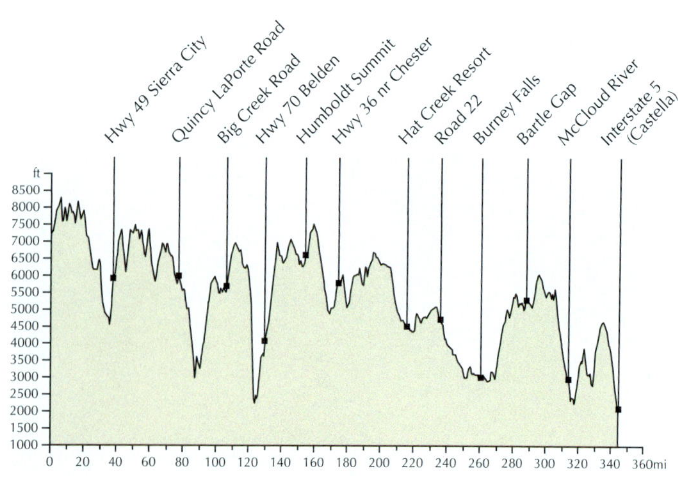

and outdoor store. While there's no bus here, the road is busy and an easy hitch. At Interstate 5 you have a range of choices from a short walk to Castella post office and Ammarati's Market, to a long hitch into the larger town of Mount Shasta.

## RESUPPLY OPTIONS

| Stage | Trail mile | Place | Off trail (miles) | Description | Facilities |
|---|---|---|---|---|---|
| 44 | 1196.6 | Sierra City | 1.4 SW | Rural community, hiker-focused store, accepts packages | |
| 46 | 1264.7 | Haskins Valley Inn | 2.7 W | Bed & breakfast Inn alongside a small but well-stocked store | |
| 46 | 1264.7 | Bucks Lake Resort | 3.6 NW | Resort with cabins, laid-back bar, restaurant and store | |
| 47 | 1269.1 | Quincy | 12.0 E | Small rural town with hospital and public transport connections | |
| 47 | 1288.1 | Belden Resort | On trail | Quirky resort, hosts festivals and RVs | |
| 47 | 1288.1 | Caribou Crossroads | 1.5 E | RV Park, Café, store and village post office | |
| 49 | 1332.3 | Chester | 7.5 E | Small town, hospital, resupply at good mid-size market | |
| 50 | 1374.4 | Hat Creek Resort | 0.2 NW | RV Park with cabins and gas station mini-mart, post office next door | |
| 51 | 1378.3 | Old Station | 0.3 W | Old Station Fill Up gas and well-stocked mini-mart, JJ's Restaurant | |
| 52 | 1412.3 | Burney | 7.7 SW | Small town along main street, useful outfitter/sports store | |
| 52 | 1420 | Burney Falls State Park | On trail | Campground with showers and store that accepts packages ($) | |

Cloud builds over Lower Twin Lake (Stage 49)

| Stage | Trail mile | Place | Off trail (miles) | Description | Facilities |
|---|---|---|---|---|---|
| 55 | 1502.2 | Castella (amenities) | 2.0 SW | State Park campground, Ammarati's Market accepts packages | |
| 55 | 1502.2 | Dunsmuir | 5.5 N | Small town, most facilities, Dollar General | |
| 55 | 1502.2 | Mount Shasta | 13.5 N | Larger town, motels, campground, outfitter | |

## PERMITS

Permits (and bear canisters) are required for overnight trips in Lassen Volcanic National Park, PCT miles 1347.4 to 1366.6, unless camping at Warner Valley Campground (mile 1351.4) where there are bear boxes. Lassen Volcanic National Park permits are non-quota and available online up to 90 days in advance.

To obtain a permit visit: www.recreation.gov/permits/4675334

For more information call the Lassen Volcanic National Park office on (530) 595-4480 or visit: www.nps.gov/lavo/planyourvisit/wilderness-permit-information.htm

## MAIL DROP INFORMATION

Sierra City Country Store
'Your Name Here'
c/o Sierra Country Store
213 Main Street
Sierra City, CA 96125
ETA: 'Your ETA'
They are open: Mon–Fri 9am–6pm, Sat–Sun 9am–7pm
Phone them on: (530) 862-1560
Visit them at: www.sierracountrystore.com

'Your Name Here'
c/o Burney Falls Camp Store
24900 Hwy. 89
Burney, CA 96013

ETA: 'Your ETA'
They are open: Mon–Sun 9am–6pm
Phone them on: (530) 335-5713
Visit them at: www.parks.ca.gov and search for McArthur-Burney Falls

'Your Name Here'
Ammarati's Market
20107 Castle Creek Road
Castella, CA 96017
ETA: 'Your ETA'
They are open: Mon–Sun 8am–8pm
Phone them on: (530) 235-2676

## POST OFFICE INFORMATION

'Your Name Here'
c\o General Delivery
Sierra City, CA 96125
Located at: 215 Main Street
Phone them on: (530) 862-1152

'Your Name Here'
c\o General Delivery
Meadow Valley, CA 95956
Located at: 7091 Bucks Lake Road
Phone them on: (530) 283-1379

'Your Name Here'
c\o General Delivery
Quincy, CA 95971
Located at: 222 Lawrence Street
Phone them on: (530) 283-3912

'Your Name Here'
c\o Caribou Crossroads
Belden, CA 95915
Located at: 16242 Highway 70
Phone them on: (415) 395-6031

'Your Name Here'
c\o General Delivery
Chester, CA 96020
Located at: 218 Laurel Lane
Phone them on: (530) 258-4184

'Your Name Here'
c\o General Delivery
Hat Creek, CA 96040
Located at: 18630 Highway 89
Phone them on: (530) 335-4744

'Your Name Here'
c\o General Delivery
Burney, CA 96013
Located at: 20655 Commerce Way
Phone them on: (530) 335-5430

'Your Name Here'
c\o General Delivery
Castella, CA 96017
Located at: 20115 Castle Creek Road
Phone them on: (530) 235-4413

'Your Name Here'
c\o General Delivery
Dunsmuir, CA 96025
Located at: 5530 Dunsmuir Avenue
Phone them on: (530) 235-0338

'Your Name Here'
c\o General Delivery
Shasta, CA 96087
Located at: 15430 Highway 299 W
Phone them on: (530) 241-9431

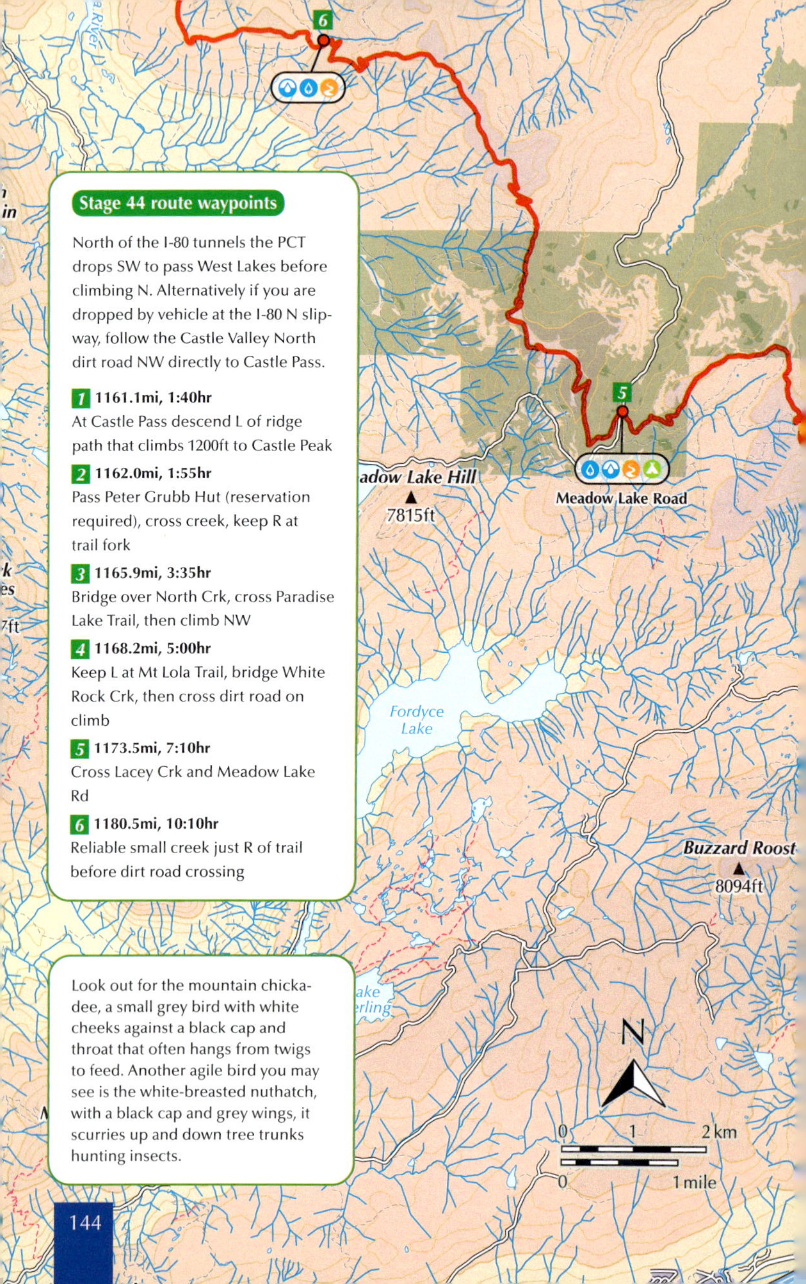


## Stage 44 route waypoints

North of the I-80 tunnels the PCT drops SW to pass West Lakes before climbing N. Alternatively if you are dropped by vehicle at the I-80 N slipway, follow the Castle Valley North dirt road NW directly to Castle Pass.

**1 1161.1mi, 1:40hr**
At Castle Pass descend L of ridge path that climbs 1200ft to Castle Peak

**2 1162.0mi, 1:55hr**
Pass Peter Grubb Hut (reservation required), cross creek, keep R at trail fork

**3 1165.9mi, 3:35hr**
Bridge over North Crk, cross Paradise Lake Trail, then climb NW

**4 1168.2mi, 5:00hr**
Keep L at Mt Lola Trail, bridge White Rock Crk, then cross dirt road on climb

**5 1173.5mi, 7:10hr**
Cross Lacey Crk and Meadow Lake Rd

**6 1180.5mi, 10:10hr**
Reliable small creek just R of trail before dirt road crossing

Look out for the mountain chickadee, a small grey bird with white cheeks against a black cap and throat that often hangs from twigs to feed. Another agile bird you may see is the white-breasted nuthatch, with a black cap and grey wings, it scurries up and down tree trunks hunting insects.

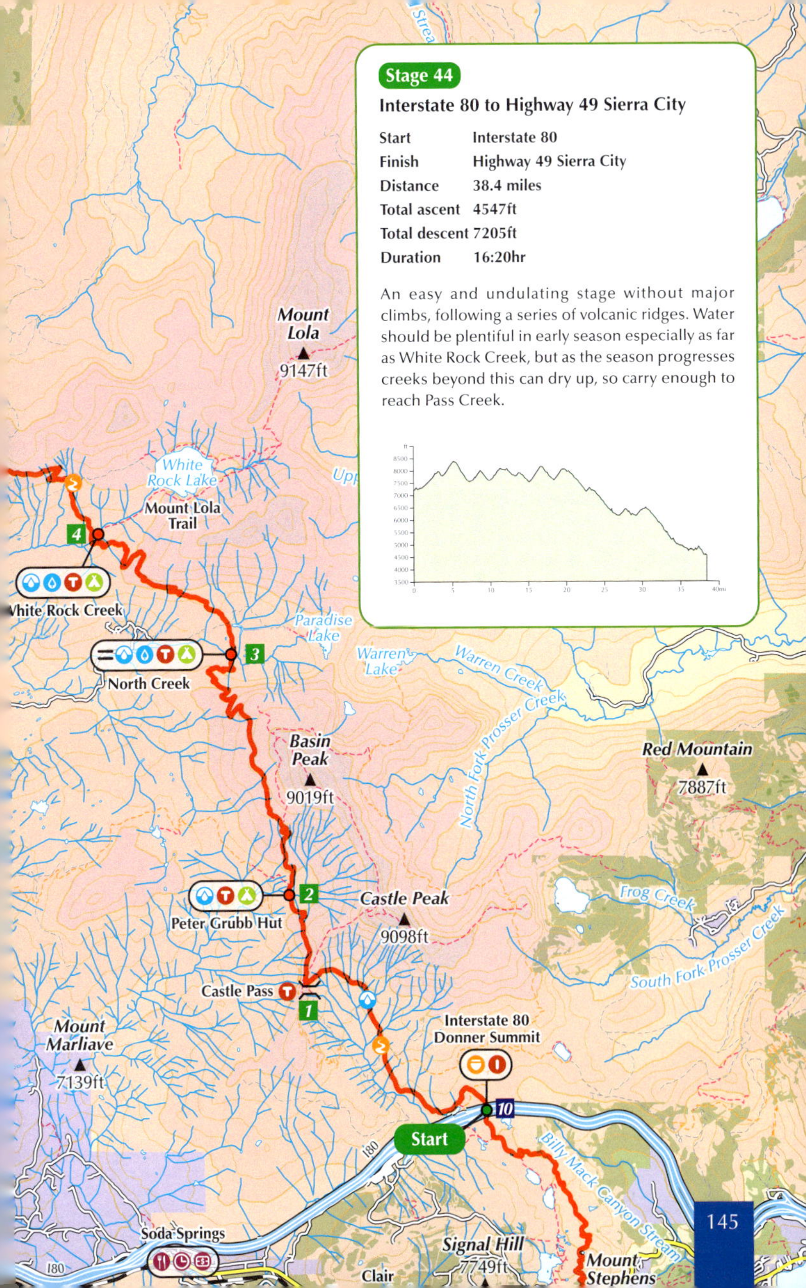


## Stage 44

### Interstate 80 to Highway 49 Sierra City

| | |
|---|---|
| Start | Interstate 80 |
| Finish | Highway 49 Sierra City |
| Distance | 38.4 miles |
| Total ascent | 4547ft |
| Total descent | 7205ft |
| Duration | 16:20hr |

An easy and undulating stage without major climbs, following a series of volcanic ridges. Water should be plentiful in early season especially as far as White Rock Creek, but as the season progresses creeks beyond this can dry up, so carry enough to reach Pass Creek.

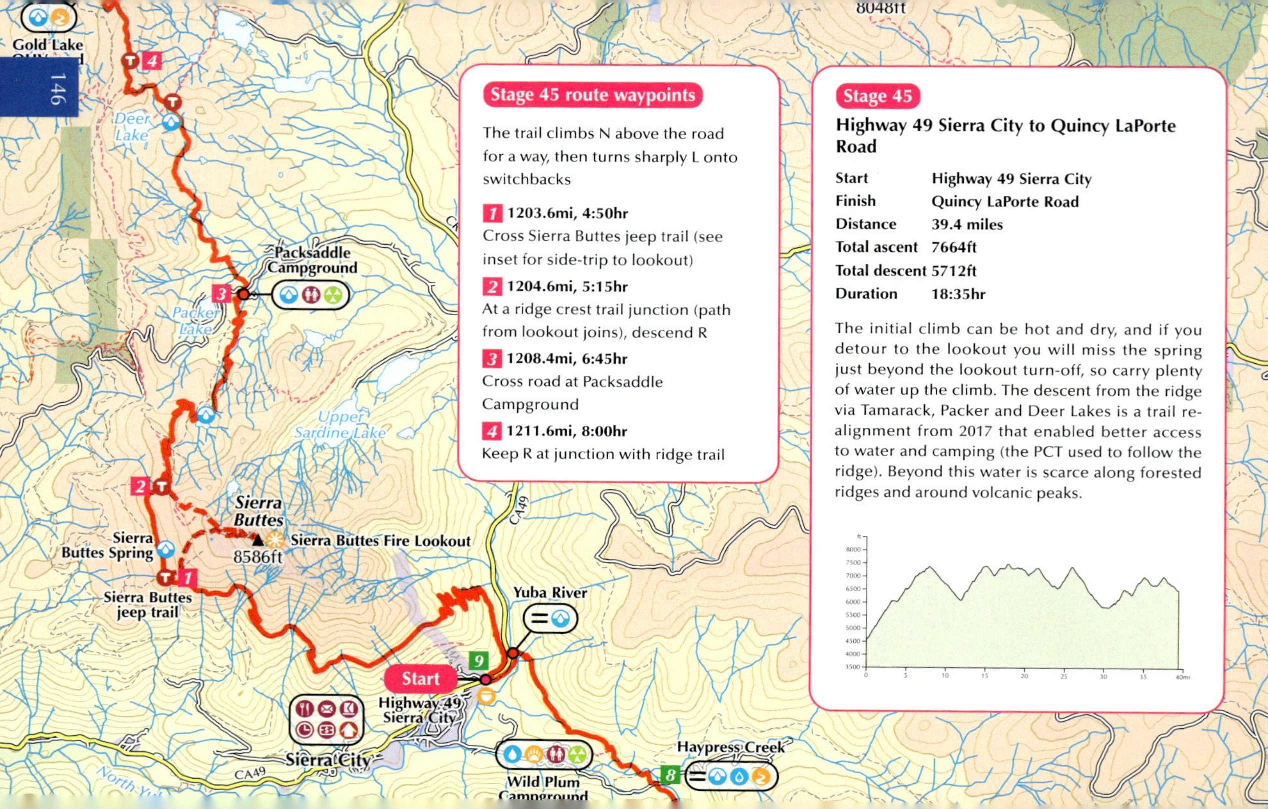


## Stage 45 route waypoints

The trail climbs N above the road for a way, then turns sharply L onto switchbacks

**1 1203.6mi, 4:50hr**
Cross Sierra Buttes jeep trail (see inset for side-trip to lookout)

**2 1204.6mi, 5:15hr**
At a ridge crest trail junction (path from lookout joins), descend R

**3 1208.4mi, 6:45hr**
Cross road at Packsaddle Campground

**4 1211.6mi, 8:00hr**
Keep R at junction with ridge trail

## Stage 45

### Highway 49 Sierra City to Quincy LaPorte Road

| | |
|---|---|
| **Start** | **Highway 49 Sierra City** |
| **Finish** | **Quincy LaPorte Road** |
| **Distance** | **39.4 miles** |
| **Total ascent** | **7664ft** |
| **Total descent** | **5712ft** |
| **Duration** | **18:35hr** |

The initial climb can be hot and dry, and if you detour to the lookout you will miss the spring just beyond the lookout turn-off, so carry plenty of water up the climb. The descent from the ridge via Tamarack, Packer and Deer Lakes is a trail re-alignment from 2017 that enabled better access to water and camping (the PCT used to follow the ridge). Beyond this water is scarce along forested ridges and around volcanic peaks.

**Stage 44 route waypoints – continued**

**7** **1185.0mi, 11:35hr**
Cross minor road, pass creek, then cross the FS07 to Jackson Meadows Reservoir

**8** **1193.9mi, 15:10hr**
Cross Wild Plum Campground road and Haypress Crk bridge, continue NW

**9** **1196.6mi, 16:20hr**
After crossing North Yuba River bridge, bear SW to cross Hwy 49 (1.4mi NE of Sierra City)

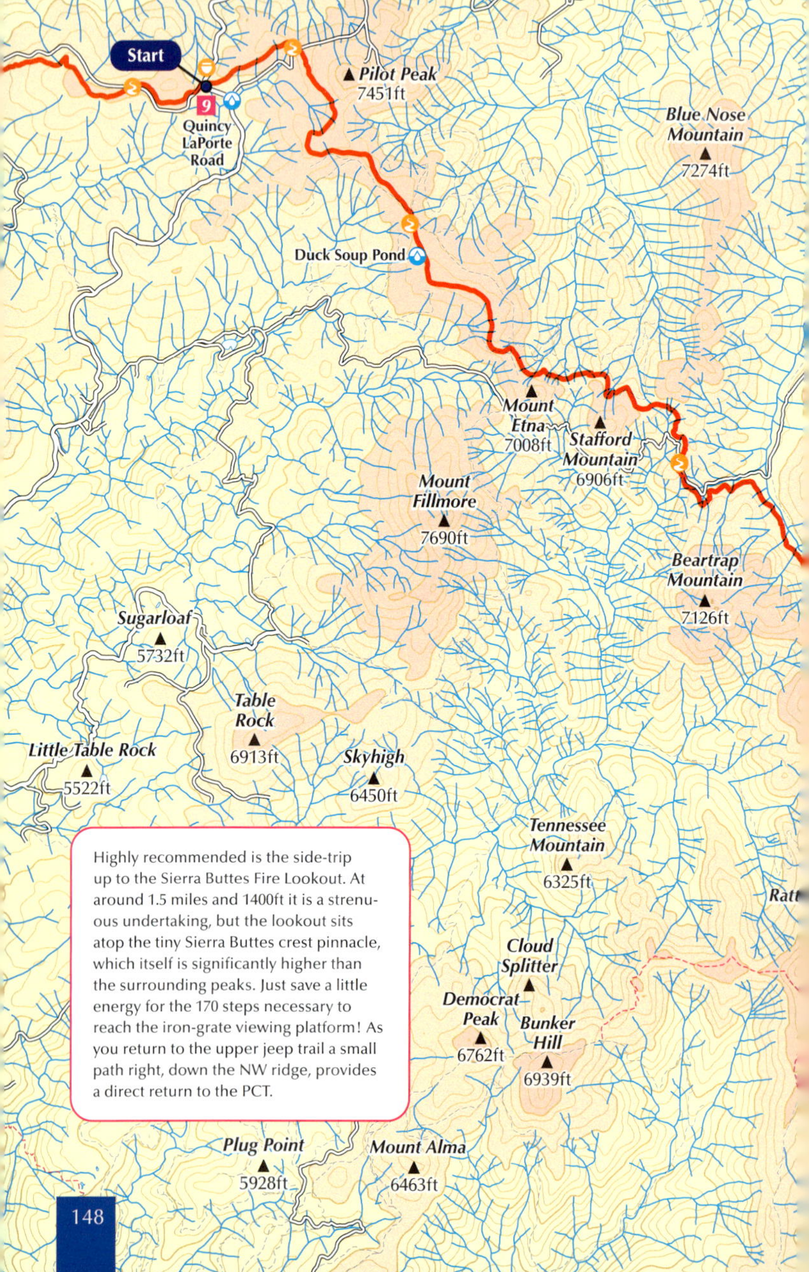


Highly recommended is the side-trip up to the Sierra Buttes Fire Lookout. At around 1.5 miles and 1400ft it is a strenuous undertaking, but the lookout sits atop the tiny Sierra Buttes crest pinnacle, which itself is significantly higher than the surrounding peaks. Just save a little energy for the 170 steps necessary to reach the iron-grate viewing platform! As you return to the upper jeep trail a small path right, down the NW ridge, provides a direct return to the PCT.

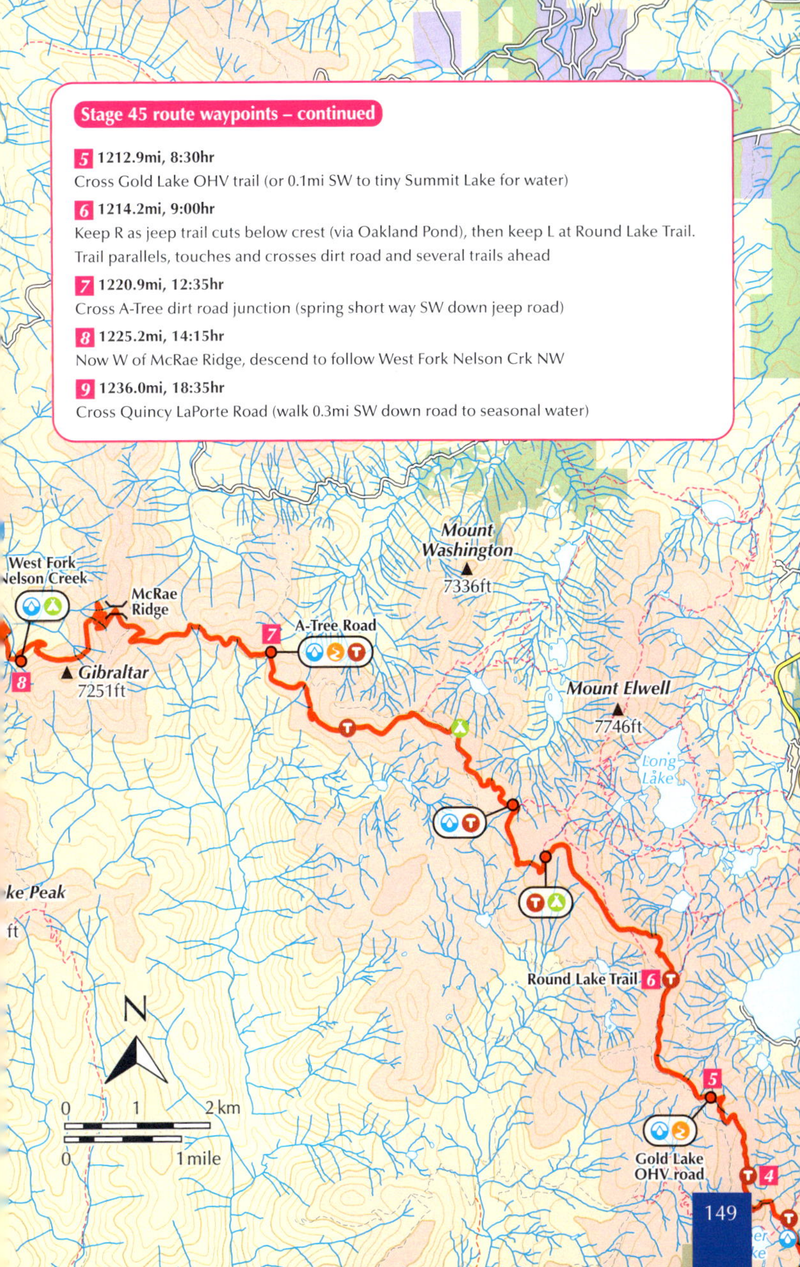


## Stage 45 route waypoints – continued

**5 1212.9mi, 8:30hr**
Cross Gold Lake OHV trail (or 0.1mi SW to tiny Summit Lake for water)

**6 1214.2mi, 9:00hr**
Keep R as jeep trail cuts below crest (via Oakland Pond), then keep L at Round Lake Trail. Trail parallels, touches and crosses dirt road and several trails ahead

**7 1220.9mi, 12:35hr**
Cross A-Tree dirt road junction (spring short way SW down jeep road)

**8 1225.2mi, 14:15hr**
Now W of McRae Ridge, descend to follow West Fork Nelson Crk NW

**9 1236.0mi, 18:35hr**
Cross Quincy LaPorte Road (walk 0.3mi SW down road to seasonal water)

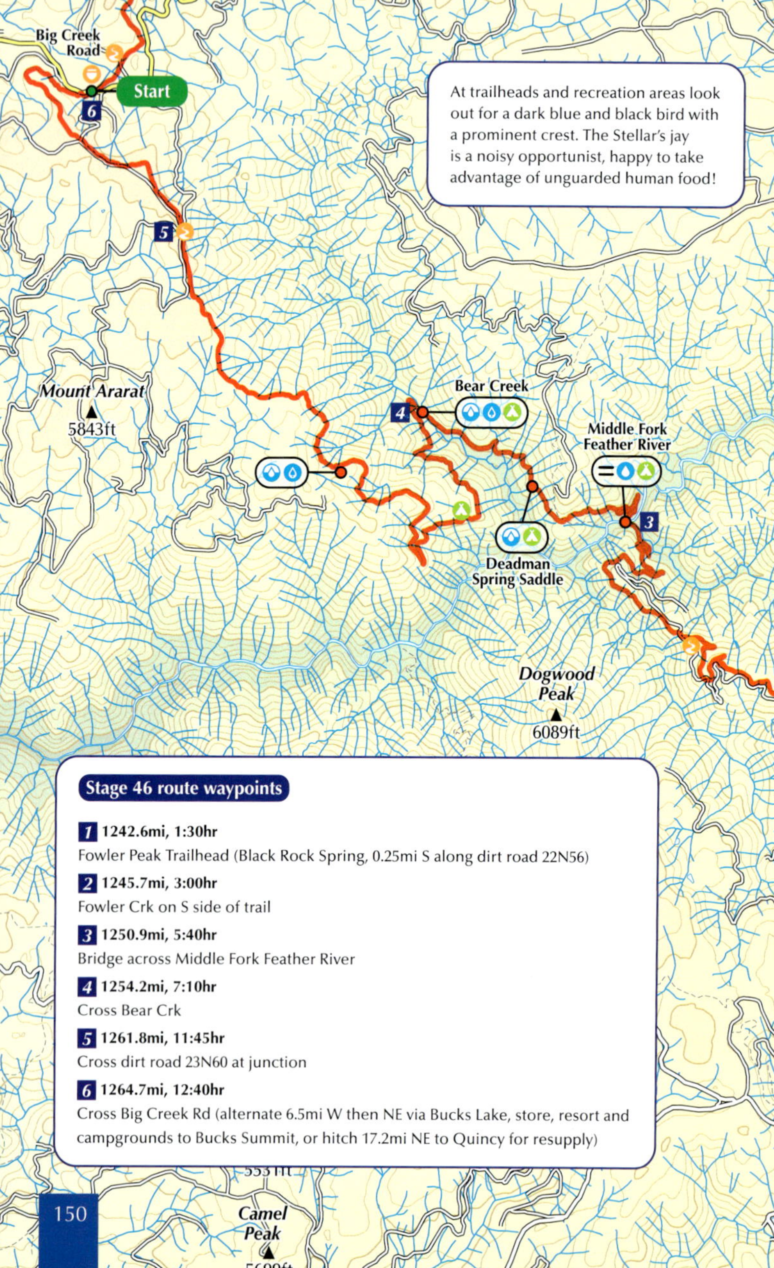


At trailheads and recreation areas look out for a dark blue and black bird with a prominent crest. The Stellar's jay is a noisy opportunist, happy to take advantage of unguarded human food!

## Stage 46 route waypoints

**1 1242.6mi, 1:30hr**
Fowler Peak Trailhead (Black Rock Spring, 0.25mi S along dirt road 22N56)

**2 1245.7mi, 3:00hr**
Fowler Crk on S side of trail

**3 1250.9mi, 5:40hr**
Bridge across Middle Fork Feather River

**4 1254.2mi, 7:10hr**
Cross Bear Crk

**5 1261.8mi, 11:45hr**
Cross dirt road 23N60 at junction

**6 1264.7mi, 12:40hr**
Cross Big Creek Rd (alternate 6.5mi W then NE via Bucks Lake, store, resort and campgrounds to Bucks Summit, or hitch 17.2mi NE to Quincy for resupply)

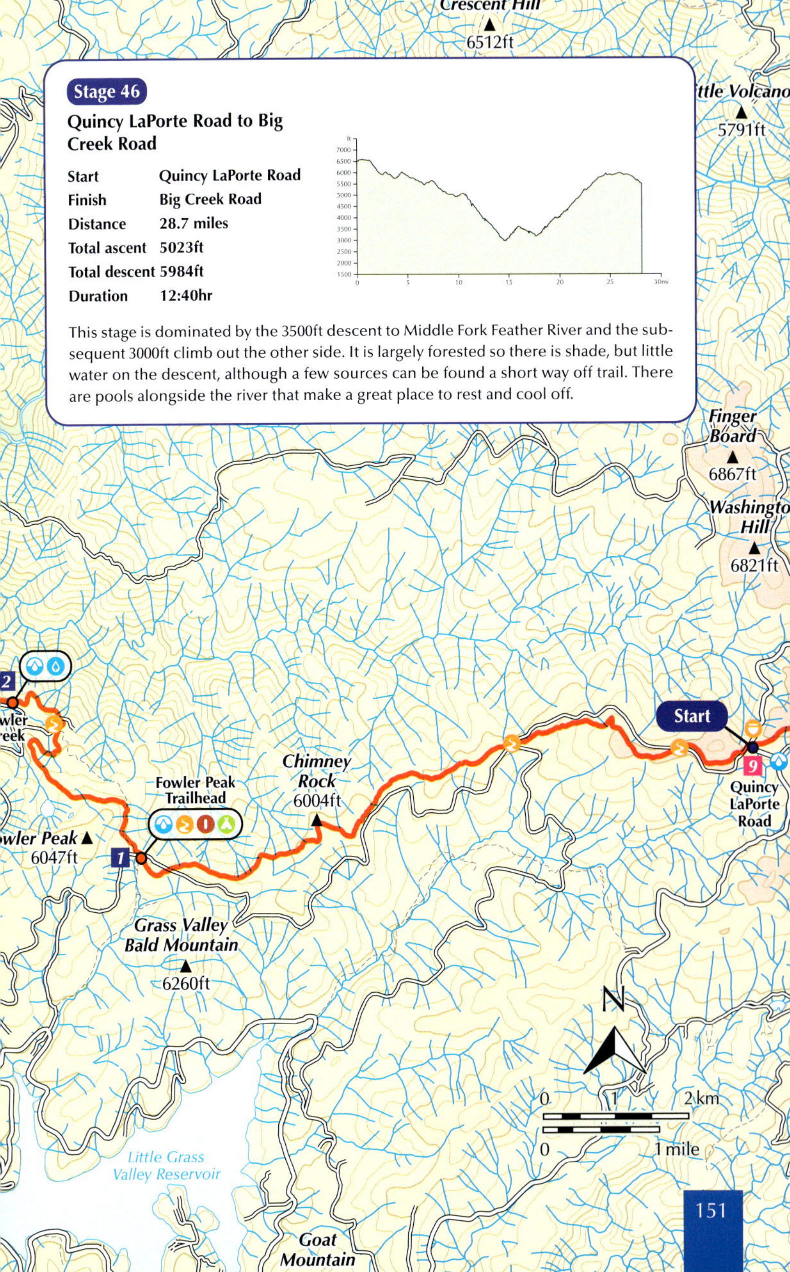


**Stage 46**

## Quincy LaPorte Road to Big Creek Road

| | |
|---|---|
| **Start** | **Quincy LaPorte Road** |
| **Finish** | **Big Creek Road** |
| **Distance** | **28.7 miles** |
| **Total ascent** | **5023ft** |
| **Total descent** | **5984ft** |
| **Duration** | **12:40hr** |

This stage is dominated by the 3500ft descent to Middle Fork Feather River and the subsequent 3000ft climb out the other side. It is largely forested so there is shade, but little water on the descent, although a few sources can be found a short way off trail. There are pools alongside the river that make a great place to rest and cool off.

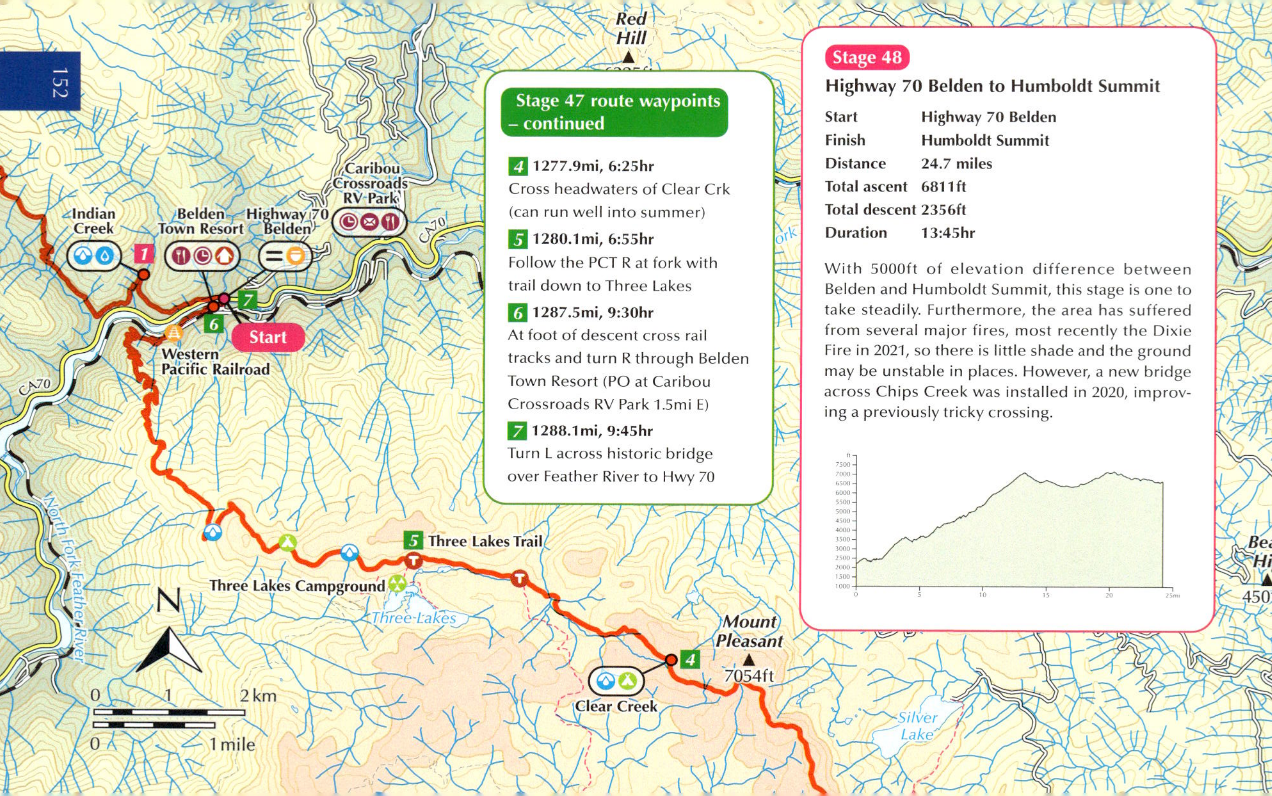


## Stage 47 route waypoints – continued

**4 1277.9mi, 6:25hr**
Cross headwaters of Clear Crk (can run well into summer)

**5 1280.1mi, 6:55hr**
Follow the PCT R at fork with trail down to Three Lakes

**6 1287.5mi, 9:30hr**
At foot of descent cross rail tracks and turn R through Belden Town Resort (PO at Caribou Crossroads RV Park 1.5mi E)

**7 1288.1mi, 9:45hr**
Turn L across historic bridge over Feather River to Hwy 70

## Stage 48

### Highway 70 Belden to Humboldt Summit

| | |
|---|---|
| **Start** | **Highway 70 Belden** |
| **Finish** | **Humboldt Summit** |
| **Distance** | **24.7 miles** |
| **Total ascent** | **6811ft** |
| **Total descent** | **2356ft** |
| **Duration** | **13:45hr** |

With 5000ft of elevation difference between Belden and Humboldt Summit, this stage is one to take steadily. Furthermore, the area has suffered from several major fires, most recently the Dixie Fire in 2021, so there is little shade and the ground may be unstable in places. However, a new bridge across Chips Creek was installed in 2020, improving a previously tricky crossing.

**Stage 47**

## Big Creek Road to Highway 70 Belden

| | |
|---|---|
| **Start** | **Big Creek Road** |
| **Finish** | **Highway 70 Belden** |
| **Distance** | **23.4 miles** |
| **Total ascent** | **2300ft** |
| **Total descent** | **5627ft** |
| **Duration** | **9:45hr** |

A straightforward stage with the initial option to turn left from Big Creek Road and detour via Bucks Lake for its camping and facilities. Surprisingly this adds just 2.3 miles over the main PCT route. Heading north from Bucks Summit, water sources can dry up in summer until Clear Creek which should still be flowing. Before descending the 36 switchbacks to Belden the 0.5 mile detour to Three Lakes Campground is highly recommended. Watch out for poison oak on the descent to Belden.

**Stage 47 route waypoints**

**1 1266.8mi, 0:50hr**
Big Crk (last of several seasonal springs)

**2 1269.1mi, 1:45hr**
Cross road at Bucks Summit Trailhead (PO 5.3mi NE at Meadow Valley, Quincy 12mi E)

**3 1273.2mi, 4:20hr**
Cross saddle, past Spanish Peak Trail on R and turn W following ridgeline

Junction to spring 0.3mi
Humboldt Summit
6841ft
8
Start
Humboldt Summit
Locke Peak
7159ft
Rock Creek
Slate Creek
Sawmill Tom Creek
Scotts John Creek
Humbug Summit
6585ft
Cold Springs
7
Butte Creek
Willow Creek
Cirby Meadows Road 26N02
6
Castle Roc
6434ft
Butte Creek
Snag Lake
Snow Mountain
6978ft
Frog Mountain Trail
5
Andesite Spring
4
Chips Creek
3
N
0
1
2km
0
1mile
Spring Valley Mountain
6827ft
Morris

## Stage 48 route waypoints

Cross road, turn L past Pacific Gas and Electric Belden Powerhouse to rest area. PCT commences W of this by the historic Eby Stamp Mill

**1 1289.1mi, 0:25hr**
Indian Crk (bridge destroyed by fire 2021, ford upstream if necessary)

**2 1294.8mi, 4:10hr**
Myrtle Flat Campground

**3 1296.8mi, 5:15hr**
Cross Chips Crk on new bridge, crossing back a little further upstream

**4 1300.5mi, 8:20hr**
Andesite Spring. Several unmarked trails ahead, take care here

**5 1301.5mi, 9:05hr**
Keep L past Frog Mountain Trail, Frog Spring 0.4mi beyond

**6 1304.8mi, 10:10hr**
Cross Cirby Meadows (dirt) Rd 26N02 bearing NW

**7 1306.4mi, 11:05hr**
Cross Humbug Summit Rd, piped Cold Springs on L, then N to ridgeline

**8 1312.8mi, 13:45hr**
Humboldt Road parking area at Humboldt Summit

At the Belden trailhead you pass the restored Eby Stamp Mill used in hard-rock gold mining. The mill was used to pulverize ore which was then amalgamated with mercury in the ball mill. This mixture was then heated to vaporize the mercury leaving concentrated gold to be extracted. During the gold rush era, millions of dollars' worth of gold was extracted along the Feather River in this way.

Belden Town Resort is an eclectic collection of buildings that variously host events, music festivals, RVs and even some hikers! There is a bar, restaurant, small convenience store and they may accept mail drops, but service can be sporadic or slow when there is not an event on. There is a small PO 1.6 miles east at the friendly Caribou Crossroads, which has a great café.

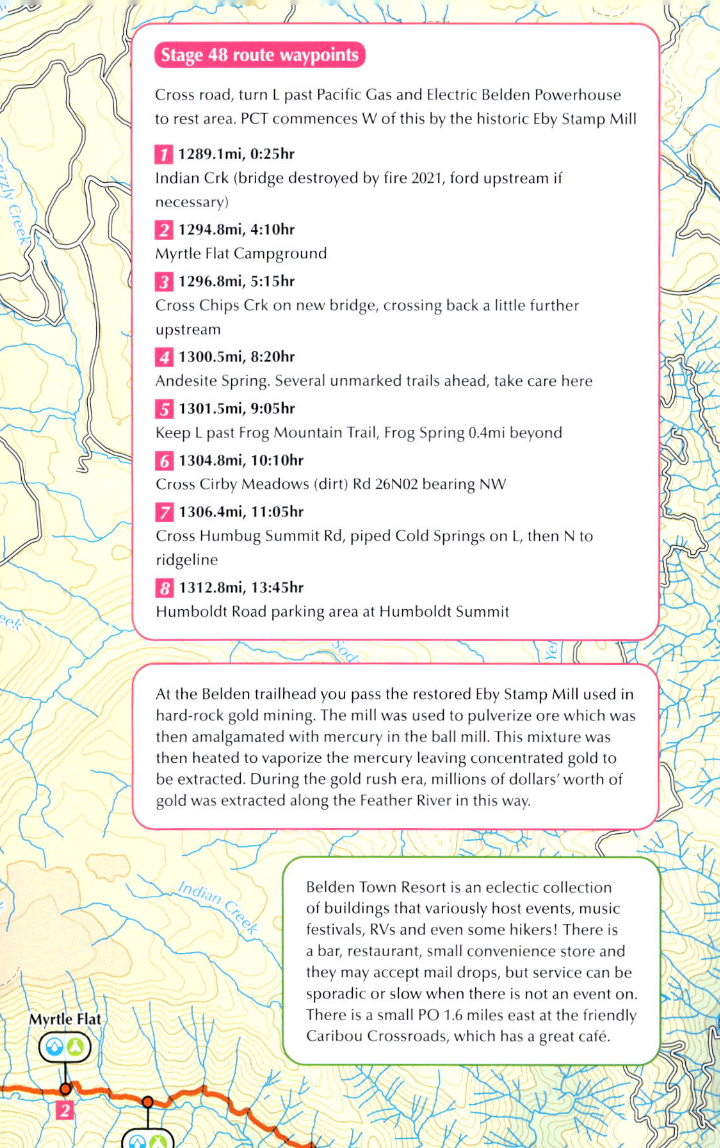

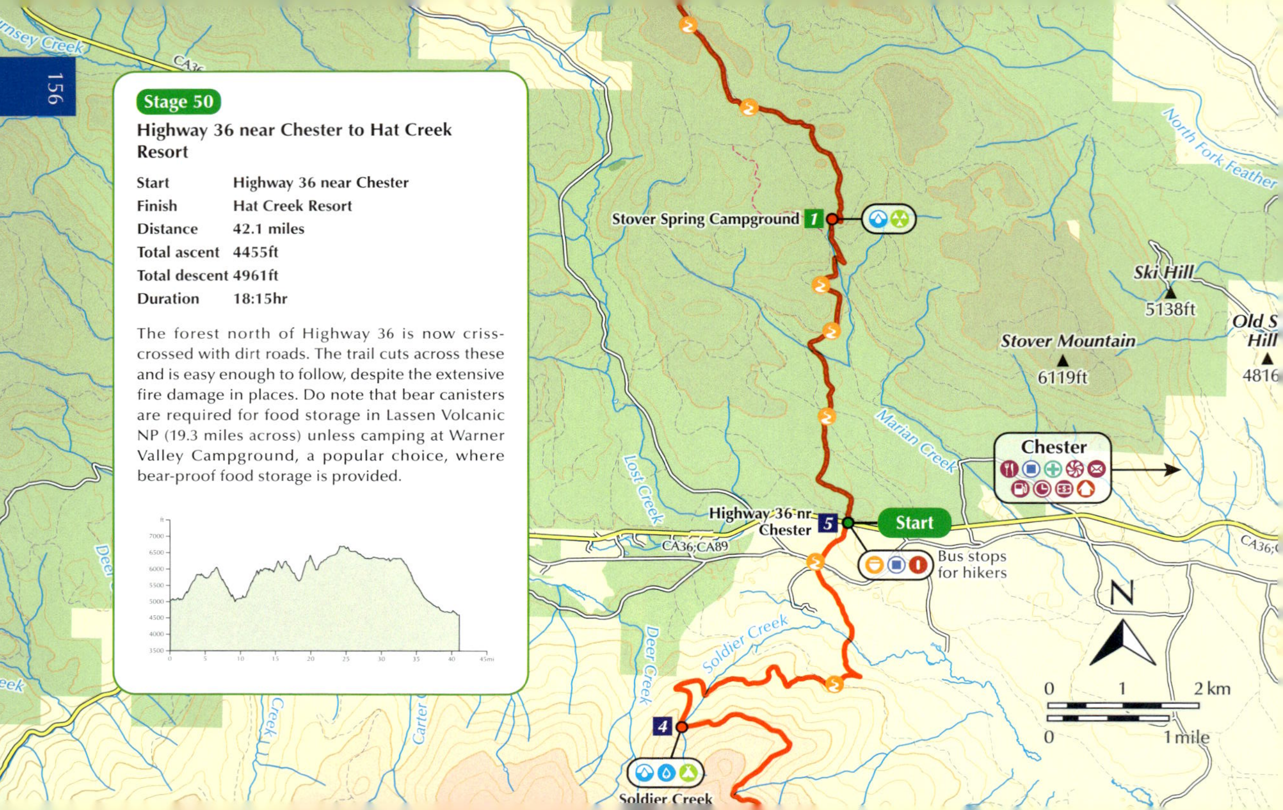


## Stage 50

### Highway 36 near Chester to Hat Creek Resort

| | |
|---|---|
| Start | Highway 36 near Chester |
| Finish | Hat Creek Resort |
| Distance | 42.1 miles |
| Total ascent | 4455ft |
| Total descent | 4961ft |
| Duration | 18:15hr |

The forest north of Highway 36 is now criss-crossed with dirt roads. The trail cuts across these and is easy enough to follow, despite the extensive fire damage in places. Do note that bear canisters are required for food storage in Lassen Volcanic NP (19.3 miles across) unless camping at Warner Valley Campground, a popular choice, where bear-proof food storage is provided.

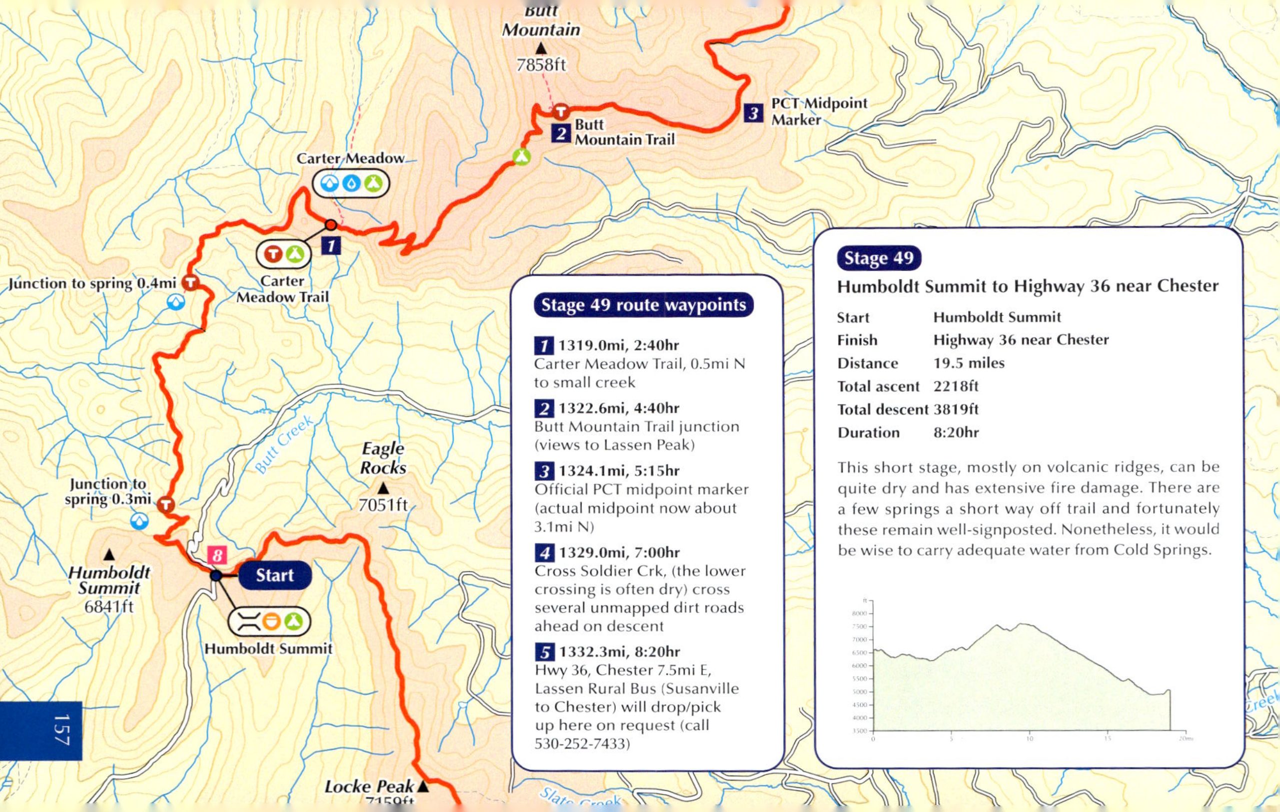
Butt Mountain
7858ft
Butt Mountain Trail
PCT Midpoint Marker
Carter Meadow
Carter Meadow Trail
Junction to spring 0.4mi
Junction to spring 0.3mi
Butt Creek
Eagle Rocks
7051ft
Humboldt Summit
6841ft
Start
Humboldt Summit
Locke Peak
Slate Creek
Stage 49 route waypoints
1 1319.0mi, 2:40hr
Carter Meadow Trail, 0.5mi N to small creek
2 1322.6mi, 4:40hr
Butt Mountain Trail junction (views to Lassen Peak)
3 1324.1mi, 5:15hr
Official PCT midpoint marker (actual midpoint now about 3.1mi N)
4 1329.0mi, 7:00hr
Cross Soldier Crk, (the lower crossing is often dry) cross several unmapped dirt roads ahead on descent
5 1332.3mi, 8:20hr
Hwy 36, Chester 7.5mi E, Lassen Rural Bus (Susanville to Chester) will drop/pick up here on request (call 530-252-7433)
Stage 49
Humboldt Summit to Highway 36 near Chester
Start Humboldt Summit
Finish Highway 36 near Chester
Distance 19.5 miles
Total ascent 2218ft
Total descent 3819ft
Duration 8:20hr
This short stage, mostly on volcanic ridges, can be quite dry and has extensive fire damage. There are a few springs a short way off trail and fortunately these remain well-signposted. Nonetheless, it would be wise to carry adequate water from Cold Springs.

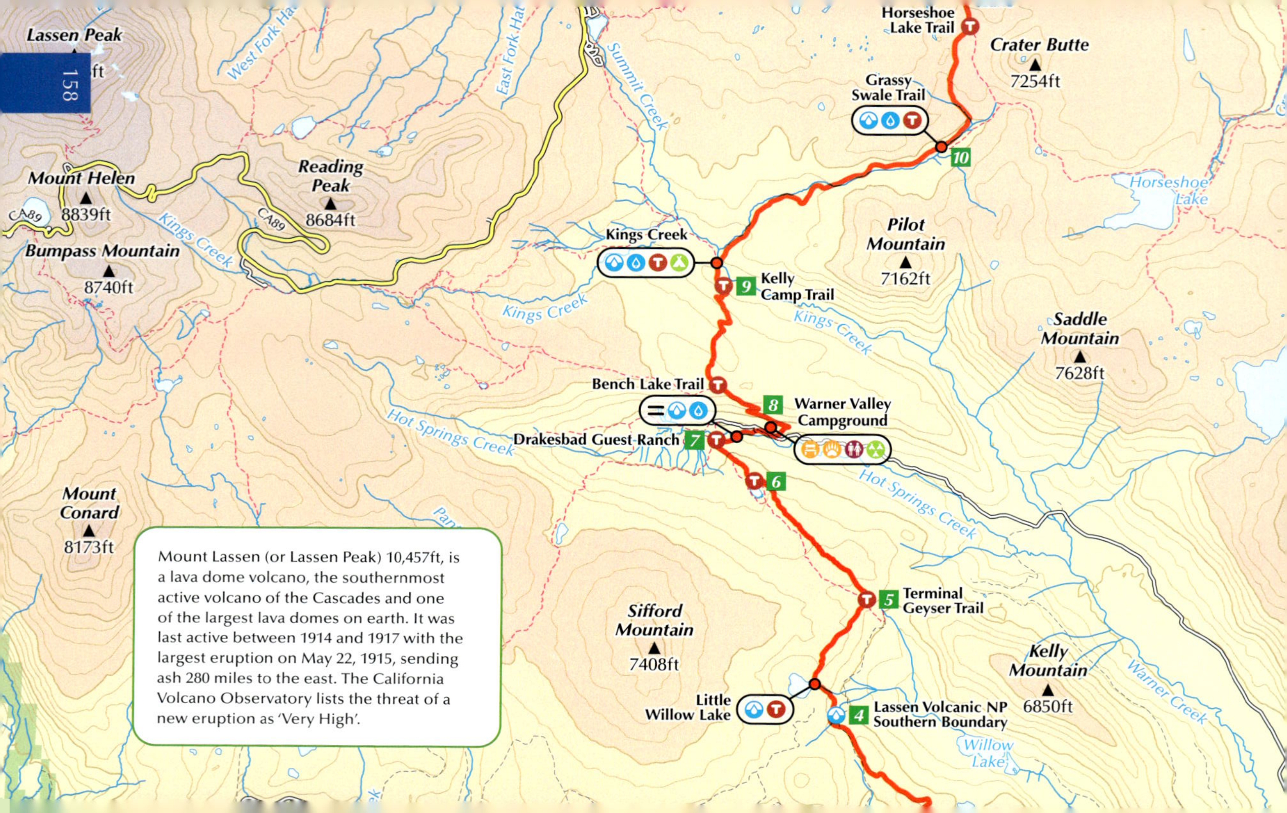


Mount Lassen (or Lassen Peak) 10,457ft, is a lava dome volcano, the southernmost active volcano of the Cascades and one of the largest lava domes on earth. It was last active between 1914 and 1917 with the largest eruption on May 22, 1915, sending ash 280 miles to the east. The California Volcano Observatory lists the threat of a new eruption as 'Very High'.

## Stage 50 route waypoints

**1 1335.7mi, 1:40hr**
Stover Spring Campground, vague trail heads SW initially, climbs, then turns N

**2 1341.6mi, 4:00hr**
Cross North Fork Feather River Bridge, then dirt road, trail R to Domingo Spring

**3 1342.6mi, 4:20hr**
Cross graded Old Red Bluff Rd (Chester 8mi E)

**4 1347.2mi, 6:40hr**
Southern boundary of Lassen Volcanic NP, spring signed 0.1mi SW

**5 1348.5mi, 7:20hr**
Keep ahead across the junction with Terminal Geyser Trail, then bear L

**6 1350.3mi, 8:00hr**
Boiling Springs Lake Circuit Trail junction, keep R for PCT N

**7 1350.6mi, 8:15hr**
Turn R at Drakesbad Guest Ranch trail junction, take bridge over creek

**8 1351.0mi, 8:30hr**
Warner Valley trailhead and campground, trail continues initially NE, then steeply NW from top of campground

**9 1353.6mi, 9:50hr**
L at Kelly Camp Trail junction, R across Kings Crk at subsequent junction

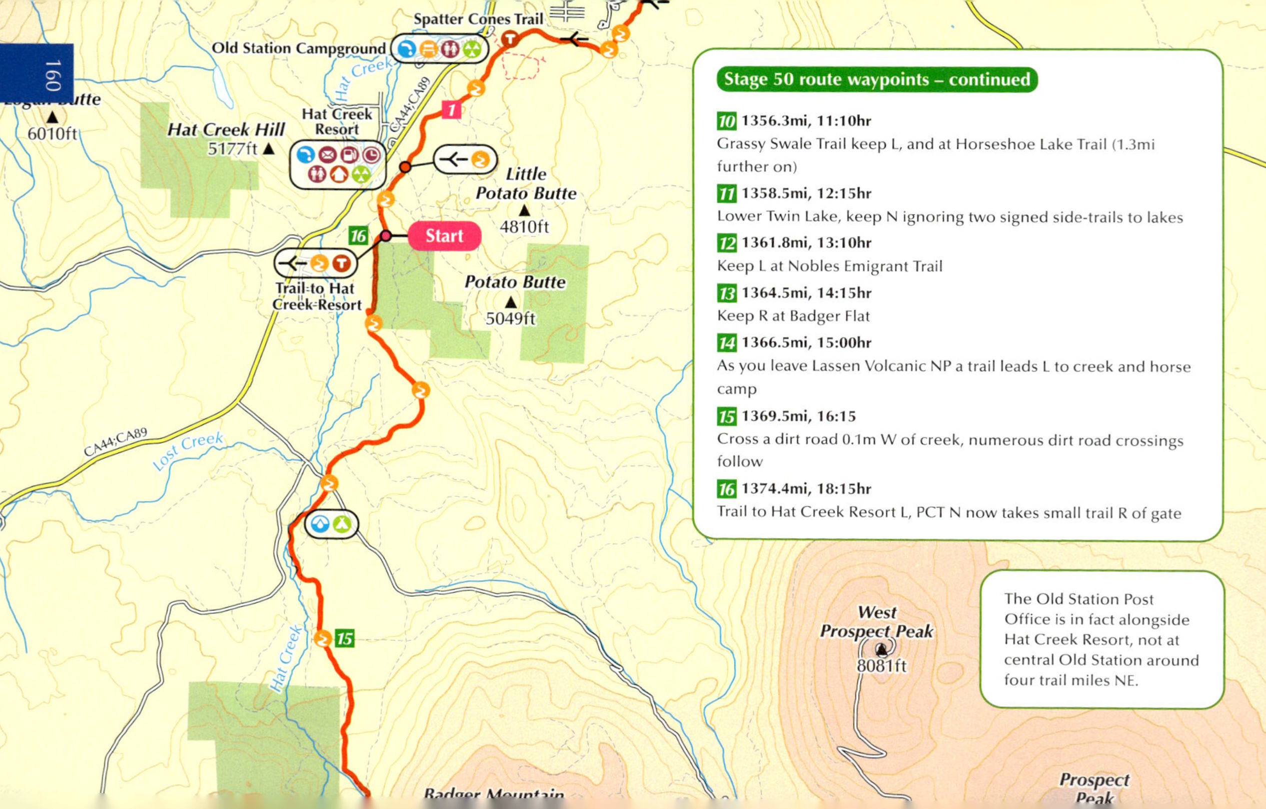


## Stage 50 route waypoints – continued

**10 1356.3mi, 11:10hr**
Grassy Swale Trail keep L, and at Horseshoe Lake Trail (1.3mi further on)

**11 1358.5mi, 12:15hr**
Lower Twin Lake, keep N ignoring two signed side-trails to lakes

**12 1361.8mi, 13:10hr**
Keep L at Nobles Emigrant Trail

**13 1364.5mi, 14:15hr**
Keep R at Badger Flat

**14 1366.5mi, 15:00hr**
As you leave Lassen Volcanic NP a trail leads L to creek and horse camp

**15 1369.5mi, 16:15**
Cross a dirt road 0.1m W of creek, numerous dirt road crossings follow

**16 1374.4mi, 18:15hr**
Trail to Hat Creek Resort L, PCT N now takes small trail R of gate

The Old Station Post Office is in fact alongside Hat Creek Resort, not at central Old Station around four trail miles NE.

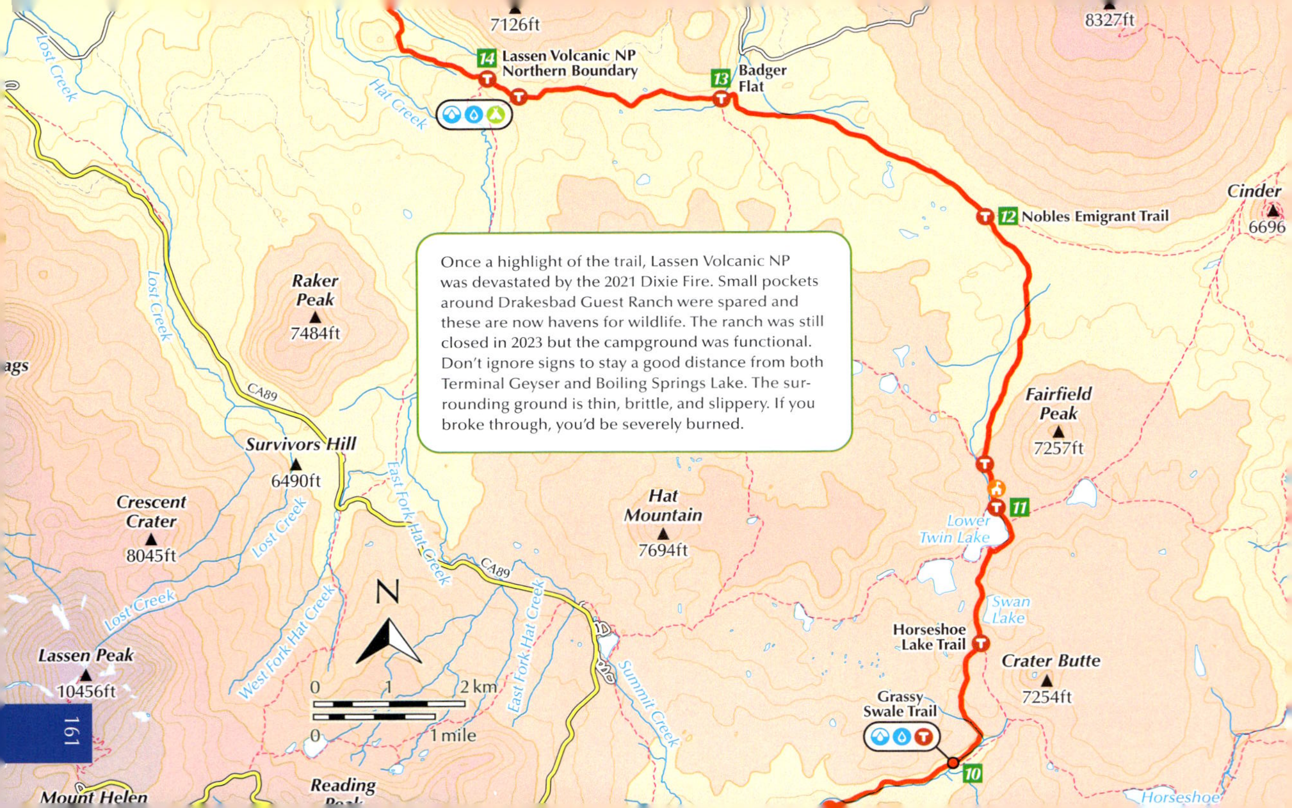


Once a highlight of the trail, Lassen Volcanic NP was devastated by the 2021 Dixie Fire. Small pockets around Drakesbad Guest Ranch were spared and these are now havens for wildlife. The ranch was still closed in 2023 but the campground was functional. Don't ignore signs to stay a good distance from both Terminal Geyser and Boiling Springs Lake. The surrounding ground is thin, brittle, and slippery. If you broke through, you'd be severely burned.

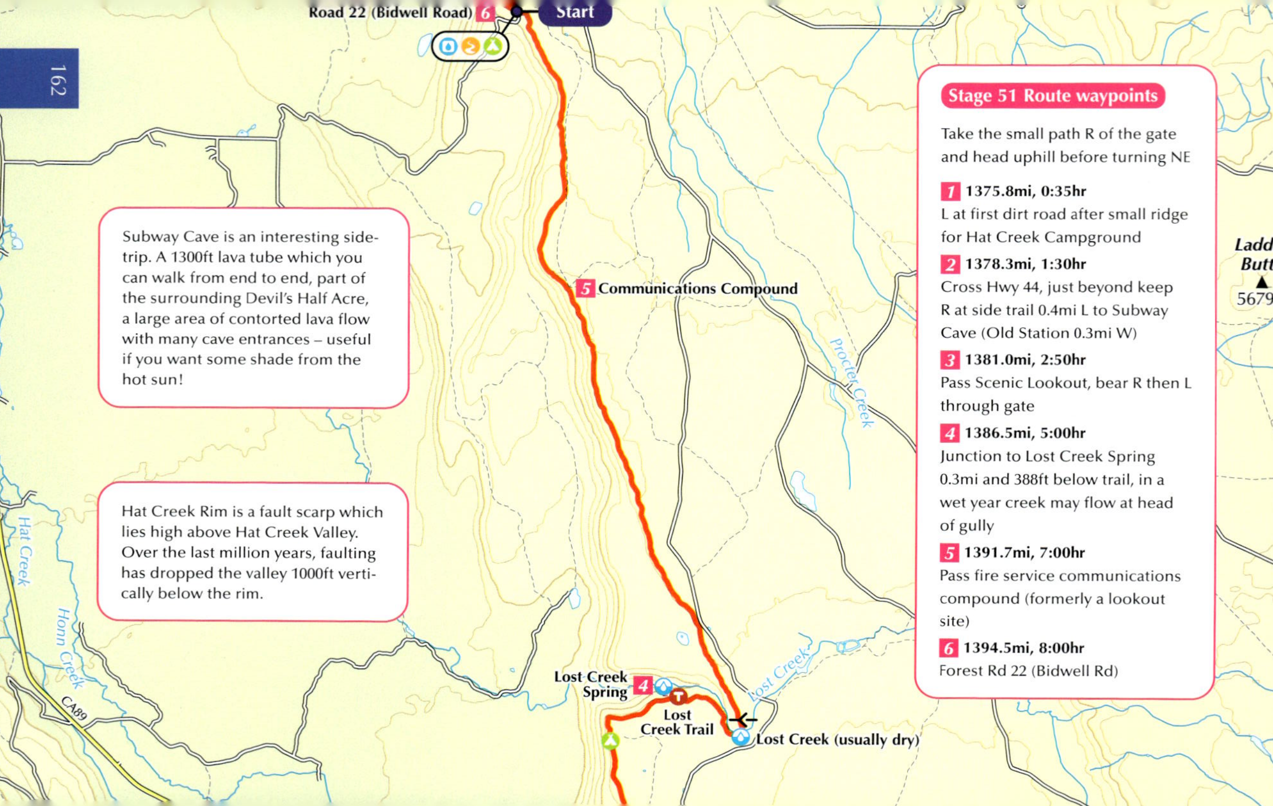


Subway Cave is an interesting side-trip. A 1300ft lava tube which you can walk from end to end, part of the surrounding Devil's Half Acre, a large area of contorted lava flow with many cave entrances – useful if you want some shade from the hot sun!

Hat Creek Rim is a fault scarp which lies high above Hat Creek Valley. Over the last million years, faulting has dropped the valley 1000ft vertically below the rim.

## Stage 51 Route waypoints

Take the small path R of the gate and head uphill before turning NE

**1 1375.8mi, 0:35hr**
L at first dirt road after small ridge for Hat Creek Campground

**2 1378.3mi, 1:30hr**
Cross Hwy 44, just beyond keep R at side trail 0.4mi L to Subway Cave (Old Station 0.3mi W)

**3 1381.0mi, 2:50hr**
Pass Scenic Lookout, bear R then L through gate

**4 1386.5mi, 5:00hr**
Junction to Lost Creek Spring 0.3mi and 388ft below trail, in a wet year creek may flow at head of gully

**5 1391.7mi, 7:00hr**
Pass fire service communications compound (formerly a lookout site)

**6 1394.5mi, 8:00hr**
Forest Rd 22 (Bidwell Rd)

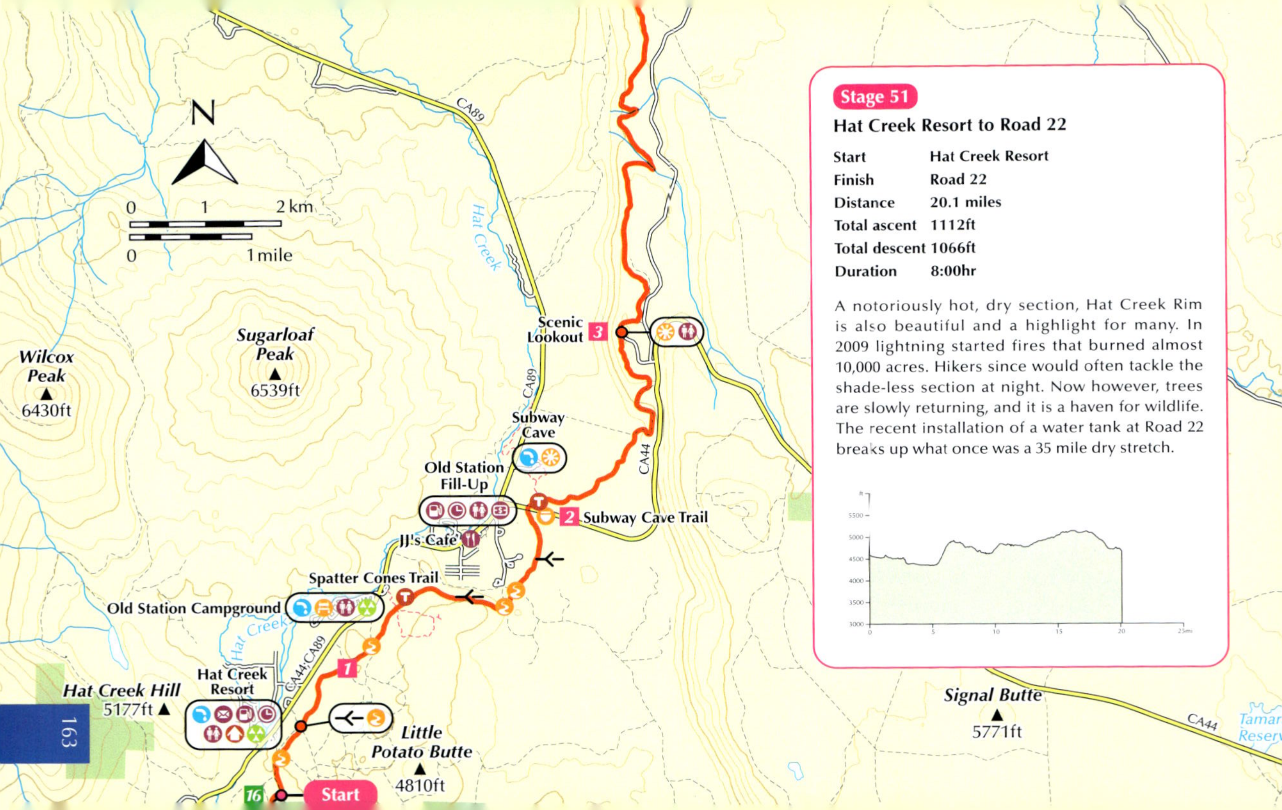


## Stage 51

### Hat Creek Resort to Road 22

| | |
|---|---|
| Start | Hat Creek Resort |
| Finish | Road 22 |
| Distance | 20.1 miles |
| Total ascent | 1112ft |
| Total descent | 1066ft |
| Duration | 8:00hr |

A notoriously hot, dry section, Hat Creek Rim is also beautiful and a highlight for many. In 2009 lightning started fires that burned almost 10,000 acres. Hikers since would often tackle the shade-less section at night. Now however, trees are slowly returning, and it is a haven for wildlife. The recent installation of a water tank at Road 22 breaks up what once was a 35 mile dry stretch.

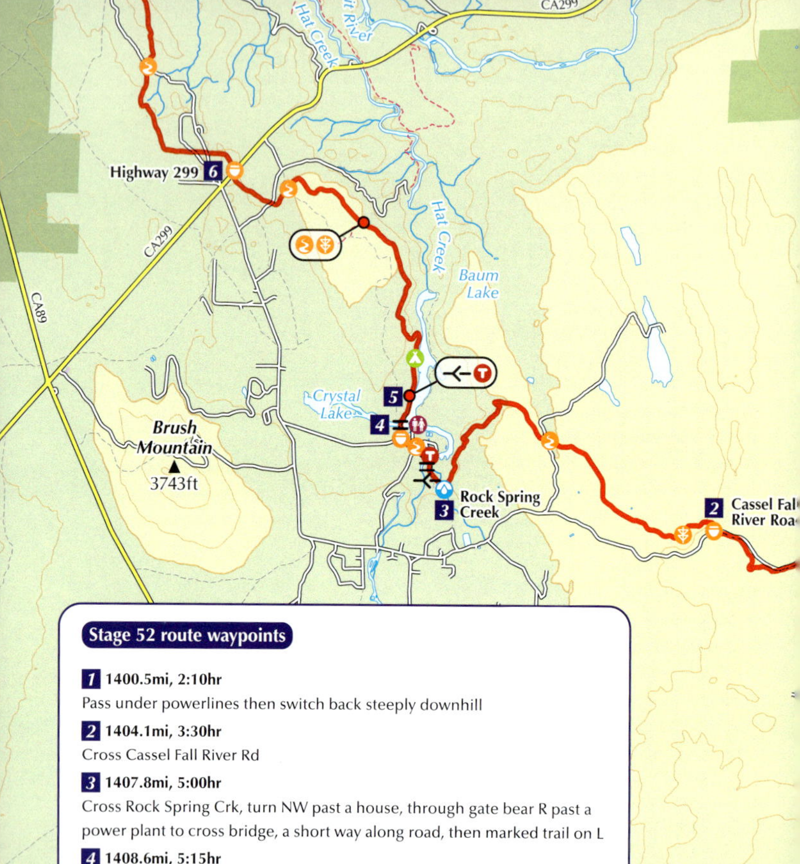


## Stage 52 route waypoints

**1 1400.5mi, 2:10hr**

Pass under powerlines then switch back steeply downhill

**2 1404.1mi, 3:30hr**

Cross Cassel Fall River Rd

**3 1407.8mi, 5:00hr**

Cross Rock Spring Crk, turn NW past a house, through gate bear R past a power plant to cross bridge, a short way along road, then marked trail on L

**4 1408.6mi, 5:15hr**

Having crossed a gravel road and paved road, cross bridge over slipway between Crystal Lake and Baum Lake (no camping in this area)

**5 1409.1mi, 5:30hr**

Keep L at trail fork then pass through gate

**6 1412.3mi, 6:50hr**

Cross Hwy 299 (Burney 7.7mi SW, walk 0.1mi SW: safer hitch at junction)

**7 1419.0mi, 9:30hr**

Cross Hwy 89, ignore Headwaters Trail, go across bridge, through campground

**8 1420.0mi, 9:50hr**

Burney Falls Trailhead (bridge across creek to campsite and store)

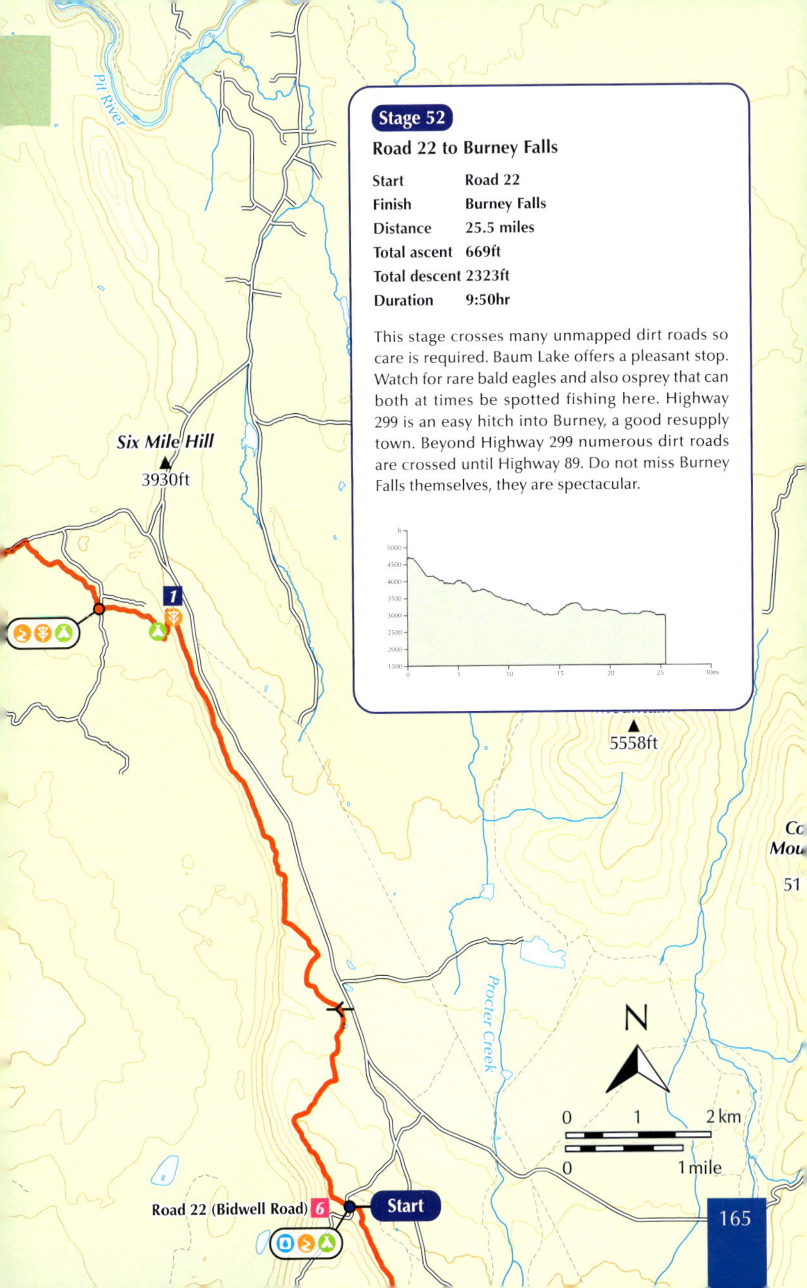


## Stage 52

### Road 22 to Burney Falls

| | |
|---|---|
| Start | Road 22 |
| Finish | Burney Falls |
| Distance | 25.5 miles |
| Total ascent | 669ft |
| Total descent | 2323ft |
| Duration | 9:50hr |

This stage crosses many unmapped dirt roads so care is required. Baum Lake offers a pleasant stop. Watch for rare bald eagles and also osprey that can both at times be spotted fishing here. Highway 299 is an easy hitch into Burney, a good resupply town. Beyond Highway 299 numerous dirt roads are crossed until Highway 89. Do not miss Burney Falls themselves, they are spectacular.

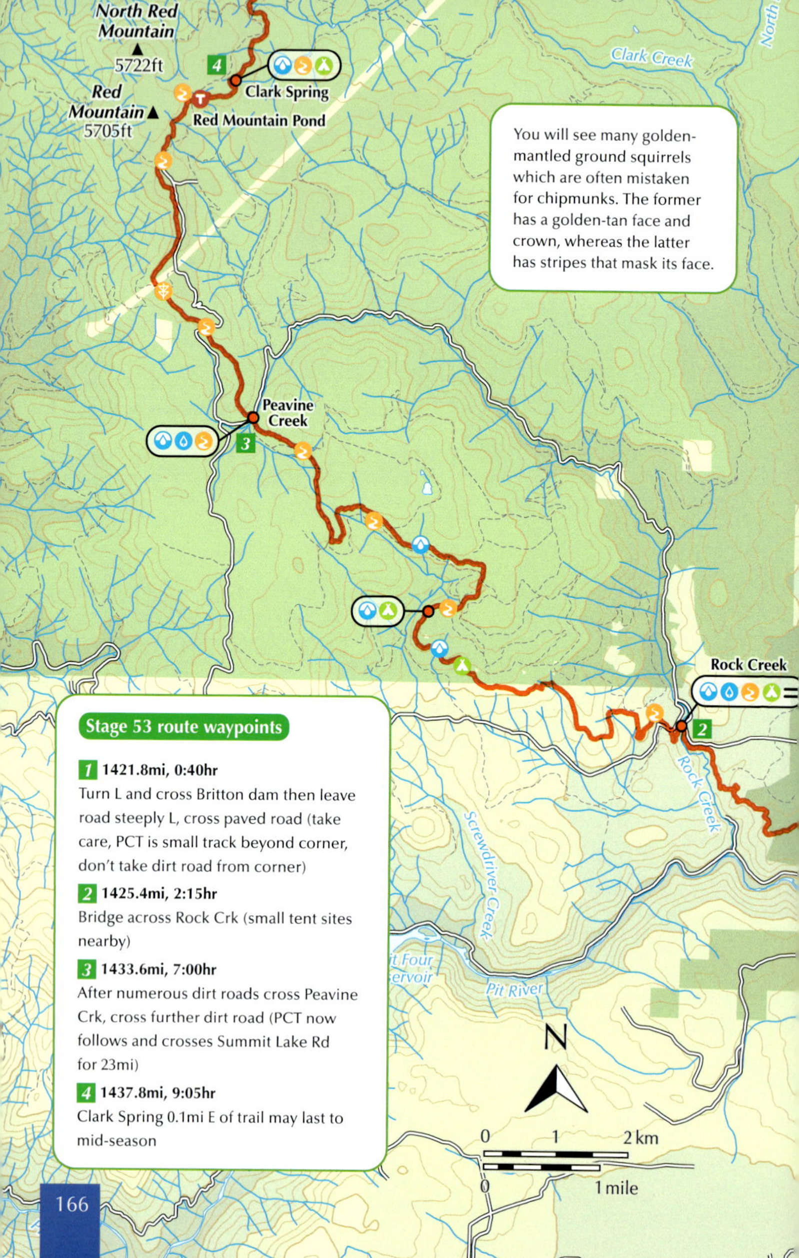


You will see many golden-mantled ground squirrels which are often mistaken for chipmunks. The former has a golden-tan face and crown, whereas the latter has stripes that mask its face.

## Stage 53 route waypoints

**1 1421.8mi, 0:40hr**
Turn L and cross Britton dam then leave road steeply L, cross paved road (take care, PCT is small track beyond corner, don't take dirt road from corner)

**2 1425.4mi, 2:15hr**
Bridge across Rock Crk (small tent sites nearby)

**3 1433.6mi, 7:00hr**
After numerous dirt roads cross Peavine Crk, cross further dirt road (PCT now follows and crosses Summit Lake Rd for 23mi)

**4 1437.8mi, 9:05hr**
Clark Spring 0.1mi E of trail may last to mid-season

## Stage 53

### Burney Falls to Bartle Gap

| | |
|---|---|
| Start | Burney Falls |
| Finish | Bartle Gap |
| Distance | 27 miles |
| Total ascent | 4678ft |
| Total descent | 2510ft |
| Duration | 13:00hr |

Ponderosa pines provide welcome shade for much of the climb, which is undertaken in the first half of the stage. You'll cross the Pit River on the Lake Britton dam (also known as the 'Pit-3 Dam') a hydro-electric structure that feeds three 23.3 MW generators. On the ridgetops of the second half, water will be scarce beyond mid-season or in a dry year.

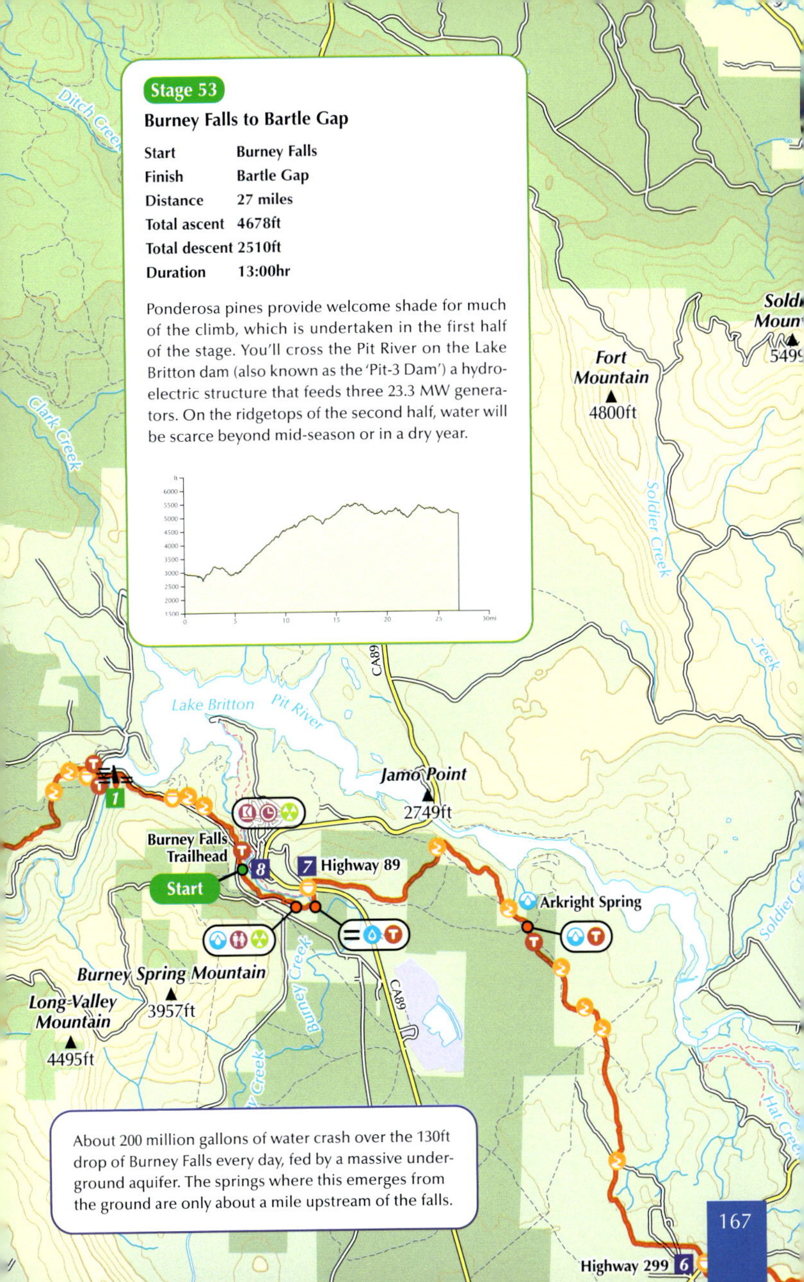


About 200 million gallons of water crash over the 130ft drop of Burney Falls every day, fed by a massive underground aquifer. The springs where this emerges from the ground are only about a mile upstream of the falls.

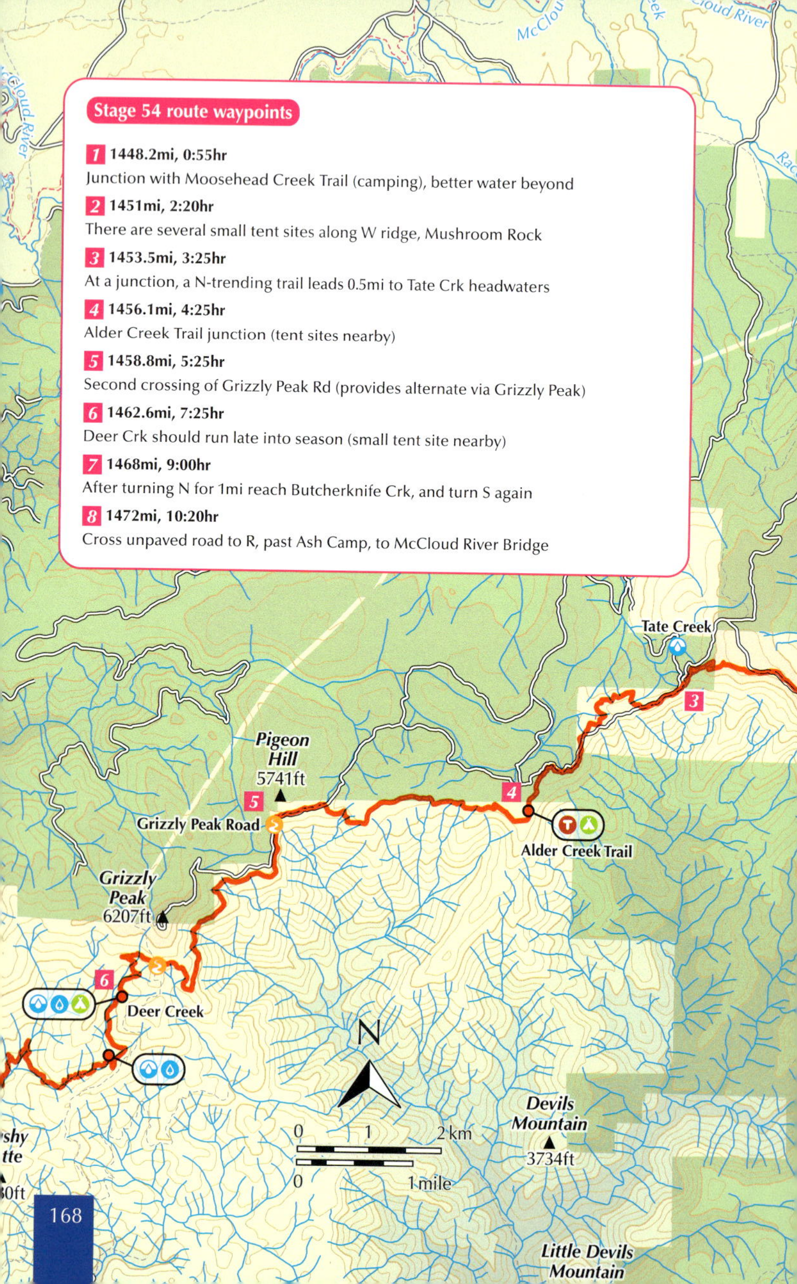
Stage 54 route waypoints
1 1448.2mi, 0:55hr
Junction with Moosehead Creek Trail (camping), better water beyond
2 1451mi, 2:20hr
There are several small tent sites along W ridge, Mushroom Rock
3 1453.5mi, 3:25hr
At a junction, a N-trending trail leads 0.5mi to Tate Crk headwaters
4 1456.1mi, 4:25hr
Alder Creek Trail junction (tent sites nearby)
5 1458.8mi, 5:25hr
Second crossing of Grizzly Peak Rd (provides alternate via Grizzly Peak)
6 1462.6mi, 7:25hr
Deer Crk should run late into season (small tent site nearby)
7 1468mi, 9:00hr
After turning N for 1mi reach Butcherknife Crk, and turn S again
8 1472mi, 10:20hr
Cross unpaved road to R, past Ash Camp, to McCloud River Bridge
Tate Creek
3
Pigeon Hill
5741ft
5
4
Grizzly Peak Road
Alder Creek Trail
Grizzly Peak
6207ft
6
Deer Creek
N
Devils Mountain
3734ft
0
1
2 km
0
1 mile
Little Devils Mountain

## Stage 54

### Bartle Gap to McCloud River

| | |
|---|---|
| Start | Bartle Gap |
| Finish | McCloud River |
| Distance | 25 miles |
| Total ascent | 2612ft |
| Total descent | 5302ft |
| Duration | 10:20hr |

A densely forested stage with glimpses of Mount Shasta north-west from the ridges between Mushroom Rock and Grizzly Peak.



### Stage 53 route waypoints – continued

**6** **1441.4mi, 10:30hr**
Cross a dirt road (0.2mi SW Kosk Spring)

**7** **1447.0mi, 13:00hr**
Cross Summit Lake Rd at Bartle Gap (5mi E to Hwy 89)

**5** **1439.8mi, 9:55hr**
Deadman Crk 0.1mi E of trail

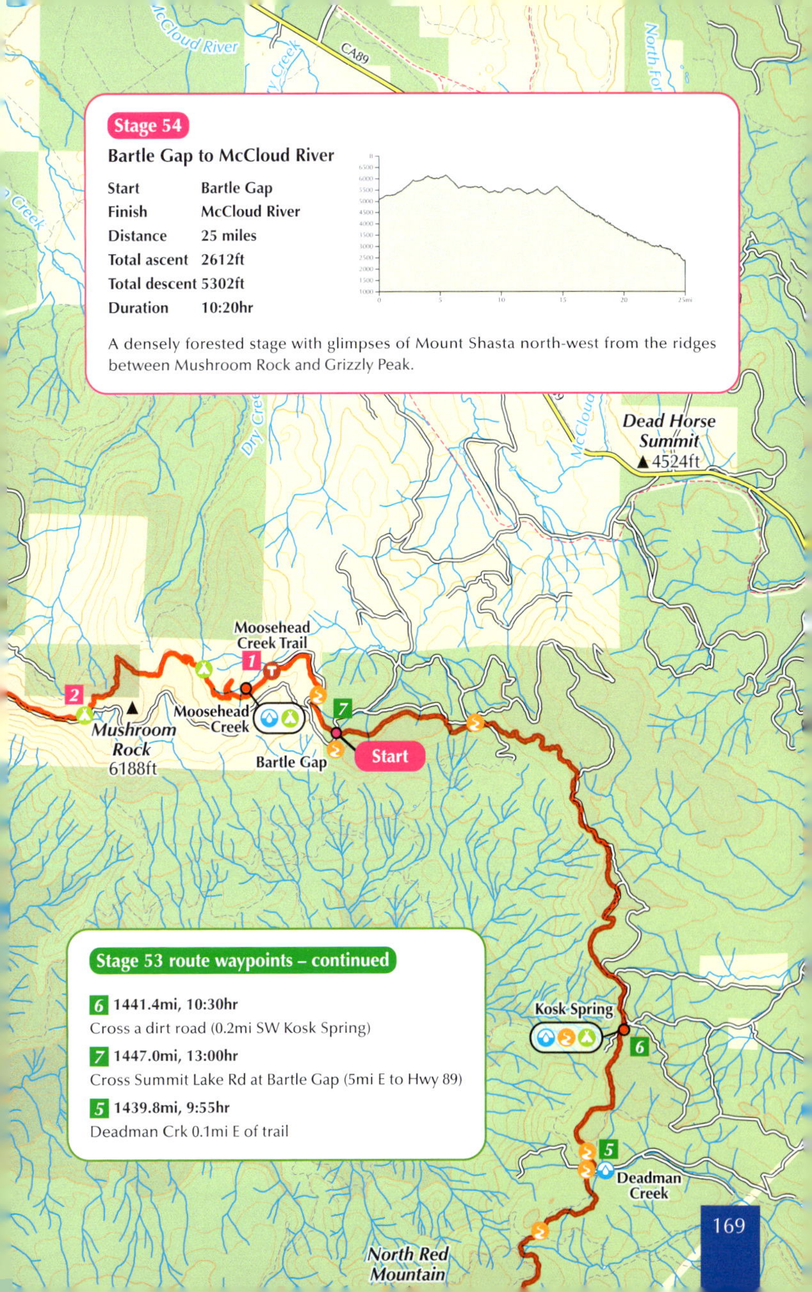

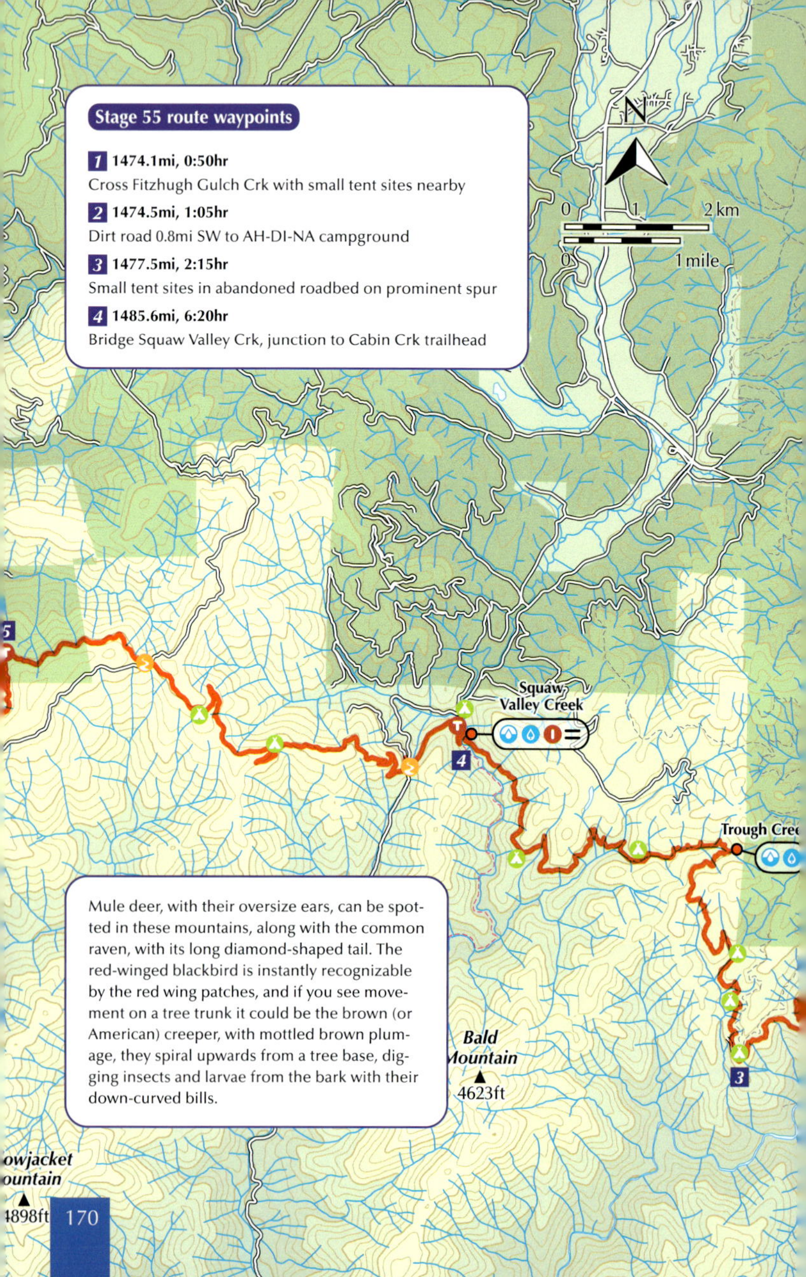


Mule deer, with their oversize ears, can be spotted in these mountains, along with the common raven, with its long diamond-shaped tail. The red-winged blackbird is instantly recognizable by the red wing patches, and if you see movement on a tree trunk it could be the brown (or American) creeper, with mottled brown plumage, they spiral upwards from a tree base, digging insects and larvae from the bark with their down-curved bills.

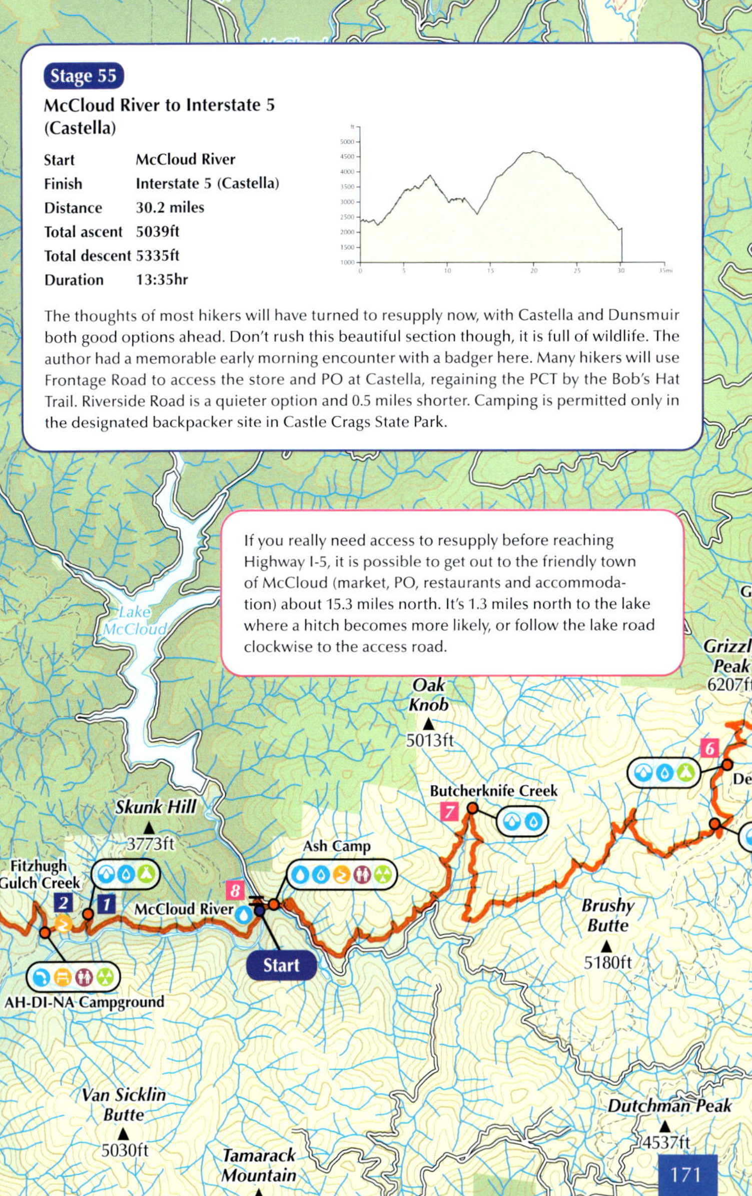

## Stage 55

### McCloud River to Interstate 5 (Castella)

| | |
|---|---|
| **Start** | McCloud River |
| **Finish** | Interstate 5 (Castella) |
| **Distance** | 30.2 miles |
| **Total ascent** | 5039ft |
| **Total descent** | 5335ft |
| **Duration** | 13:35hr |

The thoughts of most hikers will have turned to resupply now, with Castella and Dunsmuir both good options ahead. Don't rush this beautiful section though, it is full of wildlife. The author had a memorable early morning encounter with a badger here. Many hikers will use Frontage Road to access the store and PO at Castella, regaining the PCT by the Bob's Hat Trail. Riverside Road is a quieter option and 0.5 miles shorter. Camping is permitted only in the designated backpacker site in Castle Crags State Park.

If you really need access to resupply before reaching Highway I-5, it is possible to get out to the friendly town of McCloud (market, PO, restaurants and accommodation) about 15.3 miles north. It's 1.3 miles north to the lake where a hitch becomes more likely, or follow the lake road clockwise to the access road.

## Stage 55 route waypoints – continued

**5 1492.7mi, 9:50hr**
Turn L, realigned trail via Fall Crk, old PCT follows steep ridgeline

**6 1501.6mi, 13:20hr**
Join paved Riverside Rd, cross Soda Crk then L on bridge across Sacramento River and across rail tracks

**7 1502.2mi, 13:35hr**
Pass Frontage Road on L to reach Interstate-5 (Castella 2mi SW, Dunsmuir 5.5mi N, Mt Shasta 13.5mi N)

# NOTES

*Clockwise from the top: The ridge below Tinker Knob on route to Donner Pass (Stage 43); A sign reminds you just how far it is to go!(Stage 3); This Western Fence Lizard has taken to rock climbing (Stage 9)*

*Clockwise from the top: The Upper Basin below Mather Pass (Stage 32); The first way marker of many heading north (Stage 1); Looking out across the Laguna Mountains (Stage 2); Joshua Trees provide little shade in Owens Peak Wilderness (Stage 23)*

*Buckbrush, ceanothus and rabbitbrush are among the shrubs that populate Clover Meadow (Stage 28)*